NEWCASTLE'S
NEW YORK

NEWCASTLE'S NEW YORK

Anglo-American Politics, 1732-1753

Stanley Nider Katz

The Belknap Press of
Harvard University Press
Cambridge, Massachusetts

1968

Col.ᵗ Robᵗ Lurting
MAYOR

For my father and mother

Preface

This book began to take shape almost nine years ago as a doctoral dissertation. My original intention was to analyze the social basis of eighteenth-century New York politics in an attempt to get behind the formality and rhetoric preserved in the legislative journals, laws, and other official records of the colony. My question was how political power was really distributed and used, and, in particular, how the seemingly tight ruling aristocracy achieved its ends. Relatively little work had then been done on pre-revolutionary New York politics and the one truly substantial effort, by Beverly McAnear, was so rooted in the politics of the 1930's as to make its application to the 1730's unclear. The primary sources I intended to use were the personal papers of New York politicians active between 1710 and 1770, but, while reading them I found myself intrigued by their repeated disclosure of the close relationship of American politics to people and events in England. Fortunately, I was able to spend a year in England following up the leads I had uncovered in New York, working primarily with the vast collection of Newcastle Papers in the British Museum, and the result has been this inquiry into what I have called "Anglo-American" history.

Superficially, of course, the very nature of the empire guaranteed that there would be political bonds between the colonies and the mother country. Manifestly, much of colonial public life was controlled in England: most important American officials were appointed at Whitehall, many colonial political controversies were settled in royal administrative bodies such as the privy council and the board of trade, and decisions of policy were made by imperial officials in London. This organizational structure is well known, of course, but the extent to which, in practice, it forced Americans to participate in English decision-making has been underestimated. It was not always easy for New Yorkers to have personal access to the highest imperial officials, but it was quite possible for them to sway those who could. Therefore, successful colonial politicians cultivated friends in England who could influence the appointment of officeholders and the conduct of imperial administration. Conversely, purely English interests often intruded upon American politics. British merchants sought to increase their trade by improving their political connections abroad; the ruling aristocracy provided for its younger sons and importunate relatives by promoting their appointment to colonial office; changes in the ministry were reflected in changes of personnel in America.

Thus the history of Anglo-American politics in New York is the story of the selection of royal governors in accordance with the requirements of English patronage, the maneuvering of New Yorkers to displace unfriendly governors and to secure themselves jobs and favors, and the manipulation of the imperial administration in support of local interests in New York. New Yorkers strove to build up English connections so that they could exert an interest at Whitehall and they sometimes journeyed across the Atlantic to resolve conflicts which had broken out in New York City or the Mohawk Valley. At the same time, of course, they were conducting their businesses and practicing their professions, standing for election in their towns and on their manors, and arguing about local issues. The point is simply that the operation of the political system in colonial New York cannot fully be understood in terms of a closed, provincial system.

The Anglo-American cast of New York politics in the

Preface

eighteenth century was made possible by the permissive attitude of imperial officials, who were mainly concerned to see that the colonies played their economic part in maintaining a self-sufficient empire, and who were relatively uninterested in the internal regulation of colonial life so long as it remained reasonably stable. The Duke of Newcastle was the perfect administrator of such a policy, if it can be so dignified, of "salutary neglect." Newcastle was keenly aware of the subtlest political nuance, and he was devoted to the art of patronage, but he seldom intervened substantially into the conduct of American government. Thus the first half of the century witnessed the free flow of personnel, interest, and influence between England and New York. After mid-century, however, the requirements of a major war imposed specific demands upon the colonies and strict accountability on imperial officials, and the informality and flexibility of the earlier system of imperial politics began to give way to a more impersonal, rigid situation in colonial government.

Our analysis of the American Revolution is based upon virtually unexamined premises about the old regime in America, and I hope that this book will be merely one of a series of colony studies which will make possible a more sophisticated view of the crisis of the 1760's and 1770's. As it stands, however, it constitutes an examination of Anglo-American politics in their heyday in one colony. I have imposed severe chronological limits in order to study New York politics in the period after the problems of the Glorious Revolution had been resolved and before the American Revolution was clearly imminent. Governor William Cosby's arrival in New York in 1732 seems a suitable starting point, even though it comes well after Robert Hunter's resolution of the post-Leislerian turmoil, since Cosby's difficulties expose the political alignments of the Hunter and Burnet administrations. The year 1753 provides an end point, coming as it does at the close of Clinton's long governorship and immediately before the major phase of the Seven Years' War.

In transcribing from manuscript sources, the original spelling has been retained. Such punctuation as is absolutely necessary for clarity has been added, however, and all superior letters have been brought down to the line. In quotations from printed sources the spelling is unchanged, but superior letters have been lowered. All dates are in the Old Style, until the adoption of the Gregorian calendar in 1752, but in every case January 1 has been taken as the beginning of the new year. Thus, March 24, 1732/3 O.S. becomes March 24, 1733.

I should like to express my gratitude to the authorities of the following libraries and archives in this country and in England for permission to quote from manuscripts in their care: New-York Historical Society, New York Public Library, Clements Library (University of Michigan), Rutgers University Library, New Jersey Historical Society, Franklin Delano Roosevelt Library, Massachusetts Historical Society, British Museum, Public Record Office, Lincolnshire Archives Committee, National Register of Archives, Cambridge University Library, Sussex Archaeological Society, William Salt Library. I am similarly indebted to the Earl of Ancaster, the Earl of Dartmouth, Viscount Gage, the Marquess of Cholmondeley, Mr. John Rutherfurd, Jr., and Mrs. William H. Osborn. The New-York Historical Society *Quarterly* has kindly consented to the use of those portions of Chapter 2 that first appeared as an article in the *Quarterly*, LI (January 1967), pp. 7–23.

My research could not have been completed without the help of a Fulbright fellowship to King's College, University of London (1959–1960), a fellowship from the Harvard Graduate School of Arts and Sciences (1960–1961), and grants from the Graduate Research Committee, University of Wisconsin (1965) and the Charles Warren Center for Studies in American History, Harvard University (1966). Drafts of the book were typed by Mrs. Barbara H. Solakian, the final version was typed by Miss Judith A. Ryerson and proofread by Miss Claudia S. Crispin, and Miss Betsy Top of the Warren Center expedited the preparation of the manuscript.

My work in England was made possible and pleasurable by W. D. Coates, National Register of Archives; William L. Gaines and Derek V. Lawford, Fulbright Commission in the United Kingdom; Gerald S. Graham, King's College, University of London;

Preface

and the late Sir Lewis Namier. Closer to home, I have been aided by the friendly criticism of Thomas C. Barrow, Richard M. Brown, Richard Buel, Jr., Michael G. Kammen, and Eric L. McKitrick. Bernard Bailyn has been an inspiring teacher, colleague, and friend. My wife, Adria Holmes, helped with the reading and editing of the several drafts of the book. My most sincere thanks go to all of them.

Cambridge, Massachusetts   S.N.K.
May 1967

Contents

Abbreviations

Add. MSS.	Additional Manuscripts, British Museum
Adm.	Admiralty Papers, Public Record Office
ANC	Ancaster Papers, Lincolnshire Archives Committee
B.M.	British Museum, London
Bod.	Bodleian Library, Oxford
C.L.	William L. Clements Library, University of Michigan, Ann Arbor
C.O.	Colonial Office Papers, Public Record Office
C.U.L.	Cambridge University Library, Cambridge, England
F.D.R.	Franklin Delano Roosevelt Library, Hyde Park, New York
H.M.C.	Historical Manuscripts Commission
L.A.C.	Lincolnshire Archives Committee, Lincoln, England
NJHS	New Jersey Historical Society, Newark
NYHS	New-York Historical Society, New York City
NYPL	New York Public Library, New York City
P.C.	Privy Council Papers, Public Record Office
PRO	Public Record Office, London
R.U.L.	Rutgers University Library, New Brunswick, New Jersey
S.A.S.	Sussex Archaeological Society, Lewes, England
S.P. (Dom.)	State Papers (Domestic), Public Records Office
T.	Treasury Papers, Public Record Office
Wm. Salt	William Salt Library, Stafford, England
W.O.	War Office Papers, Public Record Office

PART ONE

Anglo-American Politics
in the Eighteenth Century

I

English Politics and Imperial Administration

ENGLISH POLITICAL LIFE UNDERWENT A RAD-
ical transformation during the half-century following the Glorious
Revolution of 1688–1689, as the confusion of faction and the
ephemeral demands of individual self-interest replaced party organization and questions of policy as the determinants of public affairs.
"In 1706," Sir Lewis Namier observed, "it was 'faithful service to
your country'; in 1760 'service of one's friends.' " [1] The American
colonies came of age during this transitional era and their own polit-

1. Sir Lewis B. Namier, *The Structure of Politics at the Accession of
George III* (2nd ed., London, 1957), p. 18. See also, Lucy S. Sutherland, *The
East India Company in Eighteenth-Century Politics* (London, 1952), pp. 51–52.

ical systems responded directly to the peculiarities of English politics under the first two Hanoverians.

I

Seventeenth-century English political conflict had been oriented along constitutional lines, as advocates of the common law, parliamentary independence, and religious toleration opposed supporters of a strong prerogative and the established church. These divisions, so apparent in the civil war at mid-century, were institutionalized in the Whig and Tory parties following the restoration of Stuart rule in 1660. Theoretically, Tories proclaimed the divine right of the monarchy and the supremacy of the established church, while Whigs stood for the toleration of protestant dissenters and a constitutionally limited monarchy. Party lines were not always clear and party ideology was primitive, but the existence of a disagreement on principles was generally accepted.

The Whig constitutional victory, confirmed by the Glorious Revolution, radically changed the relationship of the two parties. After 1689, the Tories could never completely cleanse themselves from the stigma of Jacobitism. Toryism managed to survive as a personal tradition and it experienced a powerful if short-lived resurgence under Queen Anne, but after 1714 it ceased to constitute a viable basis for political action.[2] A constantly shifting group of men, including died-in-the-wool Jacobite reactionaries, independent country gentlemen, and many of the London radicals, continued to call themselves Tories, but they shared neither common principles, party organization, nor national leadership and by the 1720's they no longer constituted an effective political force.[3] Sir Robert Wal-

2. Sir Roger Newdigate, described by John Brooke as the Tory archtype in this period, was "Devoted to the interests of the Church of England, zealous in defense of its privileges and prerogatives; a constant opposer of what he called 'Hanoverian measures,' by which he meant continental wars and foreign subsidies; an opponent of standing armies, government influence over the House of Commons, and Whig measures in general." Sir Lewis B. Namier and John Brooke, *The History of Parliament: The House of Commons, 1754–1790* (London, 1964), I, 187.

3. Sir Lewis B. Namier, *England in the Age of the American Revolution* (London, 1930), pp. 220, 230–231.

pole's advice to Henry Pelham in 1743 was that "what is reasonable and practicable, can only be obtained by the Whigs, and can never be hoped for by any assistance from the Tories."[4]

The withering away of the Tories and the subsidence of constitutional differences did not put an end to political controversy in England, however. Quite the contrary. It merely meant that mid-eighteenth-century political activity was conducted within the amorphous group of Whigs, and pitted Whig against Whig. The character of politics did change, however, for the revolutionary settlement of 1689 eliminated the need (or, perhaps, the opportunity) to challenge the political system itself. The constitutional problem seemed resolved, and for a time, therefore, politics became an end in itself. Men sought public office solely for the power and profit which placeholding conferred. As a result, the victorious Whigs, held together by little more than a general commitment to personal self-interest, created a political atmosphere exactly the reverse of that espoused by the greatest Whig of all, the elder William Pitt: "not men but measures."[5]

Thus, during the Whig ascendancy pursuit of office became a passion. Political power was measured in terms of patronage, and the dispensation of places was guided by a desire to curry political support or to provide for familial and political dependents. As a result, the jobs themselves became commodities. They were esteemed for their monetary value or their currency as favors and their public functions were slighted,[6] as is apparent in an undiscriminating re-

4. Lord Orford to Henry Pelham, October 20, 1743, in E. Neville Williams, *The Eighteenth-Century Constitution, 1688–1815* (Cambridge, Eng., 1960), p. 80.

5. G. H. Guttridge, *The Colonial Policy of William III in America and the West Indies* (Cambridge, Eng., 1922), p. 9. John Brooke's description of the 1754 general election may be taken as typical of politics after the death of Anne: It "was not a contest between Government and Opposition, nor was it a device for testing public opinion on political issues . . . Its outcome was the resultant of a number of local forces, personal rivalries, struggles for local consequence and importance." Namier and Brooke, *History of Parliament,* I, 62. Brooke additionally argues that we must not overestimate the importance of parliamentary patronage, and suggests that "Members were given office because they voted with Government, not that they voted with Government in order to obtain office." *Ibid.,* I, 125–126.

6. This mercenary tone is neatly caught in an observation of the mother

5

quest from one of Walpole's Herefordshire supporters for a commissionership "at the Board of Treasury, Admiralty or of Trade, as there is no man will more sincerely and heartily use his utmost endeavours to serve you." [7] A contemporary moralist pointed out, however, that there were more job-seekers than government jobs, with the result that "unsatisfied Demands, and disappointed Avarice" stimulated "the spirit of selfish Faction" in public life.[8]

The decay of traditional party organization and the increasing importance of patronage during the period of Whig supremacy shattered the seventeenth-century structure of parliamentary power. The putative Whig-Tory opposition gave way to an unclassifiable and seemingly irrational profusion of conflicting factions. The ministry was composed of an alliance of permanent royal office-holders and steady followers of the king with a group of politicians. The "opposition," insofar as one existed early in the century, drew upon other politicians and those who refused to take part in administration. Namier calls them the "ins" and the "outs." The outs included some old-style Tories, but their strength was founded upon the many country gentlemen who refused to ally themselves with any particular political faction. Finally, there was a vaguely-defined third force in parliament that consisted of politicians and political factions, out of power, contending among themselves for the opportunity to join the administration.[9] These factions, with whom the political history of the period has traditionally concerned itself, seldom embraced consistent attitudes toward public policy. They were based upon individual and family alliances and aimed primarily at

---

of a New York governor: "This is Sir Cecil's lucky year. His mother has died, by whom he has got £2,000 a year; he has also a place of £500 a year in the Ordnance; his son is page to the Prince of Wales; and his daughter to be soon so well married." Mrs. Osborn to Danvers Osborn, May 28, 1751, in John McClelland, ed., *Letters of Sarah Byng Osborn, 1721–1773* (Stanford, Calif., 1930), p. 75.

7. Sir Archer Croft to Sir Robert Walpole, July 29, 1727, quoted in J. H. Plumb, *Sir Robert Walpole* (London, 1956–1960), II, 174.

8. Rev. John Brown, *Estimate of the Manners and Principles of the Times* (7th ed., 1758), I, 107, quoted in Williams, *Eighteenth-Century Constitution*, p. 140.

9. Sir Lewis Namier, "Ford Lectures of 1934," *Crossroads of Power: Essays on Eighteenth Century England* (New York, 1963), pp. 219, 226.

placing themselves in office by becoming the king's ministers. As a contemporary newspaper essayist remarked, political conflict was not between the ministry and the people but rather among those in power (by which he meant men in politics), and in the end, "the Strife is, *Who shall be the greatest.*" [10]

The peculiar character of parliamentary activity lent to the English political scene a kaleidoscopic aspect: factions arose, merged, altered, and disappeared, and ministries were similarly affected. Individuals made alliances, transferred their allegiances, entered ministries, and left them. Since the prizes of politics were jobs and profits, the road to public success was by way of influence. Personal favor held the lesser men, particularly, to their alliances, so that when a faction had access to the ministry it was obliged to reward its own. Thus the distribution of places was made within a context of connections—those personal relationships that constituted the fabric of factional politics. David Hume put the matter neatly in advising a politically-inclined young Scotsman when he asked, "whom does the affair now depend on? . . . who does he belong to? If I knew his connections, I might probably be able by some means to facilitate your application." [11]

That such a chaotic, individualistic, and mercenary system could have provided for the administration of an empire evoked a certain amount of disbelief even among contemporaries. A prominent New Yorker, angered by his treatment in London, concluded: "that state or Kingdom must be Very ill-governed, whose officers are chose because they are relations to this or that great man or because they are able to give a large sum of money for their imployment, where a meritorious man has no Chance if he has not a good friend." [12] By the standards of the eighteenth century, however, England and the empire were not ill-governed because in fact political life was dom-

---

10. *New York Gazette*, no. 489, March 3–11, 1735.

11. David Hume to James Oswald, April 3, 1763, in [James Oswald,] *Memorials of the Public Life and Character of James Oswald of Dunnikier* (Edinburgh, 1825), pp. 79–80.

12. Beverly McAnear, ed., "R. H. Morris: An American in London, 1735–1736," *Pennsylvania Magazine of History and Biography*, LXIV (1940), p. 366.

7

inated by the great Whig magnates: the Pelhams, Grenvilles, Cavendishes, and the like. These families were not dependent upon politics for a livelihood, as many of their followers were, since they lived off the income from their landed estates. Their aristocratic pride in country was sufficient to commit them to the nation in such a way that "influence, interest and connection did not prove incompatible with ordered government." [13]

The independent power of the crown was another guarantee of stability and continuity during this period. Respect for the king and his power in parliament combined with the considerable royal prerogatives in administration and patronage to make the executive a true counterpoise to the legislature. The king's ministers were dependent upon his favor and therefore responsive to his commands in a way that distinguishes the parliamentary government of the early Hanoverians from the cabinet system as it developed in the early nineteenth century. Hume, for instance, believed that for this reason the crown prevented parliament from acting irresponsibly: "The interest of the body is here restrained by that of the individuals . . . The Crown has so many offices at its disposal, that, when assisted by the honest and disinterested part of the House, it will always command the revolutions of the whole so far, at least, as to preserve the antient constitution from danger." [14] Robert Harley argued, similarly, that no party in parliament could "carry it for themselves without the Queen's servants join with them," for "the Foundation is, persons or parties are to come in to the Queen, and not the Queen to them." [15] The nucleus of royal power in parliament consisted of permanent officeholders in the court party, generally supported by the independent country gentlemen.

The influence and prestige of the crown shaped the conduct of parliamentary affairs for, although the competence of the legislature was continually expanding, it was as yet impossible for a parlia-

13. H. J. Habakkuk, "England," in A. Goodwin, ed., *The European Nobility in the Eighteenth Century* (London, 1953), p. 15.
14. Quoted in Namier, "Ford Lectures of 1934," *Crossroads*, p. 219.
15. Quoted in Williams, *Eighteenth-Century Constitution*, p. 174.

mentary opposition to capture the ministry and pursue a policy contrary to the royal will. From time to time the king was forced to call upon ministers whom he did not like (such as George Grenville) or in whom he had little faith (such as the Marquis of Rockingham), but in the first half of the century at any rate, no administration could be formed which did not command the king's confidence. There was in fact no opposition in the modern sense of a dissenting legislative party which continually offers alternatives to policies proposed by the party in control of the government. It was of course occasionally possible for opposition factions to force the dismissal of a ministry, but since such a procedure was not yet recognized as legitimate the opposition had to justify its behavior by alleging a threat to the safety of the nation. "Opposition," proclaimed a speaker of the house of commons, was "only justifiable where the constitution is really in danger from the settled plan of an administration." [16] Even so, changes in government did not in fact come about because the electorate was convinced that national disaster was imminent, but rather because the administration majority had been undermined politically.[17]

English politics in the age of Walpole and Pelham had thus come a long way from its origins in the immediate Stuart past. The constitutional conflicts of the seventeenth century had given way to the bewildering complexity of individual competition for governmental office. Questions of patronage were public issues, and matters of more elevated concern, when they were discussed at all, were regarded skeptically by an experienced public. Such was the political system within which the British empire was governed in the eighteenth century, and, as we shall see, it was also the system with which the principal American politicians had to cope in their quest for colonial political power.

16. Arthur Onslow, in Historical Manuscripts Commission, *Fourteenth Report, Appendix, Part IX, Onslow Manuscripts* (London, 1895), p. 458.
17. Sir Lewis B. Namier, "King George III: A Study of Personality," *Personalities and Powers* (London, 1955), p. 42. For the definitive study on the subject of the development of political opposition in England, see Archibald Foord, *His Majesty's Opposition, 1714–1830* (Oxford, 1964).

II

The administration of the American colonies prior to the Seven Years' War played a very minor part in English government. In the constitutional scheme the colonies came directly under the authority of the crown,[18] since they had been settled on the basis of royal grants, but little in the way of imperial theory had been developed. Everyone supposed that the purpose of supporting colonies was to benefit the mother country in accordance with the vague precepts of mercantilist economic theory. Parliament defined the legal structure of mercantilism in the navigation acts, but the actual enforcement of the navigation system was left to royal administrative officers. Thus management of the empire lay outside the arena of parliamentary conflict, and colonial policy was not a subject of political controversy.[19]

Indeed, the most striking feature of imperial administration in the first half of the eighteenth century was the general absence of rational supervision. The old adage that the colonies were ruled by "salutary neglect" still seems apt. Imperial officials did not challenge the voluntary character of colonial participation in the imperial economic system, they were distracted by their concern for continental and military affairs, and they were not necessarily very interested in their duties. Colonial bureaucrats, after all, sought their jobs in the same spirit that other officials did, and they too were caught up in the self-interested temper of English politics. Significantly, Sir Robert Walpole's motto was "let sleeping dogs be."

The colonial administrative structure reflected this pragmatic and offhand approach to colonial affairs. The king and his privy

18. For a New Yorker's recognition of this fact, see Archibald Kennedy, *An Essay on the Government of the Colonies* (New York, 1752), pp. 15–16.
19. A. B. Keith has argued that parliament played a somewhat more decisive role in setting colonial policy earlier in the century. Arthur Berriedale Keith, *The Constitutional History of the First British Empire* (Oxford, 1930), p. 133. The contrary view is best argued by Dora Mae Clark, *The Rise of the British Treasury: Colonial Administration in the Eighteenth Century* (New Haven, 1960), passim but especially pp. 4–5, 143–145, 198.

council, for instance, who were the presumptive caretakers of colonial sovereignty, were too caught up in domestic and continental affairs to play a creative role in colonial government. They heard appeals from the colonies, passed on legislation, and called for reports on colonial questions, but in virtually all instances they followed the advice of a few officials lower in the imperial administrative hierarchy. The leading member of the ministry, whether he was Walpole, Pelham, or Newcastle, interested himself in the colonies only in so far as they influenced the conduct of foreign policy, especially in wartime.

The principal colonial administrator was the secretary of state for the southern department. His constitutional power was extensive: "Appointments, defense by land and sea, finance as connected therewith, diplomatic issues and relations with the Indians, and generally all political issues were his special care; but nothing was excluded from his sphere, and it rested virtually with him during the greater part of the life of the Board of Trade to decide the nature of its functions." [20] The secretary was supposed to perform, in sum, all of the executive functions that did not pertain to the treasury or admiralty, and he was supposed to be the official intermediary between the American governments and Whitehall. In time of war he sometimes took a leading part in both military and naval operations in America, thus adding military patronage and disposition of lucrative supply contracts to his already extensive powers.[21] In peacetime, however, the dispensation of jobs proved to be the dominating administrative interest of the secretary.

Like so many other offices, the secretaryship of state slowly evolved from an ill-defined medieval post in the royal household to fit the requirements of a modern state, and the most fundamental factor in its emergence was the character of successive secretaries. Certainly the restricted range of colonial administration in the early eighteenth century was set more by a single man than by the office itself, since for over twenty years the southern secretary was

20. Keith, *First British Empire*, p. 271.
21. Mark A. Thomson, *The Secretaries of State, 1681–1782* (Oxford, 1932), pp. 45, 88.

11

Thomas Pelham-Holles, Duke of Newcastle. The Duke, who inherited his title and vast estate from a maternal uncle, was the richest and most avidly political of the great Whig nobles of the day. He held most of the great offices (southern secretary, 1724–1748, northern secretary, 1748–1754, first lord of the treasury, 1754–1756) and devoted himself singlemindedly to the causes of traditional Whiggery. He reportedly came away from public life £400,-000 poorer for his trouble.[22]

Newcastle was a kind if slow-witted man, who was endowed with an indefatigable industry for the minutiae of public administration. "Newcastle made in politics disconnected detail his chosen province; patronage and the House of Commons, the doling out of financial advantages to importunate beggars and the engineering of elections, engrossed his thinking, which he seldom allowed to rise to the level of a political idea. Even into foreign politics he managed to infuse his habits or obsessions."[23] Shelburne accused the Duke of having the mentality of a *commis*, and it is clear that he generally mistook the details of administration for questions of policy. He was furiously busy, incredibly forgetful, and habitually tardy in his affairs. He had two aims in public life and stuck doggedly to them: support of the policies of the crown and provision for the welfare of his connection (in Pitt's words, "the disposal of employments and the confidence of the King"). Even Chesterfield, defending Newcastle against his detractors, could say no more than, "though he had no superior parts, or eminent talents, he had a most indefatigable industry, a perseverance, a court craft, and a servile compliance with the will of his sovereign for the time being."[24] Such was the man to whom the colonies were entrusted for over two decades.

As southern secretary, Newcastle had no conception of colonial policy. He viewed administration as a branch of politics, a reservoir of jobs to be distributed among parliamentary supporters of the ministry, and he selected colonial officeholders in accordance with the necessities of the English political situation. The patronage sys-

22. Namier, *England in the Age of the American Revolution*, pp. 76–78.
23. *Ibid.*, p. 82.
24. *Ibid.*, pp. 77, 74, 76; Namier, *Structure*, p. 362. It ought to be added, however, that European concerns were predominant in Newcastle's mind, and he was sophisticated in his approach to continental policy.

tem was not corrupt by contemporary standards, but the neglect of qualifications that accompanied the system had different results in America than it did at home. The effect, as Philip Haffenden has pointed out, was that "the ruling factor influencing the secretary's behavior was the strength of demands made upon him by others, rather than clear-cut objectives of his own." [25] The secretary of state, as personified by Newcastle, was therefore no more prepared to define and enforce a coherent policy for the burgeoning American empire than the crown in council.

Similarly the board of trade was an ineffective agency of colonial government because it was politically and constitutionally limited to a passive role. The board was created by William III who conceived of it as an information-gathering body that would at the same time strengthen the competence of the crown for colonial administration and prevent parliament from interfering with the royal prerogative in this sphere.[26] Accordingly, the board was given little in the way of executive responsibility, and even after the 1752 reforms won by Halifax its powers were not significantly increased.[27] The board's sole competence to act was appointive; it had a legal right to nominate governors, lieutenant governors, councillors, and colonial secretaries to the privy council, but in fact it exercised this right only in regard to councillors, forfeiting the valuable colonial patronage to the southern secretary.[28] Otherwise, the board of trade's *raison d'être* was to provide intelligence of the col-

25. Philip Haffenden, "Colonial Appointments and Patronage under the Duke of Newcastle, 1724–1739," *English Historical Review*, LXXVIII (1963), p. 428. In this passage Haffenden is concerned to defend Newcastle's dispensation of patronage. He argues that Newcastle was not unduly influenced by political pressure in making colonial appointments, and attempts to demonstrate that his gubernatorial appointees were in fact well qualified. On this point see below, Chap. 2, n. 1.

26. Keith, *First British Empire*, p. 268.

27. Arthur H. Basye, *The Lords Commissioners of Trade and Plantations, Commonly Known as the Board of Trade, 1748–1782* (New Haven, 1925), pp. 50–69. The order in council of March 1752 strengthened the hand of the president of the board of trade vis à vis the southern secretary and it enlarged the appointive powers of the board. It did not, however, give any executive supervisory powers to the board.

28. Thomson, *Secretaries of State*, p. 48; Charles M. Andrews, *The Colonial Period of American History* (New Haven, 1934–1938), IV, 311–312.

onies and of imperial trade. Accordingly, it drew up reports on colonial problems, investigated colonial disputes, and formulated commissions and instructions for colonial officers. It carried on correspondence with colonial officials (although in this connection the secretary took precedence, and officials frequently chose to communicate solely with him) and maintained close contacts in England with agents of American colonies, British merchants and planters interested in colonial ventures, and visiting colonials. The board thus had the means of formulating knowledgeable colonial policies, but since it had been delegated neither the responsibility for framing policy nor the powers of implementation, and since it faced the overwhelming competition of the secretary of state, this potential was never developed.[29]

The board of trade nevertheless played a part in colonial administration, and, carrying out its constitutional mandate, it consistently devoted itself to pursuing the goal for which it had been created in 1696: the promotion of a mercantile empire. As Charles Andrews has emphasized, the board "was primarily appointed for the consideration of trade and not for the administration of the colonies." [30] It was in close touch with the commercial interests of Great Britain, often requesting advice and information from British merchants,[31] and it steadfastly supported the traditional viewpoint that colonies existed to perform the double function of producing staple crops and consuming manufactured goods. This economic perspective

29. Beyond the fact of the secretary of state's power was the additional limitation that it was constitutionally impossible for the board to communicate with the king in council except through the secretary. Thomson, *Secretaries of State*, p. 47. Thomson correctly points out that it is unfair to criticize the secretary for usurping the board's powers. Rather, the secretary's patronage powers and the exigencies of war seriously circumscribed the board's ability to play a creative role.

30. Andrews, *Colonial Period*, IV, 300.

31. Namier, *England in the Age of the American Revolution*, p. 291; Elmer B. Russell, *The Review of American Colonial Legislation by the King in Council* (New York, 1915), pp. 75–76. See also, Michael G. Kammen, "The Colonial Agents, English Politics and the American Revolution" (unpub. Ph.D. diss., Harvard, 1964), to be published by the Cornell University Press as *Rope of Sand;* Jack M. Sosin, *Agents and Merchants: British Colonial Policy and the Origins of the American Revolution* (Lincoln, Neb., 1965).

determined the board's attitude toward the political problems of colonial administration and was, for instance, the reason behind its insistence upon the creation of royal governments in America. Colonies which were directly responsive to the demands of the king in council could be supervised and disciplined more easily.

The board's preoccupation with trade led it to a very precise notion of the "proper position that a colony should occupy in the English colonial world." "It had to see that royal orders were carried out, not so much for the sake of keeping colonial administration in the right path as for seeing that the colonies were doing what England expected them to do." [32] Thus the board adopted a negative, regulatory approach to colonial administration and hesitated to recommend intervention in the domestic affairs of the colonies. This approach was, in effect, the theoretical justification for a policy of "neglect." The weakness of mercantilist domination of colonial thinking became manifest as the century passed its mid-point, however. Americans felt that their interests had been "sacrificed on the altar of England's moneyed prosperity," [33] while Englishmen realized that their indifference to the details of colonial government in America had permitted the development of small pockets of power that no longer responded to the demands of parliament and the crown.

The selection of personnel was another factor which, as much as its mercantilist viewpoint, prevented the board of trade from developing into a more sensitive institution of colonial administration. William Blathwayt once discouraged a clerk at the board of trade from aspiring to membership on the grounds that he had "neither age, knowledge, nor interest, three of the requisites for a successful commissioner of trade." [34] An examination of the board membership from the appointment of Westmoreland in 1719 to the accession of George III, however, would seem to rule out any significant alternative to interest as a criterion for selection. Charles Town-

32. Andrews, *Colonial Period*, IV, 315.
33. *Ibid.*, IV, 295.
34. Gertrude A. Jacobsen, *William Blathwayt: A Late Seventeenth Century English Administrator* (New Haven, 1932), pp. 301–302.

shend and Thomas Pelham, Jr., for instance, solicited Newcastle directly: Townshend's father asked the Duke for "some place of business" for his difficult son, and Pelham pleaded with his uncle for a post "that I may be able to go on." [35] Sir Archer Croft was a constant supplicant of Walpole's favor who adduced his reliability in parliament as a sufficient qualification for appointment to office.[36] Likewise, Sir Orlando Bridgeman probably owed his appointment to his Leicester House connection, Sir John Hobart to the fact that his sister was mistress to the Prince of Wales, James Brudenell to his brother, the Earl of Cardigan, and the Duke of Richmond, Sir Charles Gilmour to Carteret, James Grenville to Pitt, James Oswald to Halifax, and Richard Rigby to Bedford.[37] Edward Ashe, Sir Thomas Frankland, Sir Richard Edgcumbe, and Edward Elliot were all rewarded with places at the board of trade because of their control of several parliamentary seats.[38] Even Tories were appointed to the board when their parliamentary support was needed by the administration. Sir John Phillips, John Pitt, and Baptist Leveson Gower were all brought in during the organization of the Broad-Bottom administration in December 1744.[39] Others, like Sir Benjamin Keene, Lord Dupplin, Francis Fane (the long-time counsellor to the board of trade), and Sir Thomas Robinson received their places in reward for the considerable services they had rendered to the ministry.[40] Thus the board of trade, like those of admiralty,

35. Namier and Brooke, *History of Parliament*, III, 540, 258.

36. Plumb, *Walpole*, II, 172–174.

37. Sir John Bernard Burke et al., eds., *Genealogical and Heraldic History of the Extinct and Dormant Baronetcies of England, Ireland, and Scotland* (London, 1841), p. 82; [George Edward Cokayne, ed.,] *The Complete Peerage of England Scotland Ireland Great Britain and the United Kingdom Extant Extinct or Dormant by G.E.C.*, ed. Vicary Gibbs et al. (new ed., London, 1910–1959), II, 401; John B. Owen, *The Rise of the Pelhams* (London, 1957), pp. 49n2, 245; Namier and Brooke, *History of Parliament*, II, 546, III, 237–240, III, 354–360.

38. Owen, *Pelhams*, p. 49; Namier and Brooke, *History of Parliament*, I, 53, II, 379–380, 386–390.

39. Owen, *Pelhams*, pp. 72, 215, 66n1. Both Pitt and Gower gradually came to be regarded as Whigs during their tenures in office. *Ibid.*, p. 258.

40. Sir Leslie Stephen and Sir Sidney Lee, eds., *The Dictionary of National Biography* (London, 1885–1901), X, 1189–1190 (hereafter, *DNB*); Namier and Brooke, *History of Parliament*, II, 600–601, II, 412; *DNB*, XVII, 47–49.

treasury, and the lesser organizations, was the creature of successive Whig administrations and was considered a refuge for needy politicians rather than a professional department requiring proved competence of its members. As a result, board members were placemen who considered colonial questions to be problems of English politics rather than of imperial policy.[41]

Although places at the board were openly considered political plums, they were not the most desirable ones, for the board of trade ranked third to treasury and admiralty among the large executive boards.[42] Eight members of the board of trade were promoted to the higher boards: four to the admiralty and four (including Charles Townshend, who served on both) to the most desirable, the treasury.[43] No board of trade member had previously served on the admiralty or treasury, and thus colonial problems were generally attended to by men of lower political standing and less high-level administrative experience than were naval and treasury affairs. Other board of trade members resigned in favor of more lucrative posts: Walter Carey and William Gerard Hamilton for the secretaryship to the lord lieutenant of Ireland, Robert Sawyer Herbert to the surveyorship of crown lands, Benjamin Keene to the paymastership of pensions, Sir Thomas Robinson to the mastership of the great wardrobe, Andrew Stone to the treasurership of Queen Charlotte, and James Grenville to the joint-vice-treasurership of Ireland.[44] Indeed, Grenville chose the latter post in preference to the presidency of the board of trade.[45] Occasionally, places at the board of trade were treated with no more respect than pawns, to be traded for the

41. For an early, although exaggerated, view of the political character of the board of trade, see Keith, *First British Empire*, pp. 274–276.

42. Namier and Brooke, *History of Parliament*, III, 541, 237; Oswald, *Memorials*, p. 341.

43. Richard Edgcumbe (1755), Sir Thomas Frankland (1730–1741), Thomas Pelham, Jr. (1761–1763), John Pitt (1756), and Charles Townshend (1754) served on the admiralty board. Thomas Hay (1754–1755), James Grenville (1756–1761), James Oswald (1759–1762), and Charles Townshend (1766, 1770–1774) served at the treasury.

44. Namier and Brooke, *History of Parliament*, II, 193, III, 356, II, 614; Owen, *Pelhams*, p. 245; Namier and Brooke, *History of Parliament*, III, 366–367, III, 484, II, 546.

45. *Ibid.*, II, 546. This occurred in July 1766 when Pitt offered Grenville his choice of the two administrative boards or the pay office.

slightest advantage. Francis Fane, for instance, resigned his place in 1756 to make way for William Gerard Hamilton, whose patron, Henry Fox, had been promised the post when he joined the ministry. In the same complicated strategem, Fox's follower William Sloper was added to the board of trade, resigning his parliamentary seat to Charles Townshend, whom the administration was anxious to accommodate.[46]

This expedient and mercenary attitude toward appointments accounts at least partially for the steadfastly Anglo-centric, frequently negligent, and generally inconsistent quality of English imperial administration. It is also true, however, that the board of trade was very like the other branches of English government in an age when efficiency was seldom a criterion for the conduct of public business.[47] By contemporary standards, in fact, the board of trade had a great deal to recommend it. During the era of the Whig supremacy all the members of the board were at the same time members of parliament, and therefore well rehearsed in the problems of politics, finance, and foreign affairs that occupied the legislature.[48] Many board members had previously held other public offices and were experienced in the conduct of affairs. Moreover, the fact that most of them secured their offices as tokens of ministerial favor should not be interpreted to mean that they were necessarily unqualified or uninterested officials. On the contrary, many members who had little to recommend them as colonial administrators prior to their appointment served long and well in the employ of the board. For the thirty-four members who served between 1720 and 1765, the average length of service was slightly over ten years and the median slightly under ten.[49] Five men (Paul Doc-

46. Namier and Brooke, *History of Parliament*, III, 444–445. Sloper later wanted to exchange his board of trade post for the sinecure of deputy paymaster at Gibraltar, a position he subsequently obtained. *Ibid.*

47. For example, see Piers Mackesy's extensive argument that the British lost the revolutionary war mainly because of the inefficiency inherent in their governmental system. *The War for America, 1775–1783* (Cambridge, Mass., 1964).

48. A partial exception is the previously mentioned arrangement by which William Sloper traded his parliamentary seat for a place at the board.

49. For a list of board of trade members, see Appendix A.

minique, Thomas Pelham, Sr., Martin Bladen, Edward Ashe, and Soame Jenyns) sat at the board of trade more than twenty years and four (Westmoreland, Richard Plumer, Sir Orlando Bridgeman, and James Brudenell) remained fifteen or more. With some exceptions, the meetings of the board were fairly well attended, although it was also generally true that a few diligent and influential members handled the bulk of the business.[50]

Finally, it should be pointed out that although board of trade appointments were treated primarily as matters of political patronage, for nearly a half-century the board itself was not greatly affected by changes of administration. The period of Newcastle's long southern secretaryship and Walpole's tranquil ministry insulated government departments from political raiding. During these years (and, to a certain extent, throughout the period before 1760) board of trade members were not held strictly accountable for their ministerial loyalty in parliament. "Practice was extremely lax and a good deal of latitude was allowed to Members, which accorded with contemporary political theory, that an M.P. ought to give his vote independent of Crown or party." [51] With Walpole's fall from power in 1742, however, political factionalism and ministerial instability forced the increased exploitation of government departments in political maneuvering. Hence the flurry of new appointments, transfers of place, and dismissals at the formation of the Broad-Bottom in December 1744 and after Pelham's death in 1754. In 1746, when Pelham and Newcastle were attempting to force Bath and Grenville out of their positions of influence with George II, junior members of all three boards authorized their superiors to inform the king of their willingness to quit office.[52] This active involvement of the board of trade in national politics undoubtedly diverted energy and attention from colonial affairs, but the fact remains that at no time did the board as a whole resign, nor was there ever a turnover of more than three members in any one year. This stability, plus the longevity of the permanent staff, ensured a continuity which might

50. Andrews, *Colonial Period*, IV, 306.
51. Namier and Brooke, *History of Parliament*, I, 119.
52. Owen, *Pelhams*, p. 295.

have blossomed into a maturing and competent administration of the empire, despite the character of recruitment to the board of trade, if it had been endowed with executive power. In the end the board failed both because of the weakness of its conception and the nature of its personnel.

On the whole, the Hanoverians governed their empire in an offhand manner, reacting pragmatically to colonial questions as they arose, and generally failing to create special institutions or policies for colonial government.[53] Therefore the character of individuals and the quality of specific decisions determined the nature of imperial control. Furthermore, American posts and American problems were dealt with in the context of English political life, a fact that colored every aspect of colonial public affairs in the first half of the eighteenth century.

53. For the pragmatic, Anglo-centric character of English policy formulation in the pre-revolutionary period, see Jack M. Sosin, *Whitehall and the Wilderness: The Middle West in British Colonial Policy, 1760–1775* (Lincoln, Neb., 1961), pp. 52–78.

2

The Royal Governors
of New York

HIS NOMINATIONS TO AMERICAN GOVERNOR-
ships, Lord Halifax assured the Duke of Newcastle when he took
charge of the board of trade, would be "founded on no other mo-
tive than the good of His Majesty's service, and a Desire of doing
what may be agreable to you." [1] In putting the northern secretary's

1. For an interpretation of imperial administration quite the opposite of
that presented here, see Philip Haffenden, "Colonial Appointments and Patronage under the Duke of Newcastle, 1724–1739," *English Historical Review,*
LXXVIII (1963), pp. 417–435. Haffenden stresses the experience and fitness of
the governors appointed by Newcastle, as well as the qualifications of inferior
imperial officers. He denies that British politics had much to do with such appointments, and argues that even the poorest choice for an American post

pleasure on an equal footing with the public good, Halifax acknowledged that in the staffing of English government, a man's acquaintances were as important as his ability to perform his office. New Yorkers, in particular, were aware of the fact that the way to appointment as a royal governor lay through the favor of the king and his principal officers.

The process was exemplified in the fall of 1727 when John Montgomerie was selected to supplant William Burnet as New York's governor. The change appears in some respects to be for the worse.[2] Burnet was an intelligent, vigorous executive who had championed the interests of the empire against the selfish schemes of the New York fur traders. Montgomerie, a Scottish soldier and member of parliament who had once been a Leicester House groom of the bedchamber for George II, was a man of few convictions who unhesitatingly abandoned Burnet's contest with the local fur interests in favor of an alliance with their political leaders, the Philipse and DeLancey families, which afforded him a quiet administration.[3]

(William Cosby) "was possessed of qualities which were long considered fundamental in a good colonial governor. In due course, when he fell below the requirements expected of him, he was suspended" (p. 424). Cosby was in fact never suspended, and "the requirements expected of him" were anything but consistent and clear. Haffenden has based his research upon the highly formalized records of the board of trade and the privy council in the preparation of this article, thus slighting the interaction of administrative routine and practical politics. The issue is not, however, whether Newcastle was stupid or corrupt—it is what effect the patronage system had upon the conduct of imperial administration.

For a list of English politicians Haffenden considers interested in colonial appointments, see *ibid.*, p. 131. For the study of colonial governors generally, see Leonard Labaree, "The Early Careers of the Royal Governors," *Essays in Colonial History Presented to Charles McLean Andrews by His Students* (New Haven, 1931), pp. 145–168; Louise B. Dunbar, "The Royal Governors in the Middle and Southern Colonies on the Eve of the Revolution: A Study in Imperial Personnel," in Richard B. Morris, ed., *Era of the American Revolution* (New York, 1939), pp. 214–268.

2. See William Smith, *The History of the Province of New-York* . . . (New-York Historical Society, *Collections*, 1st ser., IV–V [1826]), I, 240. (Hereafter, NYHS, *Colls.*)

3. See the drafts of various letters by James Alexander, 1728–1731, in the Rutherfurd Collection, I, New-York Historical Society, New York, N.Y.,

The Royal Governors of New York

Burnet resented his transfer to Massachusetts Bay, believing the governments of New York and New Jersey (linked until 1738) more profitable than that of the Bible Commonwealth, and Thomas Burnet later protested to Newcastle that his brother's removal from New York was due to the "spleen" of well-placed enemies. Thomas Hutchinson came nearer the truth in suggesting that Montgomerie was selected on account of the "particular esteem" in which he was held by George II. In fact, the governorship of New York was Montgomerie's reward for his loyalty to the then Prince of Wales during a 1716 quarrel with his father. In 1727, according to Cadwallader Colden, the newly enthroned George II "thought it proper to recompense those servants more particularly who had suffered by adhering to him. For these reasons Coll. Mont. had his choice of several offices both at home and abroad. He made choice of the Government of New York as the most lucrative and attended with the least trouble." [4] Royal intervention in the selection of a colonial governor was unusual, but the personal character of Montgomerie's appointment was in keeping with the ordinary procedure.

Four New York governors were chosen in the quarter century following 1727, each of them a client of the incumbent southern secretary or president of the board of trade. Colonel William Cosby, Montgomerie's successor, was a Newcastle appointee. His connection to the Duke was marital—his wife, Grace Montague, was Newcastle's first cousin and the sister of the first Earl of Halifax —and he flaunted his influence in New York, boasting the protec-

especially I, 77. See also Cadwallader Colden's undated essay (post–1728), Rutherfurd Collection, I, 63.

4. Cadwallader Colden, "Letters on Smith's History of New York, [1759]," NYHS, *Colls.*, 1868, p. 217; David Nichol Smith, ed., *The Letters of Thomas Burnet to George Duckett, 1712–1722* (Oxford, 1914), pp. 199–200; Thomas Hutchinson, *The History of the Colony and Province of Massachusetts-Bay*, ed. Lawrence Shaw Mayo (Cambridge, Mass., 1936), II, 246. It is worth noting that Burnet, having lost heavily in the South Sea calamity of 1720, gave up his post in the customs service in favor of the governorship of New York, "with a view to his retrieving his fortune in a course of years." Hutchinson, *History of Massachusetts-Bay*, II, 247. Haffenden concludes that Townshend was responsible for the Montgomerie appointment ("Colonial Appointments," p. 420), but it would seem more likely that Townshend intervened in behalf of the king.

tion of "the great interest of the Dukes of New Castle, Montague and Lord Halifax." [5] So powerful were Cosby's connections that he, like Montgomerie, was given a choice of colonial governorships. He had already boarded ship and was about to set sail for the government of the Leeward Islands, when he learned of Montgomerie's death and returned to London so that Newcastle might secure for him the more lucrative mainland governorship. Cosby retained his office in New York until he died in 1736, despite his ineptitude and the rumor that "the King personally hates him." [6] According to one of his enemies, Cosby bluntly asserted his confidence in the strength of his patrons in rejecting an accusation that he had violated the law: "how, gentlemen, do you think I mind that: alas! I have a great interest in England." [7] Even after his death, Newcastle and Henry Pelham continued to provide for his widow and family.[8]

John West, seventh Baron De la Warr, was the absentee gover-

5. Cadwallader Colden and James Alexander both considered Cosby's relationship to Halifax to be the reason for his appointment in New York. [Cadwallader Colden,] *History of Gov. William Cosby's Administration and of Lt.-Gov. George Clarke's Administration through 1737*, NYHS, *Colls.*, 1935, p. 283; Alexander to Colden, February 21, 1732, NYHS, *Colls.*, 1918, pp. 49–50. For the genealogical implications of Cosby's marriage, see G.E.C.'s *Complete Peerage*, VI, 245–247; Mark Antony Lower, *Historical and Genealogical Notices of the Pelham Family* (n.p., 1873), pp. 44–54; Robert Walcott, *English Politics in the Early Eighteenth Century* (Oxford, 1956), p. 42. There was at least one connection Cosby did not benefit from, however. His daughter Grace married Lord Augustus Fitzroy, son of the Duke of Grafton. Grafton did not approve of the hasty and secret marriage, and was not reconciled with his daughter-in-law until after Cosby's death. H.M.C., *Manuscripts of the Earl of Egmont: Diary of . . . the Earl of Egmont* (London, 1920–1923), II, 421; see below, Chap. 4, n. 78.

6. Lewis Morris, Jr., to R. H. Morris, July 26, 1735, Morris MSS., Box 2, Rutgers University Library, New Brunswick, N.J.

7. Smith, *History*, II, 26. Haffenden adds Martin Bladen of the board of trade to the list of Cosby's patrons. Haffenden, "Colonial Appointments," p. 422n6, 430.

8. Grace Cosby to Newcastle, December 2, [1737], n.d. [1737?], February 11, 1737, December 27, 1750, Add. MSS. 32992, foll. 187, 185, Add. MSS. 32690, fol. 237, Add. MSS. 32723, fol. 442, British Museum, London. The first two letters are from Mrs. Cosby, and the last three are from her daughter, also named Grace. See also the efforts of Henry Pelham and Lord Sandwich (a Montague) for the Cosby family: Henry Pelham to Robert Walpole, n.d., Cholmondeley-Houghton MSS., Correspondence, no. 3306, Cambridge Uni-

nor of New York from 1737 to 1741, and he was the only peer to hold the New York office during Newcastle's secretaryship. Like Montgomerie a court functionary and former army officer, he owed his appointment to the patronage of Newcastle. De la Warr was a friend of the secretary's confidante, Lord Chancellor Hardwicke, and he served as a political lieutenant for Newcastle in the house of lords, at times taking a leading part for the Walpole ministry. De la Warr openly solicited favors in return for his service, and New York was a token of Newcastle's esteem for him.[9]

Of all the governors during this period, however, Admiral George Clinton, who held the office from 1743 to 1753, was most directly a protégé of Newcastle's. Clinton was the younger brother of the seventh Earl of Lincoln, who married the sister of Newcastle and Henry Pelham.[10] Lincoln died in 1728, but his widow kept Clinton's claims to preferment constantly before her influential brothers, and the story of the admiral's quest for an American post reveals a lot about appointment to colonial office in the mid-eighteenth century.

For several years Lady Lincoln prodded Newcastle to secure Clinton's promotion in the navy, but the Duke was hampered by the formalism of the naval promotion ladder, the limited opportunity for advancement in peacetime, and his relative's lack of aptitude for sea command. Clinton acknowledged the dilemma in a laconic note to Newcastle: "[I] must acknowledge your Grace's favour to me in

versity Library, Cambridge, Eng.; Sandwich to Admiral Anson, September 13, 1748, N.S., Add. MSS. 15957, fol. 82, B.M. A copy of Cosby's will is preserved in the Gage Papers (GA 1305a), Sussex Archaeological Society, Lewes, Eng.

9. Hardwicke to Newcastle, May 23, 1741, Add. MSS. 32697, fol. 55; De la Warr to Newcastle, May 21, 1741, February 3, 1737, January 21, 1738, Add. MSS. 32697, foll. 31, 56, Add. MSS. 32691, fol. 34, B.M.; State Papers (Domestic) 36:45, fol. 40, Public Record Office, London; Namier, *Structure*, p. 48n3.

10. Allen Johnson and Dumas Malone, eds., *The Dictionary of American Biography* (New York, 1928–1944), IV, 225; John Charnock, *Biographia Navalis* . . . (London, 1794–1798), IV, 59–60; Egerton Brydges, ed., *Arthur Collins's Peerage of England* . . . (London, 1812), II, 214–215; L. G. Pine, ed., *Burke's Genealogical and Heraldic History of the Peerage, Baronetage and Knightage* (102nd ed., London, 1959), p. 1663; Clinton to Henry Clinton, December 14, 1752, Clinton MSS., XII, William L. Clements Library, Ann Arbor, Mich.

getting me always the stations I have desired, but I like an unfortunate fellow have always met with some disappointment." [11] By 1739 Clinton was seeking civil employment as the best means of meeting his increasing indebtedness to London merchants. In August 1739 he wrote Newcastle that he had heard reports of his appointment to the governorship of New York, and offered his thanks: "I know very well if such a thing was to have happen'd it must have been by your Grace's favour." [12] The rumor proved false, however, and we can imagine Clinton's chagrin in April 1740 when he wrote his patron "how terrible was I shock'd when your Grace told me you had no such thoughts, I must stick to the sea." [13] He declared his willingness to pursue his naval career, but ten months later once more pleaded for help. His creditor was falling into bankruptcy: "he has been obliged to put me into severall peoples hands, and draws on me every day, nothing but the prospect I have thro' your Graces Kindness to me of New York keeps their hands off." [14] In April 1741 he hysterically reminded Newcastle that only the possibility of the New York appointment stood between him and financial disaster. Within a week, however, he was able to write Newcastle a letter of gratitude for securing him the governorship.[15] Characteristically, the news had reached the future governor before it reached the board of trade.

Sir Danvers Osborn, Clinton's successor, resembled him only in

11. Clinton to Newcastle, September 23, 1739, Add. MSS. 32692, fol. 316, B.M. For examples of Lady Lincoln's intervention on Clinton's behalf, see Add. MSS. 32687, fol. 332; Add. MSS. 33064, foll. 322, 327, 359, 417, 421, 423, 435; Add. MSS. 33065, fol. 8, B.M.; S.P. (Dom.) 36:35, fol. 58; S.P. (Dom.) 36:36, foll. 74, 113, 201, 205, PRO.

12. Clinton to Newcastle, August 28, 1739, Add. MSS. 32692, foll. 260–261, B.M.

13. Clinton to Newcastle, April 30, 1740, Add. MSS. 32693, foll. 245–248, B.M.

14. Clinton to Newcastle, June, 26, 1740, Add. MSS. 32693, fol. 414; Clinton to Newcastle, February 19, 1741, Add. MSS. 32696, fol. 107, B.M.

15. Clinton to Newcastle, April 23 and 29, 1741, Add. MSS. 32696, foll. 353, 420, B.M. The board of trade did not read Secretary of State Newcastle's orders (dated April 30) to draft a commission and instructions for Clinton until May 14. *Journal of the Commissioners of Trade and Plantations, 1735–1741* (London, 1920–1938), pp. 382–383.

that his sole qualification for the post was his relation by marriage to a leading colonial administrator. Osborn was a young Bedfordshire baronet whose only accomplishment at the time of his appointment in 1753 seems to have been his representation of the county in parliament from 1747. He was the descendant of a governor of Guernsey and a distinguished judge, but, like his father, aspired to be no more than a country gentleman. He was brought out into the world, however, by an aggressive, well-connected mother and the interest his own marriage had created for him.

Mrs. Osborn, his mother, was a daughter of the influential admiral, Viscount Torrington, and sister of the ill-fated Admiral George Byng. She was an intelligent, politically-sophisticated woman, well liked at court, who assumed much of the responsibility for the fortunes and careers of her numerous family.[16] Sir Danvers' wife was the daughter of the first Earl of Halifax, whose son became president of the reinvigorated board of trade in 1748. Lady Osborn died in 1743 at the tender age of twenty-three, and her death left the young baronet a psychological cripple. But her brother Halifax remained Osborn's close friend and was responsible for his appointment in New York—or so the provincials thought.[17]

Cosby, De la Warr, Clinton, Osborn. If New York was at all typical of the royal colonies, we may suspect that during this period objective administrative criteria were generally neglected in the selection of governors. All four of them gained their appointments through political interest, three being actually related to English administrators. The road to the governorship lay through the favor

16. [George Edward Cokayne], *Complete Baronetage, edited by G.E.C.* (Exeter, 1900–1906), III, 243–244; Emily F. D. Osborn, ed., *Political and Social Letters of a Lady of the Eighteenth Century, 1721–1771* (New York, 1891), p. 11. On Mrs. Osborn see *DNB*, III, 570; Osborn, *Letters*, p. 8. For some idea of Mrs. Osborn's connections, see John McClelland, ed., *Letters of Sarah Byng Osborn, 1721–1773* (Stanford, Calif., 1930), pp. 37, 43, 57. Her sagacity and foresightedness are illustrated in a letter of 1767 to Sir Danvers' son: "Lord and Lady North dined with me the day before they went out of town. As he would be a great man soon, I began my solicitations before he was so, and put in my claim with regard to you." *Ibid.*, pp. 133–134.

17. G.E.C.'s *Complete Peerage*, VI, 247; Smith, *History*, II, 151; Osborn, *Letters*, p. 11.

of the king and his principal officers, and especially by way of connection to Newcastle, for whom personal friendship or political obligation constituted sufficient grounds for preferment.

I

Why did these four men seek colonial employment? The answer is simple: They hoped to improve their fortunes in America. The historian William Smith tartly observed of De la Warr's motives that "a peer of the realm was only to be induced to accept so humiliating a station by the prospect of a speedy repair of his finances." [18] For Clinton the job was a last-minute expedient to stave off legal action against him for indebtedness, and we shall see that Cosby's finances were also in considerable disrepair. The New York assembly condemned the characteristic avarice of governors in 1749: "as they know the Time of the Continuance in their Governments to be uncertain, all Methods are used, and all Engines set to work to raise Estates to themselves." [19] It is only fair to add that Osborn's motives were more complex, not to say confused, but in general we must agree with the eighteenth-century Virginian who observed that American governorships were distributed as "the last Rewards for past Services," with the result that the governors "expecting nothing after that, were almost necessitated to make Provision for their whole Lives, whereby they were in a manner forced upon such Methods (whether Good or evil) as would compass those Ends." [20] Most contemporary Americans would have accepted this assessment.

Governorships, like most public offices in England, were a form of personal property, a commodity which could be bought and sold, so the cash value of the government of New York may be estimated

18. Smith, *History*, II, 33.
19. Reply to Governor Clinton's message, July 14, 1749, *Journal of the Votes and Proceedings of the General Assembly of the Colony of New-York* [*1691–1765*] (New York, 1764–1766), II, 267. (Hereafter, *Assemb. Jour.*)
20. [Anon.,] *An Essay Upon the Government of the English Plantations on the Continent of America* (1701), ed. Louis B. Wright (San Marino, Calif., 1945), p. 37.

in terms not only of its income, but also of its sale price. Surviving documents offer evidence of two unsuccessful attempts to purchase the government in the 1740's. The first occurred in June 1740 and involved the offer of £1,100 to De la Warr by George Clarke, the lieutenant governor of the colony.[21] The second, in the form of a protracted negotiation between Admiral Peter Warren and the incumbent, Admiral Clinton, took place in 1745 and 1746. Clinton began by asking £5,500 for the job, but gradually came down to the £3,000 which Warren proferred, protesting all the while that Lieutenant Governor Clarke had offered him £500 a year for the governorship even before he had set sail for America to begin his assignment: "but I was lead to believe the Government was a [?] four thousand pounds a year sterling." [22] Whether Clarke or Warren would have received Newcastle's official blessing as governor is unclear—what is certain is that contemporaries thought of the office in terms of its material value.

Estimates of the annual income of the post varied as widely as those of its net worth. In 1736, one New Yorker estimated the annual profits at £10,000, but this unquestionably inflated figure was intended as a lure to a prospective governor.[23] In the 1730's, to be sure, the governor was able to accumulate fees and acreage from his participation in the prerogative to grant lands, and Governor Cosby certainly did so. In succeeding administrations, however, the amount of land available for disposition decreased rapidly, thus rendering the office less lucrative.[24] De la Warr, for instance, com-

21. G. Clarke, Jr., to De la Warr, June 20, 1740, in E. B. O'Callaghan and Berthold Fernow, eds., *Documents Relative to the Colonial History of the State of New York* (Albany, 1856–1887), VI, 163–164. (Hereafter, *New York Col. Docs.*)

22. Clinton to [?], August 27, 1745, incomplete; Clinton's memo, "A scheme how to get home"; Warren to Clinton, August 28, 1745, Clinton MSS., II; Warren to Clinton, June 24, 1746; Warren to Clinton, July 14, 1746; Clinton to Warren, July 1746, Clinton MSS., III, C.L. For a detailed account of the Clinton-Warren negotiation, see below, Chap. 8.

23. R. H. Morris to Lewis Morris, Jr., February 13, 1736, Morris MSS., Box 2, R.U.L.

24. Smith, *History*, I, 304. The ordinary income of the New York governor falls into three categories: salary, fees and gifts, and the income of the New Jersey government. The salary in New York, appropriated by the

plained that he had never profited from the government, and, in May 1741, he urged Newcastle to delay Clinton's appointment until December so that he might collect a perquisite accruing to the governor in November. Else, he protested, he would not even recoup the £600 he had expended in "the passing my Commission for that

assembly in a series of five-year revenue acts from 1703 through 1737, was £1,560 New York currency in lieu of £1,200 sterling. It remained constant until 1770, when Governor John Murray, Earl of Dunmore was instructed to pay himself £2,000 per annum out of the revenues from the tea duty. The increasingly independent assembly insisted upon annual appropriations after 1737, however, and governors were threatened with salaryless years in times of disagreement with the legislature. Leonard W. Labaree, *Royal Government in America* (New Haven, 1958), pp. 337–341. The governor received fees for appointments to office, condemnation of ships and goods which contravened the navigation acts, and several other sources, but the largest single fund derived from his role in granting lands. He received regular fees for approving land grants, generally received supplementary gratuities for his favor, and not infrequently was given a share of the lands themselves. As has been noted above, this form of income began to disappear as the ungranted lands diminished. The governor also received gifts for performing many of the other functions of his office.

The government of New Jersey, which was not separated from New York until 1738, provided an annual salary of £1,000, as well as sources of occasional income similar to those of New York. F. W. Ricord and W. Nelson, eds., *Documents Relating to the Colonial History of the State of New Jersey* (1st series, Trenton, 1890), XIV (*Journal of the Governor and Council*, vol. II, 1715-38), pp. 234, 319, 401, 546, etc. For an argument for the poverty of the New Jersey office, see Lewis Morris to Newcastle, June 2, 1732, in William A. Whitehead, ed., *Documents Relating to the Colonial History of the State of New Jersey* (1st series, Newark, 1882), V (1720–1737), p. 314.

The income of the government of New York increased in time of peace, when the governor could keep the Independent Companies at less than full strength, retaining the salaries and clothing allowances for the missing soldiers. Clinton to Warren, [July 1746], Clinton MSS., III, C.L. Cosby, for instance, estimated that if he were allowed to keep the pay for twenty-five men for each of the four companies, he would increase his profits by £1,289.3.4, New York currency. Cosby's estimates of the profits arising from the Independent Companies, September 17, 1730, Clinton MSS., I, C.L. In time of war, on the other hand, the governor's income could be augmented by his skill in negotiating contracts to supply provincial troops. In short, no precise figure can be quoted for the governor's annual income. It generally declined after the 1730's as the ungranted lands were depleted, but it varied according to the shrewdness and complacency of the colonial executive.

Government." [25] Profits were necessarily slimmer for a nonresident like De la Warr, who had to forfeit his salary and most fees to the lieutenant governor who presided over the colony in his absence. Clarke, as we have noted, thought the government worth an offer of £500 a year. Clinton was told it was worth £4,000 per annum, but estimated his own profits as something less than half of that figure.[26] In 1753 the governorship was worth much less than it was in 1732, but it was still profitable enough for needy men to seek it out.

II

Unfortunately, there was no guarantee that a man chosen for reasons of patronage and serving for economically self-interested motives should be competent to govern an American colony. Since the common criterion of selection was "negative merit," [27] or the knowledge that a prospective appointee had no demerit severe enough to disqualify him, executive ability was an unanticipated dividend in a colonial governor. In fact, the royal governors of New York during this period were inexperienced, ill-informed, poorly-motivated, and generally unsuited to hold public office. The absentee De la Warr can be exempted from consideration because he never exercised the privileges and responsibilities of office, but the other three governors appointed during this period were conspic-

25. De la Warr to Hardwicke, May 21, 1741; De la Warr to Newcastle, May 21, 1741; Hardwicke to Newcastle, May 23, 1741, Add. MSS. 32697, foll. 56, 31, 55, B.M.

26. See above, n. 22. In 1741, Clinton argued that "the whole perquisite of the government to me wont exceed £1,600 a year" due to the fact that the governor was obliged to spend at least £1,200 a year on living expenses "for they must have show and be entertained especially the time the assembly setts." Clinton to Newcastle, London, June 30, 1741, Add. MSS. 32697, fol. 261, B.M. There is some confirmation of this figure in the fact that Governor Horatio Sharpe of Maryland was informed in 1757 that the government of New York was worth £1,600 sterling per annum. Gov. Sharpe to William Sharpe, July 6, 1757, in William Hand Browne, ed., *Correspondence of Governor Horatio Sharpe* (Baltimore, 1890), II, 47.

27. "Negative merit" is Lord Elibank's phrase in a May 12, 1752, letter to James Oswald. Oswald, *Memorials*, p. 168.

uous failures, as anyone who had studied their earlier careers might have guessed they would be.

Governor Cosby was the sixth of seven sons in a gentle Anglo-Irish family, and the sixth son to become a soldier. He entered the army in 1704, served in Flanders and Spain, and achieved a colonelcy of the 18th Royal Irish in 1717. His promotion was, no doubt, hastened by his marriage into the Montague family. Cosby's regiment was transferred to Minorca in 1718, and for the next decade the colonel exercised the additional responsibilities of the civil and military governorship of that little British outpost in the Mediterranean.[28]

Cosby remains an obscure figure in the official records of Minorca, but stories of his misdeeds there became current in New York after he assumed the government. The most vicious account was that of Cosby's dealings with a Portuguese merchant, Bonaventura Capedevilla. According to Cadwallader Colden (an opponent, to be sure), Cosby condemned as contraband a £9,000 cargo of snuff consigned by Capedevilla to Minorca in 1718, cowed the local judiciary into confirming his action while refusing to allow the local courts to investigate many of the relevant documents, and tried to falsify some records which he sent to the privy council when it investigated the affair in 1722. Colden states that the privy council found for Capedevilla and forced Cosby to pay £10,000 damages, so that "the Government of New York by the death of Coll Montgomerie came seasonably in his way to repair his broken fortune."[29]

28. Dalton, *George the First's Army, 1714–1727*, p. 304 and n. 1; G. leM. Gretton, *The Campaigns and History of the Royal Irish Regiment, 1684–1902* (Edinburgh, 1911), pp. 69, 425; "List of Colonels with the Dates of their Commissions," October 19, 1734, Add. MSS. 33046, fol. 97, B.M.; Robert Beatson, *A Political Index* (3rd ed., London, 1806), II, 217. Cosby relinquished his regimental command in 1732, upon becoming captain general of New York, but he was allowed to retain his rank as colonel. Instead of a regiment in the army records, his "provision" was listed as "Governour of New York."

29. Colden, *History of Cosby and Clarke*, pp. 283, 286. The Capedevilla episode remains obscure, escaping mention in the published records of the board of trade, privy council, and secretary of state. Lewis Morris had 250 copies of "Capedevillas case" printed in London in March 1735 as part of his

The Royal Governors of New York

Colden may well have exaggerated the Capedevilla story, but Governor Cosby's hunger for land and his apparent ruthless intent to increase his own estate led many New Yorkers to believe it. William Smith accused him of illicitly acquiring lands on Long Island and in the Mohawk Valley, but sadly reflected that public protestations were pointless: "no representation repugnant to his avarice had any influence upon Mr. Cosby. The weakness of his understanding rendered him reprehensible even to fear." [30] Cupidity and stupidity were the sins most frequently ascribed to Cosby by his opponents (Lewis Morris called him "that weak madman"), and it was generally agreed that he was the dupe of his wife and his local political advisers.[31] Neither by training, aptitude, nor temperament was he a wise choice for governor of New York.

Prior to his appointment George Clinton, like his predecessor, displayed few signs of a talent for leadership which might have qualified him for the governorship of New York. As the younger son of a nobleman, Clinton was sent out into the world with only an annuity of £100 a year and the hope of his family's support in the pursuit of a naval career. He went to sea in 1707 at the comparatively late age of twenty-one or twenty-two, and rose slowly but steadily through the ranks over the next twenty-five years, even though in 1720 he contrived to lose a fifty-gun ship in a storm at sea.[32] By the early 1730's, however, Captain Clinton found it hard

---

attack on Cosby, and it is clear that the New York opposition was convinced of the reality of the governor's misdeeds in Minorca. Lewis Morris to James Alexander, March 31, 1735, Rutherfurd Collection, II, 115, NYHS.

30. Smith, *History*, II, 26. See also, *ibid.*, II, 24–26.

31. Lewis Morris to Sir Charles Wager, October 12, 1739, in *The Papers of Lewis Morris, Governor of the Province of New Jersey from 1738 to 1746*, New Jersey Historical Society, *Collections*, IV (New York, 1852), p. 67; Smith, *History*, I, 26.

32. *DAB*, IV, 225; Charnock, *Biographia*, IV, 59–60; Will of the Earl of Lincoln, August 26, 1693, extract, Clinton MSS., I, C.L. Clinton's first officially recorded commission was that of fourth lieutenant of the *Blenheim*, but the same document mentions a November 22, 1712, commission as second lieutenant of the *Nottingham*. Adm. 6:11, fol. 280, PRO. His naval career can be traced in the PRO: Index to the Admiralty Commissions and Warrants Book (Adm. 6), Part I, 1695–1734 and 1735–1742, and in the Adm. 8

to secure important and profitable naval assignments, and he began to harass Lady Lincoln and Newcastle with pleas for their help. Newcastle obliged Clinton in 1731 with an assignment as commander of the squadron annually sent to Newfoundland, a post that carried the additional responsibility of the civil government, but the Duke's impatience is manifest in a letter to Sir Robert Walpole: "You know why I interest my self for him; he is indeed very importunate, but very poor, and if the little thing he proposes could be done for him, I should be infinitely obliged to you, and it would rid me of him at once." [33] Clinton could not be shrugged off so easily, as we have seen, and he began threatening to refuse to accept poor naval assignments at all, presenting Newcastle and his sister with the prospect of a totally impoverished supplicant. Through Newcastle's influence in naval affairs, Clinton was assigned to even larger ships, and, finally, in 1736 he was appointed naval commander in chief in the Mediterranean with the full powers of an admiral.[34] During the next four years he commanded a number of men of war, but peacetime service was not very lucrative and even when the European war began he never seemed to be where prizes were taken.[35] His indebtedness increased precipitously, and he pleaded with Newcastle to put him "in some way to live by the sea, and not only barely to subsist by it but to enable me to pay my debts." [36] Soon, as we have seen, both Clinton and his patron gave up the hope that Clinton could support his family as a sailor, and Newcastle arranged to turn the captain into the presumably greener pastures of New York government.

series, especially Adm. 8:20 and 21. See also, Clinton memorial, Add. MSS. 33055, fol. 244, B.M.; Charnock, *Biographia*, IV, 60–61.

33. Newcastle to [R. Walpole], n.d., Cholmondeley-Houghton MSS., Correspondence, no. 3296, C.U.L.; Add. MSS. 33055, fol. 244, B.M. Charnock Add. MSS. 33055, fol. 244, B.M. Charnock places this event in 1732. *Bio-* places this event in 1732. *Biographia*, IV, 61.

34. Add. MSS. 33055, fol. 244, B.M.; Charnock, *Biographia*, IV, 61. He commanded the *Gloucester* on this assignment.

35. On the unprofitability of peacetime naval duty, see Mrs. Clinton to Newcastle, November 14, 1738, Add. MSS. 32691, fol. 466, B.M.

36. Clinton to Newcastle, April 30, 1740, add. MSS. 32693, foll. 245–248, B.M.

Clinton's accomplishments as governor were as few as his naval successes, and his ineptitude rendered the office much less profitable than his family had hoped it would be. His introverted and seemingly paranoiac personality did not lend itself to strong leadership. He therefore surrendered himself to the management of his strong-willed wife and a succession of political favorites. Contemporaries faulted him for his inability to meet the social demands of the governorship: "In a province given to hospitality, he erred by immuring himself in the fort, or retiring to a grotto in the country, where his time was spent with his bottle and a little trifling circle . . . He was seldom abroad; many of the citizens never saw him; he did not even attend divine worship above three or four times during his whole administration." [37] Worse, the governor's weakness was aggravated by his avarice. Smith alleged that "Mrs. Clinton prompted her husband, whose good nature gave place to her superior understanding, to every plausible device for enhancing the profits of his government . . . [and he] boldly relied upon the interest of his patrons to screen him from reprehension." [38]

As we shall see, neither Cosby nor Clinton was the sort of official who could gracefully combine his own interests with those of the province and the empire. They had a lot in common, including the initial "C," which to some New Yorkers betokened bad luck in a governor: Richard Coote, Earl of Bellomont, and Edward Hyde, Viscount Cornbury, had preceded them.[39] Both Clinton and Cosby were sons and sons-in-law of gentle (or noble) families for whom pampered military or naval careers had not provided sufficient

37. Smith, *History*, II, 158. Dr. Alexander Hamilton must have fallen in with Clinton's clique. The traveler recorded that, while visiting New York, he "was tired of nothing here but their excessive drinking." "Govr. Cn himself is a jolly good toaper and gives good example and, for one quality, is esteemed among these dons." Carl Bridenbaugh, ed., *Gentleman's Progress: The Itinerarium of Dr. Alexander Hamilton, 1744* (Chapel Hill, 1948), pp. 88–89. Many of Clinton's psychological difficulties were reflected in those of his son. See Frederick Wyatt and William B. Willcox, "Sir Henry Clinton: A Psychological Exploration in History," *William and Mary Quarterly*, 3rd ser., XVI (1959), 3–26.

38. Smith, *History*, II, 158.

39. See *New York Weekly Journal*, no. 8, December 24, 1733, and the rejoinder in *New York Gazette*, no. 428, December 31–January 7, 1734.

income, and they were appointed on the strength of their connections to the Duke of Newcastle. Although each had had some small gubernatorial experience, they shared (and here they were not typical) a lack of political finesse, undisguised avariciousness, subservience to the advice of their wives and political advisers, and a generally slothful, unintelligent approach to their official duties.

Sir Danvers Osborn completes the unhappy list of the mid-century governors of New York. The Osborn family motto, "Quantum in rebus inane" ("How much in life is foolish") was especially appropriate to the introverted nobleman. Despite reports of unruly behavior at Oxford, Osborn was ordinarily cautious and taciturn, and quite the typical country gentleman in his indifference to the public affairs of the day. Shattered by the death of his young wife in childbirth, he spent the succeeding ten years wandering about England, sharing the hospitality of his mother in London and his brother-in-law Halifax in Northampton, unable to come to terms with the world about him.[40]

Halifax, when at the board of trade, assured Governor Clinton that "none but a Nobleman of Fortune" would be his successor, whereupon he dispatched Sir Danvers to New York. Newcastle himself described the new governor as "a proper Person of Weight." [41] In a sense Osborn was a "proper person," for he was fairly rich, sensitive, and conscientious, although inexperienced in government. But he proved to be much too sensitive, as his melancholy response to Lady Osborn's death might have suggested. He was joyously received in New York, but he quickly became aware that the assembly intended to resume the intractable attitude it had developed under his predecessors and, within a week of his arrival, he took matters into his own hands and was found "in Mr. Murray's garden hanging in his hankerchief fastened to the nails at the top of the fence." [42] The coroner's jury, investigating the tragedy, gauged the "great disorder of the unhappy gentleman's mind" by the brief note he had left, and branded him a "lunatic." The note read: "Quos

40. Osborn, *Letters*, p. 11; McClelland, ed., *Osborn*, pp. 29, 33, 38.
41. Ayscough to R. H. Morris, November 24, 1752, Clinton Letterbook, p. 126, C.L.; Newcastle to H. Walpole, June 29, 1754, Add. MSS. 32735, fol. 598, B.M.
42. Smith, *History*, II, 155.

Deus vult perdere, prius dementat [What God wishes to destroy, he first makes mad]; Have Mercy on me God! and blessed Jesus!" [43] Halifax evidently had yet to learn that a mature talent for leadership was a necessary qualification for the governor of the increasingly complex and recalcitrant province of New York.

The governors of New York from 1732 to 1753 were, then, typical products of the English patronage system. They were all appointed through the influence of their patrons, and they were selected for personal and political reasons rather than on the basis of administrative ability. With the exception of Osborn, they sought the post for its financial rewards. We may accept the fact that patronage was a legitimate political practice in the eighteenth century, and we may also assume that the motives of these men for seeking office were no worse than those of their contemporaries in English posts. Unfortunately, however, the governors were pivotal figures in colonial politics. They were endowed with a considerable range of executive, legislative, military, and judicial power. Furthermore, they were, for the most part, on their own once they arrived in America, since the difficulties of transatlantic communication and the vagaries of imperial decision-making in London forced them to act independently. Generally restrained by the terms of their commissions and instructions and guided by the advice of the local royal council, the governors were nevertheless virtually unrestricted in the day by day, month by month, exercise of power. William Blathwayt, a faithful royal official, recognized the problem early in the eighteenth century: "The sending of good Governors to the Plantations is much insisted on with good reason, for where his Majesty has so few officers of his own appointment they ought to be the more careful of their Duty and at so great a distance from his Majesty's eye great Temptations happen whereby his Majesty's service does often suffer." [44]

Ideally, the governors should have been chosen more carefully

43. *Ibid.*, II, 152–157. See also, DeLancey to Archbishop Herring, October 15, 1753, William Smith MSS., vol. I, no. 4, NYHS.
44. [Anon.,] *Of the American Plantations* (1714), in William L. Saunders, ed., *The Colonial Records of North Carolina* (Raleigh, N.C., 1886–1890), II, 158.

than their domestic counterparts. They should have been skilled in law, military science, and government. They should have been selflessly dedicated to the interests of the empire, and possessed of subtle political skill. All this was impossible in an eighteenth-century context, of course, but it is hard to escape the suspicion that, far from meeting the ideal, the governors of New York would have performed poorly even as domestic officeholders at a similar level, since they were almost totally incapable of keeping the ship of state on an even keel. Perhaps little more could be expected of them, however, because they had acquired their jobs as a direct result of the failures of their earlier careers. The fault, ultimately, was as much in the system which chose them as in the governors themselves.

3
New York Government and Anglo-American Politics

THE HAPHAZARD RECRUITMENT OF GOVER-
nors in England had an immediate effect on the practice of politics
in America. As a New Yorker remarked during the Stamp Act
crisis: "Government will never recover any Strength here, till it is
in other hands, and in general will be loosing Ground as the Colonys
increse, till other people are sent out to fill the most interesting
Officers, than such as are fit for nothing at Home." [1] At the beginning of the eighteenth century, in the absence of formal party
organization, the royal governor was the pivot of political life.

1. John Watts to Moses Franks, November 9, 1765, NYHS, *Colls.*, 1928,
p. 399.

Local politicians oriented their behavior in accordance with his preferences and foibles.

I

The governor of New York stood at the center of its governmental system, participating as he did in the executive, legislature, and judiciary.[2] His formal powers were considerable. As legislator he possessed an absolute veto over laws passed by the assembly, whose very existence depended upon his summoning it into being. As judge, he also exercised the power to pardon and chancery jurisdiction, and he acted with the council as the highest court of appeal in the province. As executive, he was the principal instrument for expression of the royal will and power in America and the military commander in chief. Cutting across his constitutional roles, moreover, were the powers of appointment and financial prerogatives which translated his legal authority into meaningful political terms. The governor appointed innumerable local officials as well as the principal governmental officers of Albany and New York City. He chose the members of the supreme court and exercised a *de facto* power to name the members of the provincial council, the naval officer, and the officers of the Independent Military Companies stationed at New York. This patronage was the governor's most important financial prerogative. At the same time, however, he shared with his council the power to grant the unsettled lands of the province, received numerous fees for performing governmental acts, and, especially in time of war, exercised considerable discretion in the distribution of military supply contracts.

The provincial council provided the institutional nucleus for the governor's local allies, both because of its political role and because seats at the council board were the most valuable sinecures

2. For the powers of the governor, see Evarts B. Greene, *The Provincial Governor in the English Colonies of North America* (New York, 1898), passim, and Leonard W. Labaree, *Royal Government in America* (New York, 1958), pp. 92–133. For the structure of New York government generally, see Rex M. Naylor, "The Royal Prerogative in New York, 1691–1775," New York State Historical Association, *Quarterly Journal*, V (1924), pp. 221–255.

in New York. The councillors were not, as the assembly pointed out early in the century, "another distinct state or Rank of People, in the Constitution . . . , being all Commons." [3] They were appointed by the board of trade upon the recommendation of the governor as being "men of estate and ability, and not necessitous people or much in debt, . . . well affected to our government" and of "good life." [4] In short, the analogy to the house of lords will not do, for there was no necessary social distinction between councillors and assemblymen. The council was not, as ideally it should have been, a mobilization of the rich, wise, and just members of the community to help the governor to govern. Rather, the councillors were intended to be reliable supporters of the governor, and one of their functions was to bolster the administration against the encroachment of adverse political factions and the assembly.

The constitutional powers of the council were not extensive, but they were critical. It was an advisory body to the governor and the upper house of the colonial legislature. The advice and consent of the council were required for the calling, proroguing, and dissolving of assemblies, payment of public money, erection of courts of justice, granting of unsettled lands, and appointment to many offices.[5] The council served with the governor as the highest court of appeal in New York, and it acted on its own as a legislature. It exercised little of the financial prerogative which was gradually bolstering the power of the assembly, but its functions were important enough to provide a rudimentary counterpoise to the increasingly aggressive lower house.[6] Since councillors stood to gain from a strengthened royal prerogative, they were generally firm sup-

3. Quoted in H. Hale Bellot, "Council and Cabinet in the Mainland Colonies," Royal Historical Society, *Transactions,* 5th ser., V (1955), p. 168.
4. Charles W. Spencer, *Phases of Royal Government in New York, 1691–1719* (Columbus, O., 1905), p. 46; Charles Z. Lincoln, *The Constitutional History of New York* (Rochester, N.Y., 1906), I, 34.
5. Spencer, *Phases of Royal Government,* p. 52; Lincoln, *Constitutional History,* I, 443–447.
6. Spencer dates the transference of the dominant role from the council to the assembly during Hunter's administration (1709–1719), with "the imperious necessity for a working relation between the governor and the revenue-granting body." *Phases of Royal Government,* p. 96.

porters of the administration and royal instructions even when they were not philosophical imperialists.

Only a few adherents of the governor could be provided with places on the New York council, however, because its membership fluctuated between seven and twelve. Even in this small body, a few places were taken up by professional officers of the crown (who could be counted on to support the governor anyway) and by English members who never came to America.[7] Absenteeism and distance from New York City frequently made it difficult even to achieve a quorum,[8] but the council nevertheless served as the symbolic rallying-point for the governor's faction. It was the patronage most ardently sought, and it played the double role of bringing men to the governor's side and serving as his foremost institutional ally.

The most rapidly changing institution in the New York political system was of course the assembly, whose power in regard to money bills afforded it a constantly expanding part in the control of public affairs.[9] This prerogative caused real concern among contemporary placeholders, such as Archibald Kennedy: "From an Assembly, if we value our Constitution, we have every Thing to dread; they have the purse on their Side, which greatly preponderates in the Balance, and will be doing (I wish I could say fairly) what every other monied Person does; that is, turn it to their own particular Advantage." [10] Although the assembly steadily increased the sphere of its competency throughout the first half of the century, it did not achieve its majority until the onset of the Seven Years' War, when command of the disposition of men and money

7. Examples of the former are Archibald Kennedy, George Clarke, and Richard Bradley. Examples of absentee membership are George Clarke, Jr., and Sir Peter Warren.

8. James Alexander to Cadwallader Colden, April 14, 1729, NYHS *Colls.*, 1917, p. 278; Colden to Peter Collinson, January 10, 1761, *ibid.*, 1876, p. 56; John Watts to Monckton, October 11, 1764, *ibid.*, 1928, p. 298.

9. For the traditional interpretation see Charles W. Spencer, "The Rise of the Assembly, 1691–1760," in Alexander C. Flick, ed., *History of the State of New York*, II (New York, 1933), pp. 151–198. A more sophisticated account of assembly development is Jack P. Greene, *The Quest for Power: The Lower Houses of Assembly in the Southern Royal Colonies, 1689–1776* (Chapel Hill, N.C., 1963).

10. Archibald Kennedy, *Essay*, p. 17.

vastly strengthened its bargaining power, and when the internal affairs of the colonies finally captured the attention of English officials.

The assembly met for two brief sessions each year, spring and fall, to deal with appropriations and the minor legislation that constituted the bulk of its business. It was an intimate body, which gradually grew from a membership of twenty-two in 1698 to one of twenty-seven in 1769,[11] and thus it behaved quite differently from the large legislatures of the present day or even the English parliament of the eighteenth century. English constitutional experience was doubtless responsible for allowing the assembly to monopolize the power of the purse, which was the foundation of the emerging importance of the lower house. The assemblymen learned how to employ their financial prerogative against the executive by withholding passage of the appropriation bill in return for concessions from the governor. They also established the practice, even more damaging to royal government in America, of allotting salaries to individuals rather than to their offices, thereby acquiring "in effect the Nomination of all the Officers who are not immediately appointed by the King." [12]

New York governors were able to deal successfully with most legislatures for about forty years after the arrival of Governor Robert Hunter in 1710. The device they used was a system of barter pioneered by Hunter, whereby the assembly appropriated money for the governor's salary and crucial governmental and military expenditures in return for the governor's assent to acts that contravened his instructions, his acquiescence in appointments to provincial office, and, especially, his control of county patronage.[13] In this way the governor financed his operations and the leading assemblymen gained office, local power, and legislative freedom. From time to time, as subsequent chapters will demonstrate, governors were too

11. For the assembly, see Spencer, *Phases of Royal Government,* pp. 70, 77; Lincoln, *Constitutional History,* I, 447–454.
12. Colden to Secretary Popple, December 15, 1727, *New York Col. Docs.,* V, 844.
13. Spencer, *Phases of Royal Government,* p. 155; Greene, *Provincial Governor,* p. 158.

loyal, proud, or inept to deal successfully with the increasing demands of the assembly, but until the onset of the great war for empire at mid-century the system generally worked to everyone's benefit.

Although the constitutional role and political effectiveness of the assembly were expanding throughout the eighteenth century, to speak of the "rise of the assembly" as the determining factor in colonial politics in this period is to distort its importance. Nor, except in the broadest sense, should the rise of the assembly in America be equated with the "winning of the initiative" by the house of commons, for the American development was inherently unselfconscious.[14] The New York assembly jealously guarded its privileges and strove to increase its power throughout the eighteenth century, but before mid-century its aggressiveness had no consistent ideological basis. Assemblymen sought to improve the position of the legislature for its own sake and for their own advantage, rather than in purposeful opposition to competitors within the colonial constitution. Indeed, the assembly's rivalry with the governor was frequently seen as a personal contest, an attitude derived largely from the primitive character of party organization. As Carl Becker noted: "there were no political parties; there were rather two centers of influence, and the only division that was permanent was that between the men who at any time were attached to the governor's interest and the men who made use of the assembly to thwart that interest." Furthermore, the governor's "interest" was inherently unstable: "there was no constant factor operating to hold any group of men to the governor's interest. Not being thoroughly identified with the colony, only while he was in a position to grant favors or insure the continuance of those already granted, could the governor hold individuals or factions, and the so-called popular party was likewise not a permanent group, but a residuum, as it were, composed at any time of those without the sphere of executive influence."[15] The political scene in eighteenth-century New

14. Wallace Notestein, *The Winning of the Initiative by the House of Commons* (London, 1924), Raleigh Lecture on History.

15. Carl L. Becker, *The History of Political Parties in the Province of New York* (Madison, Wis., 1960), pp. 7–8.

York was therefore in a constant state of flux. True political parties had not yet emerged, and the stage was occupied by transitory factions formed about certain individuals, families, and issues, unable to develop the stable organizational mechanisms which would have rendered them self-perpetuating.

It is important at this point to remember that, although a considerable percentage of the adult male population of New York voted, a much smaller group participated in politics and exercised public office. This political elite was drawn from among the merchants and lawyers of New York City and Albany and the principal landholders of the Hudson Valley. It did not constitute an aristocracy, as Becker thought,[16] for access to the group was easily obtained, and newcomers to America and obscure New Yorkers freely participated in it. A few socially and economically prominent families remained dominant, however, families whose names still sound familiar—the Beekmans, DeLanceys, Livingstons, Morrises, Philipses, Schuylers, Van Rensselaers, and Van Cortlandts. Members of such families generally operated in unison, since the rewards of politics were considered familial rather than personal property. Likewise, intermarriage among the leading families created the binding ties of many political factions. The group was also united by economic interests, particularly those which arose from the fur trade, Hudson River Valley agriculture, and the mercantile life of New York City.

The power of great families was thus noticeable within the provincial ruling group, but by 1730 the bonds of family alliance which had characterized Leislerian New York were giving way to a more flexible system in which "interest often connects people who are entire strangers and it sometimes separates those who have the strongest natural connections." [17] The political elite thereafter played a multiple role. According to Becker: "The leaders within

16. *Ibid.*, pp. 8–10, 12–14.
17. William Alexander to Robert Livingston, Jr. [?], March 1, 1756, in Livingston Rutherfurd, *Family Record and Events* . . . (New York, 1894), pp. 57–58. See also, Beverly McAnear, "Politics in Provincial New York, 1689–1761" (unpub. Ph.D. diss., Stanford, 1935), 954–955; Milton M. Klein, "Democracy and Politics in Colonial New York," *New York History*, XL (1959), 228.

this class stood, as it were, between the governor and the assembly, using either as occasion demanded. When the governor was the real center of influence, with lands to grant or sinecures to offer, ambitious men with favors to ask turned to him and supported him. But with titles secure and position assured, their dependence upon the governor decreased; and in the later period the leaders of the aristocracy in increasing numbers identified themselves with the assembly." [18] The leading politicians seldom acted together, however. Those New Yorkers favored by the governor's policies and patronage generally lent him their support, while the "outs" formed cliques against him, and attempted to use the assembly as a counterpoise to executive power. Neither group was stable, for men ceased to follow the governor when he treated them less well than they expected, and his opponents easily crossed into his camp after a bit of wooing. During any one administration, however, there was likely to be a fairly continuous division between the "outs" and the "ins," although of course there were frequently several different factions arrayed in opposition to the governor.

The assembly was composed of representatives from the several counties, New York City, Albany, Schenectady, a few smaller towns, and several of the great manors, such as Rensselaerswyck, Cortlandt Manor, and Livingston Manor. The leading families of the colony superintended the selection of candidates to stand for the legislature,[19] took the lead in securing election of these candidates, and controlled the assembly itself by means of their own votes and their influence over other representatives. To Cadwallader Colden's somewhat jaundiced eye, representation was scattered among "the owners of these extravagant Grants, the Merchants of New York, the principal of them strongly connected with the Owners of these great Tracts, by family Interest, and of Common Farmers, which last are Men easily deluded and led always with popular Arguments of Liberty and Privilege." [20] The merchants and landowners were

18. Becker, *Political Parties*, pp. 11–12.

19. Carl L. Becker, "Nominations in Colonial New York," *American Historical Review*, VI (1900–1901), p. 265.

20. Colden to Board of Trade, September 20, 1764, NYHS, *Colls.*, 1876, p. 363. See also Colden to Dr. John Mitchell, July 6, 1749, *ibid.*, 1935, p. 33.

indeed an interconnecting elite which had little difficulty in over-coming the numerical superiority of the "common farmers." [21] They acted, however, in a manner which does not fully accord either with Carl Becker's aristocratic interpretation of New York politics or with Milton Klein's democratic reading—opposing views which nevertheless agree that the lower house was the breeding ground of the American democratic tradition.[22] On the one hand, Becker exaggerates the degree to which an upper "social class" directly controlled New York politics until it was supplanted by popular masses using the techniques of modern political democracy. Klein, however, while correctly emphasizing the breadth of the franchise in colonial New York, overestimates the degree to which control of political activity was popularly based.

Klein admits that "the local aristocracy did occupy a commanding position in the colony's politics, and they continued to do so after independence," and he offers the explanation that: "Undoubtedly the landed aristocrats exercised great influence in the colony's politics, but their influence is better ascribed to voter illiteracy and indifference than to open balloting or the landlord-tenant relationship." [23] "Illiteracy" unquestionably played a part in restricting the popular basis of politics, but "indifference" was surely the prevailing temper. Contemporaries also caught the mood, as William Smith did when he remarked "that torpor which generally prevails when [the multitude] are uninfluenced by the arts and intrigues of the restless and designing sons of ambition." [24] "Deference" is probably an even better term than "indifference" to

21. Charles W. Spencer, "Sectional Aspects of New York Provincial Politics," *Political Science Quarterly*, XXX (1915), pp. 423, 424.
22. Carl L. Becker, "Growth of Revolutionary Parties and Methods in New York, 1765–1774," *American Historical Review*, VII (1901–1902), p. 57; Becker, *Political Parties*, pp. 5–22; Klein, "Democracy and Politics," pp. 223–240. George Chalmers was probably the first historian to find that the government of New York was "democratical," in 1714. Quoted in Greene, *Provincial Governor*, p. 194. For a general discussion of "democracy" in colonial America, see J.R. Pole, "Historians and the Problem of Early American Democracy," *American Historical Review*, LXVII (1962), pp. 626–646.
23. Klein, "Democracy and Politics," pp. 240, 232.
24. Smith, *History*, II, 69.

describe the behavior of an electorate which uncomplainingly forfeited its prerogatives of self-government to a few of its members.[25]

In the first part of the eighteenth century, New York political
life was, as we have noted, more often based upon economic and
family connections and interests than ideological concerns. This was
also the case in mid-century England, where, to paraphrase the contemporary writer John Douglas, the infrequent occasions when the
king's government could be overturned occurred when political
opposition arose out of "an honest disapprobation of the public plan
of government."[26] Ordinarily, however, opposition failed because
the electorate recognized that it sprang from the disappointed ambitions of politicians. Voters therefore seldom believed that policy
issues, rather than internecine struggles for power, were at stake.
The public, as represented by a narrow electorate, was cynical and
uninterested in the conduct of public affairs. The comparison between English and American politics in this regard is not exact,
however, for on this side of the Atlantic, from the end of the seventeenth century, the public accepted the reality and pertinence of
political conflict. The American electorate was deferential and naïve
rather than deferential and cynical.

For Americans, politics were primarily the concern of politicians, although the electorate occasionally took the rhetoric of
public life at face value and reacted as though ideological issues
were at stake. Essentially petty and self-interested opposition to
governors by those members of the political elite who were out of
favor therefore tended to take on a popular aspect, using the "popular Arguments of Liberty and Privilege."[27] The outs argued for
access to power in the name of the people, and hence historians have
traditionally referred to the conflict of the "court" party and the

25. See Pole, "Early American Democracy," pp. 628–629, 642.

26. John Douglas, *Seasonable Hints from an Honest Man* (1761), p. 7,
quoted in Williams, *Eighteenth-Century Constitution*, p. 88. For English
attitudes similar to those of America see Foord, *His Majesty's Opposition*,
p. 238.

27. The phrase is Colden's: see above, n. 20. The best example of this
phenomenon in early New York history is the public uproar during the
Zenger trial of 1735. See Stanley N. Katz, ed., *A Brief Narrative of the Case
and Trial of John Peter Zenger* (Cambridge, Mass., 1963), pp. 5–17.

"popular" party. Once in office, however, the so-called popular leaders behaved no differently than had their erstwhile opponents, many of whom were now their allies.[28]

In New York, prior to the French and Indian War, local issues and the clash of personalities set the tone of public life. On a few occasions, such as in the Cosby administration, the public was genuinely aroused by broader issues and politicians took strong stands on principle. Even at these times, however, the underlying divisions seem to have been ephemeral, personal, and narrowly economic. Ideological Morrisites of the early 1730's, for instance, must have been horrified by the "courtly" conduct of their former leader when he became governor of New Jersey in 1738.

The keynote of politics in this period was flexibility. Governors came and went, and so did councillors. The assembly, although jealous of its prerogatives, responded freely to its fluctuating leadership. Power circulated widely among the ruling group. In many ways, then, New York politics mirrored the factionalism and confusion of early Georgian England. And to some extent, of course, New York responded directly to the English situation.

II

The Anglo-American nature of colonial politics has generally been neglected by historians,[29] although it is only from an Atlantic perspective that the intricacies of the characteristic political factionalism of the early years of the eighteenth century can clearly be

28. Note the behavior, to name the two most striking examples, of Lewis Morris as governor of New Jersey, and James DeLancey as lieutenant-governor of New York.

29. More recently a broader approach has been taken by a number of colonial historians: Bernard Bailyn, *The New England Merchants in the Seventeenth Century* (Cambridge, Mass., 1955); Lawrence H. Leder, *Robert Livingston, 1654–1728, and the Politics of Colonial New York* (Chapel Hill, N.C., 1961); John A. Schutz, *William Shirley: King's Governor of Massachusetts* (Chapel Hill, N.C., 1961). "Anglo-American politics, 1675–1765" was the subject of the October 1966 session of the Conference on Early American History, the outgrowth of which is the forthcoming volume of essays edited by Alison G. Olson and Richard M. Brown to be published by the Rutgers University Press.

seen. Royal governors and colonial politicians contended for the tangible rewards of place and power on this continent, but although the stakes of the game were in America, many of the best hands were not. Access to the principal jobs, favors, and policies sought by New York politicians more often than not lay through Whitehall rather than City Hall or Fort George. The powers of appointment and decision-making that were vested in the officers of state and imperial officials in England made a direct impact upon the conduct of politics in America.

Charles Andrews has observed that "the tendency to center colonial patronage in England" was a fundamental factor in "the growing centralization of the entire British system as we advance toward the climax of the Revolution."[30] Certainly this is so, although the process of centralization in itself was not as important as the growing necessity, after about 1750, to make appointments serve the needs of newly-formulated imperial policy. During the first half of the century, there were many sources of colonial patronage in England and there were no clearly formulated standards for its use, so that American posts could be distributed according to the pragmatic and self-interested canons of eighteenth-century English political life. Thus, in order to gain or retain their offices, Americans were obliged to enter into the politics of the mother country.

London was also the source of judicial, administrative, financial, military, and, occasionally, legislative activity that affected colonial life. The privy council was a court of last resort for major legal disputes as well as for questions of colonial policy. It resolved conflicts over land grants, as in the case of the Oblong, and displacements from office, as when Lewis Morris was replaced as chief justice, and disallowed colonial statutes.[31] The legal officers of the crown made decisions that changed the course of colonial politics, such as the 1735 opinion that the governor should not take part in the activities of the legislative council. The treasury, customs commissioners, admiralty, and other agencies were responsible for hundreds of de-

30. Andrews, *Colonial Period*, IV, 187.
31. See above, Chap. 4, for the Oblong case. For the comparative rarity of disallowance of statutes see Russell, *Review . . . in Council*, p. 57n2.

cisions affecting New York: administering the navigation system, assigning military and civil officers, reimbursing Americans for imperial expenses, bringing business into the New World. Parliament was less likely to be involved with colonial administration prior to the Seven Years' War, but it was a factor in questions of trade and finance.[32]

For Englishmen holding colonial posts and ambitious colonists alike, then, the challenge of Anglo-American politics was to have "a good stake in the Hedge"[33]—to establish an influential English connection. Colonials and English placemen sought out every avenue of approach to the great officers of state, members of the administrative boards and of parliament, as well as leaders of the military and the church. They appealed to formal organizations, such as the Protestant Dissenting Deputies, and informal groups, such as the American merchants resident in London.[34] They sought help in moments of crisis, but even more urgently, they tried to establish English connections that would spring to action of their own accord when they could be of service. For English placemen, who came to office through the interest of their friends and relatives, connections were already in existence and needed only to be tended and strengthened. For many Americans, however, especially when they were acting in opposition to such placemen, the problem was to establish contacts in an essentially alien ground, which, as a practitioner of the art complained, entailed "a pretty deal of pains."[35]

It was a complex, unsystematic business, which, in the first part of the century, was carried on largely without benefit of a formal

32. On the treasury, see Clark, *Rise of the British Treasury;* on the customs, see Thomas C. Barrow, *Trade & Empire: The British Customs in Colonial America, 1660–1775* (Cambridge, Mass., 1967).

33. Quoted in Andrews, *Colonial Period,* IV, 309.

34. See, for instance, N. C. Hunt, *Two Early Political Associations: The Quakers and the Dissenting Deputies in the Age of Sir Robert Walpole* (Oxford, 1961); Bernard L. Manning, *The Protestant Dissenting Deputies,* ed. Ormerod Greenwood (Cambridge, Eng., 1952); Maurice W. Armstrong, "The Dissenting Deputies and the American Colonies," *Church History,* XXIX (1960), p. 316n6.

35. Carl R. Woodward, *Ploughs and Politicks: Charles Read of New Jersey and His Notes on Agriculture, 1715–1774* (New Brunswick, N.J., 1941), p. 97.

colonial agency. New York employed no agent from 1730 to 1748, but even if it had he would not have solved the problem for most New Yorkers. The agent was, among other things, ill-paid and subject to the vicissitudes of assembly politics. Often he did act informally in behalf of an individual or faction, as George Bampfield did for the Livingstons and Robert Charles for James DeLancey, but since he was also ostensibly the agent of the whole colony (or, more accurately, the assembly) he had to take care whose personal interests he represented. There were, however, more compelling reasons for looking beyond the agent for a means of establishing a continuing personal contact in England. The most important was that it was difficult to find competent agents who were familiar enough with New York and loyal enough to their employers to be trusted with such weighty business. Moreover, the complexities of British politics were such that the formal representations to which an agent was likely to restrict himself were of little specific use to individual New Yorkers. In the words of Lewis Morris, "As to agents, unless the Court is dispos'd to do us service, no agent can do us much." [36]

Imperial placemen and New York politicians, faced with the need to protect or improve their positions in England, had therefore to establish personal channels of communication. Their efforts were of three (frequently concurrent) types: personal missions, the employment of private agents, and the mobilization of English friends and relatives in their behalf.

In moments of political crisis, the first instinct of English officials and American politicians who were losing their grasp in New York was to set off for London. There, they felt, it was possible to present their case more successfully than any English representative could. One of the first personal trips to England for political purposes was made by Lewis Morris in 1702 in order to wrest the

36. Lewis Morris to Mrs. Norris, May 14, 1742, *Governor Lewis Morris Papers*, p. 145. For the history of the New York agency, see Edward P. Lilly, *The Colonial Agents of New York and New Jersey* (Washington, 1936). For Morris' survey of potential New York agents, see his letter to James Alexander, February 25, 1736, Rutherfurd Collection, II, 177, NYHS.

government of New Jersey from the proprietors, although Robert Livingston had gone home as early as 1695 to claim reimbursement for his expenses in provisioning British troops during King William's War. Governor Hunter determined to return to England in 1719 when he received word of an organized attempt to secure disallowance of the most recent New York money bill. He was eager "that nothing may be resolved till I am brought Face to Face to answer these or any other men, as to what I Have done in my station," for he felt that only he could conduct an adequate defense: "I know not the objections but I forsee an inevitable necessity of my coming home for that very purpose for it is impossible to answer as one should at this distance or to instruct another." [37] When in 1725 Governor Burnet unwisely and unsuccessfully attempted to remove Stephen DeLancey from the political scene by questioning the validity of his citizenship, word traveled across the province that DeLancey was "Resolved to go for England if the Chief Justice gives his opinion that he is an alien." [38]

The best known of eighteenth-century New York political missions was of course that made by Lewis and Robert Hunter Morris in 1735, and recorded by the younger Morris in his diary,[39] but for a number of reasons it was also the last of its kind. A pamphleteer of 1714 had long before pointed out the inconvenience and inefficiency of such trips, noting "the great charge, vexation, and loss of time and damage to their Estates [of those] who are forced to take long and dangerous voyages." Such voyages were seldom successful: "Thus after two or three, sometimes four or five Years excessive

37. Robert Hunter to A. Philipse, August 15, 1718, *New York Col. Docs.*, V, 516.

38. Philip Livingston to Robert Livingston, September 23, 1725, Livingston-Redmond Papers, Franklin Delano Roosevelt Library, Hyde Park, N.Y.; see also, William L. Sachse, *The Colonial American in Britain* (Madison, Wis., 1956), pp. 93–115, 132–153. For a typical letter of advice to an American in London, see [Lt. John Ormsby Donnellan,] "Advice to a Stranger in London, 1763," *Pennsylvania Magazine of History and Biography*, LXXIII (1949), 85–87.

39. Beverly McAnear, ed., "R. H. Morris: An American in London, 1735-1736," *Pennsylvania Magazine of History and Biography*, LXIV (1940), pp. 164–217, 356–406. (Hereafter, R. H. Morris, "Diary.")

charge and trouble, and severall long voyages from the other part of the World, the unhappy American Subjects are forced to bear their oppression." [40] The irrascible Lewis Morris failed in London and became extremely disgruntled when he considered the time, money, and effort he had expended there.[41] Henceforth, New Yorkers turned to methods of communication with England that did not require them to leave their local interests unprotected.

One alternative to private missions to England was the employment of private agents—personal representatives either sent from America or already resident in England. This technique was, of course, employed throughout the century, but it took on an added importance as the stakes of colonial politics grew higher with the onset of the imperial crisis. William Shirley, the experienced governor of Massachusetts, Robert Hunter Morris, veteran of his father's 1735 adventure and the ex-soldier John Catherwood, for example, were among other things the personal representatives of Governor Clinton when he was hard-pressed by the strong DeLancey connection at mid-century. Costs of transporation and maintenance in England were prohibitive, however, and colonials could afford representations in London only to a limited extent. It was also generally true that private agents, particularly Americans, stood outside the channels of English political power, and so were less useful as a "stake in the Hedge" than a continuing English connection.

Family connections were the strongest bonds to England a New Yorker could have, since they did not depend upon considerations of business or friendship that required reciprocity. As a leading New York politician put it in a letter to the English cousin who was his firmest supporter, "You will always find in me a gratefull mind, the only return can be made you from this quarter of the world." [42] It might, for instance, be argued that the DeLancey family's domination of New York politics at mid-century was a function of the strength of their family connection in England and a

40. [Anon.,] *Of the American Plantations* (1714), in *Colonial Records of North Carolina*, II, 159.
41. R. H. Morris, "Diary," pp. 213–214, 403.
42. James DeLancey to John Heathcote, June 17, 1736, 1 ANC XI/B/5 "0," Lincolnshire Archives Committee, Lincoln, Eng.

reflection of the failure of the Livingstons to establish such a relationship.[43] During the revolutionary crisis, conversely, when the English political situation became constricted by the requirements of imperial policy and the focus of American politics narrowed to this side of the Atlantic, the Livingstons had their day. Failing family, however, most New Yorkers nurtured any and all contacts they could muster. Cadwallader Colden, for instance, appealed to his old Scottish patron, the Marquis of Lothian, as well as his scientific correspondent, Peter Collinson.[44] The great task was simply to mobilize anyone with the slightest political influence in England.

The American governors generally had the strongest political interests in England, since it was through these connections that they were appointed. The same was true of many of the principal imperial placemen. If their influence in London had been sufficient to put them in office, it often remained strong enough to keep them there. One need only think of Clinton's relationship with Newcastle, Cosby's with Halifax and Newcastle, or George Clarke's with Blathwayt and Horatio Walpole to understand how hard it was for an opposition to displace them. American politicians had frequently to start from scratch in forming a connection, but it is characteristic of English politics at this time that there was sufficient mobility for even a rank outsider to work his way into the system.

The seeming triviality of the contest for English influence

43. Controversy over the character of the DeLancey-Livingston rivalry has taken a new lease on life. See Roger Champagne, "Family Politics versus Constitutional Principles: The New York Assembly Elections of 1768 and 1769," *William and Mary Quarterly*, 3rd ser., XX (1963), pp. 57–79; Lawrence H. Leder, "The New York Elections of 1769: An Assault on Privilege," *Mississippi Valley Historical Review*, XLIX (1962–1963), pp. 675–682; Bernard Friedman, "The New York Assembly Elections of 1768 and 1769: The Disruption of Family Politics," *New York History*, XLVI (1965), pp. 3–24; Patricia U. Bonomi, "Political Patterns in Colonial New York City: The General Assembly Election of 1768," *Political Science Quarterly*, LXXXI (1966), pp. 432–447. For evidence that the Livingstons were not entirely insensitive to the need for English representation, see Robert Charles to Philip Livingston, August 31, 1742, Rutherfurd Collection, II, 207, NYHS.

44. Lewis Morris to Marquis of Lothian, March 26, 1735, NYHS, *Colls.*, 1918, pp. 126–127; Collinson to Colden, March 27, 1747, *ibid.*, 1919, p. 369, and various other letters in NYHS Colden Papers and the British Museum Collinson Papers.

should not, however, obscure the importance of the long-range aims of Anglo-American politics. In contending for immediate objectives such as jobs, political favors, and changes of policy, colonists and imperial officials were really disputing the control of political power in New York. From a broader point of view, Anglo-American politics had two interconnected aspects: the demonstration of American power to impress imperial officials in England, and the display of English influence in order to maintain American political power.

Everyone active in colonial public life was continually aware of the scrutiny of English officials. Imperial administrators were seldom insistent upon the precise execution of detailed policies, but for a variety of reasons they were strongly committed to the maintenance of stability in colonial politics. Thus it was vital that the governor, when confronted with a vigorous colonial opposition, should convince his superiors at home that he was in control of the situation in America. When Lewis Morris was governor in New Jersey, for instance, his daughter warned him from England to maintain an orderly administration at all costs since, if he should "have any difference [he] would find no redress from hence, since they would leave [him] to fight it out" alone in New Jersey.[45] The governor had to restrain the assertive tendencies of the local assembly and use his domination of the council to demonstrate that he had local support. At the same time, of course, the opposition attempted to show the governor's incompetence to control the government of the colony in the hope that the English authorities would lose confidence in him and that he would be replaced, allowing a reallocation of offices and a redistribution of power.

Even more important, however, evidence of political influence in England was the prerequisite for political mastery in America, whether for the administration or for its opponents. For the governor and his adherents, the ins of colonial politics, signs of favor with the imperial administration provided a hedge against local political disaffection. So long as the governor's appointees and policies were confirmed in England, New Yorkers looked to him for places and

45. Euphemia Norris to Lewis Morris, June 15, 1742, Morris Family Papers, R.U.L.

favors. The New York governors were all intensely aware of this phenomenon, and George Clinton was virtually paranoid on the subject. As Cadwallader Colden explained the situation, Clinton decided against returning to England in 1749 because "The Faction had endeavour'd to persuade the people that the Governors conduct was so blamed that his freinds could not support him and that the Chief Justice [James DeLancey] has a better Interest at Court than the Govr and had he gon people would have been confirm'd in this opinion . . . which was exceedingly strengthen'd by the Govrs not having been able to procure any thing directly from the ministry in vindication of his conduct." [46] New Yorkers were incredibly sensitive to the winds of political favor in England, and when the administration showed signs of having weaker English influence than its challengers (as was the case with Clinton and DeLancey in 1746), it was extremely difficult for the governor to retain control of the political situation in New York. Local families active in politics began to search out alternative sources of favor, the assembly increased its recalcitrance, and even the council was likely to waver. Thus the continuing contest for English attention was not simply a series of random private transactions, but a constant test of strength for the indications of imperial favor which were ultimately the determinants of political power in the royal colonies of America.

New York politics were thus factional and Anglo-American. Within the colony, they were oriented around the governor, for it was to his instructions, patronage, and attitudes that local politicians and the assembly responded. Neither continuing lines of party organization nor consistent ideological divisions had yet emerged. At the same time, there was a direct involvement with English politics. Here again the governor provided the focal point, since he was the direct link not only to the prerogative of the crown but also to the king's ministers. His supporters sought to bolster his standing while those New Yorkers outside of his circle beseeched Whitehall to turn him out. Moreover, New Yorkers engaged in a perpetual

46. Colden to John Catherwood, November 21, 1749, NYHS, *Colls.*, 1920, p. 159. See also, Clinton to R. H. Morris, November 28, 1751, R. H. Morris Papers, I, 33, New Jersey Historical Society, Newark, N.J.

competition for favor in London. Thus the interaction of two poly-centric systems of politics intensified and complicated the characteristic public life of the royal colonies in America. The political history of New York in the early eighteenth century, as the following chapters attempt to demonstrate, is one of governors and factions contending for power in an Anglo-American context.

PART TWO

The Conduct of Politics in New York, 1732-1753

4
Governor Cosby: New York,
1732-1735

GOVERNOR WILLIAM COSBY'S ENTRANCE INTO New York was auspicious. Heralded as "a gentleman of good character, . . . married to the Earl of Hallifaxe's Sister & has Children," he had already flattered New Yorkers by rejecting his appointment as governor of the Leeward Islands in favor of the mainland colony.[1]

1. Alexander to Colden, February 21, 1732, NYHS, *Colls.*, 1918, pp. 49-50. Newcastle notified the board of trade of Cosby's appointment as governor of the Leeward Islands on April 30, 1731, and his commission was sealed on May 11. The board received Van Dam's report of Montgomerie's death on December 23. On January 13, 1732, the board received a second letter from Newcastle concerning Cosby; the king had appointed him governor and captain general of New York and New Jersey. The board completed its drafts of

The Conduct of Politics in New York, 1732–1753

Arriving on the first day of August 1732, Cosby claimed that he had delayed his departure from England in order "to give the best Assistance I was able, towards defeating the Bill then depending in Parliament, in favour of the Sugar Islands." Despite his doubtful worth as a lobbyist, the Governor's good intentions were gratefully acknowledged by the New York assembly, which voted him a gift of £1,000.[2] The Cosby administration thus seemed destined to prove equally beneficial for New Yorkers and for their new executive. The board of trade must have been similarly optimistic, since, when drafting Cosby's instructions, they omitted an article that had been required since the beginning of the century, directing the New York governor not to "engage in any party." The instruction had originally been directed at the "unhappy" divisions in Leislerian New York, but by 1732 at least one prominent New York politician, James Alexander, argued to the board that "party differences seemed over and every thing seemed to promise an easier administration than any governor had ever met with in this place."[3] Alexander was exaggerating for effect, but he had a point. Mont-

---

Cosby's instructions on April 28, 1732, and by May 19 both the commission and the instructions had been confirmed by the king in council. *Journal of the Commissioners for Trade and Plantations*, January 1728/9–December 1734 (London, 1928), pp. 101, 261, 265–266, 287–288, 293–294, 315–316; W. L. Grant and James Munro, eds., *Acts of the Privy Council of England, Colonial Series* (Hereford, 1910), III (1720–1745), 817; Van Dam to Lords of Trade, July 1, 1731, *New York Col. Docs.*, V, 921; Lords of Trade to the king, April 28, 1732, *ibid.*, V, 934–935. (Hereafter, *Board of Trade Journal; Acts, Privy Coun., Col.*)

2. Speech of the governor, August 10, 1732, *Assemb. Jour.*, I, 633. Governor Cosby's instructions forbade him to accept gifts from the assembly. Smith contended that the legislators originally voted to offer the governor only £750, which he refused, demanding £1,000. Smith, *History*, II, 2. There is no mention of Cosby's participation in the parliamentary consideration of the Molasses Act in Leo Francis Stock, ed., *Proceedings and Debates of the British Parliaments respecting North America* (Washington, D.C., 1924–1941), IV, passim. For the Governor's account of his service as a lobbyist, see Cosby to Van Dam, January 27, 173[2], Rutherfurd Collection, IV, 33, NYHS.

3. Lords of Trade to the king, April 28, 1732, *New York Col. Docs.*, V, 934; James Alexander to Alured Popple, December 4, 1733, in William A. Whitehead, ed., *Documents Relating to the Colonial History of the State of New Jersey* (Newark, 1882), 1st series, V, 360. (Hereafter, *New Jersey Archives.*)

gomerie's administration of New York from 1728 to 1731 had witnessed the continuation of traditional rivalries, but avoided the emergence of a major crisis that would disrupt the political life of the colony.

The apparently stable condition of New York political life which awaited Cosby did not long survive his arrival, however, for within a year the Governor's headstrong behavior fostered the birth of an opposition party more vigorous than any since those arising out of Leisler's Rebellion. Historians have traditionally ascribed the birth of opposition in the 1730's to Governor Cosby's behavior in the affair of "Van Dam's salary," although the Van Dam incident was merely symptomatic of the profoundly divisive impact of the new governor upon the political structure of the colony.[4]

I

The difficulties began on November 14, 1732, when Cosby presented the council with an additional instruction, "Relating to moities of salary and perquisites" owed him by senior councillor Rip Van Dam, who had governed New York since Montgomerie's death on July 1, 1731.[5] Cosby's instruction declared that he was entitled to half the governor's salary paid Van Dam between July 1, 1731, and his own arrival thirteen months later: £1,975.8.10. At the council meeting of November 27 Van Dam refused to return the half-salary, reasoning "That where the King or the Law casts an office on any man which is not in his power to refuse & no body else dare execute that in such case all the Sallary & Prequisites annexed to such Office pass with Such Office And that the Person on whom the Burden of the Office is cast is by the Law entituled to the Benefits

4. See especially Herbert L. Osgood, *The American Colonies in the Eighteenth Century* (New York, 1904–1907), II, 446–451.

5. W. N. Sainsbury, J. W. Fortescue, and Cecil Headlam, eds., *Calendar of State Papers, Colonial Series, America and West Indies* (London, 1860–1953), 1933, p. 279 (hereafter, *Cal. State Papers, Col., Am.*); Berthold Fernow, ed., *Calendar of Council Minutes, 1668–1783* (Albany, 1902), p. 318 (hereafter, *Cal. Coun. Min.*). See also, Lewis Morris to Alexander, February 24, 1735, Rutherfurd Collection, II, 113, NYHS.

of it." [6] When the council rejected his argument, Van Dam took a new tack, offering to return the half-salary if Cosby would give him half of the perquisites he had received in England: £6,407.18.10. The Governor, who had the stronger claim, refused Van Dam's terms and began legal action in order to recover the salary.[7] Cosby cannot be faulted for pressing his rights, but his tactless manner alienated several of the leading figures in New York politics and aroused the suspicions of important segments of the population.

Cosby's initial problem was to find a court in which he could successfully prosecute his suit. His chances at common law, which required jury trial, must have seemed slim, since New York City juries would not be likely to side with a newly-arrived Irish governor against a respected and aging Dutch merchant. Furthermore, since the governor was also the chancellor in New York, he could not proceed in chancery, where he would be the judge of his own cause. Cosby therefore required a juryless court in which he would not have to take part, and his solution was to ask the supreme court of the province to sit as a court of exchequer, hearing his suit on the equity side. The supreme court justices' commissions made it clear that they were empowered to sit as a court of exchequer, and such a court had previously been convened in New York, although it is not certain that it had exercised an equitable jurisdiction. The council's ordinance of December 4, 1732, establishing an exchequer court may well, therefore, have seemed reasonable to the Governor and his friends.[8] As Cadwallader Colden pointed out: "It is probable that if the first Bill had been brought upon any other occasion than at the suit of a Governor or perhaps of any other Governor than Coll Cosby it had passed without opposition." [9] As it was, however, it could be objected that the supreme court could not exercise

6. Colden, *History of Cosby and Clarke*, p. 290.

7. Smith, *History*, II, 4; Alexander to Governor Hunter, draft, February 7, 1732, Rutherfurd Collection, I, 151, NYHS.

8. *Cal. Coun. Min.*, pp. 318–319; Colden, *History of Cosby and Clarke*, p. 290; Smith, *History*, II, 4; Katz, ed., *Brief Narrative*, p. 205n8. For the texts of the supreme court judges' commissions, see *ibid.*, pp. 50–52.

9. Colden, *History of Cosby and Clarke*, p. 291.

exchequer jurisdiction, or that a legislative act rather than an ordinance was necessary to erect such a court. To his opponents, it appears that Governor Cosby had erected a court of dubious constitutionality for the purpose of recovering a sum of less than £1,000 to which he was not absolutely clearly entitled. The risk must have been obvious.[10]

The case of Cosby vs. Van Dam was argued on April 9, 1733, before the three justices of the supreme court: Chief Justice Lewis Morris, James DeLancey, and Frederick Philipse. Van Dam's lawyers, James Alexander and William Smith, questioned the jurisdiction of the court while Attorney General Richard Bradley, for the Governor, tried to argue the merits of the case. Chief Justice Morris overruled Bradley, who had objected to the narrow basis of the defense, and listened to the jurisdictional arguments, whereupon he read a long prepared statement declaring that the supreme court could not exercise equity jurisdiction. Second Justice DeLancey took the opposite view the following day (as did Philipse at the beginning of the next court term), and Morris severely upbraided his junior associates before stalking out of the courtroom. The case could not, therefore, be resolved.[11] To all intents and purposes, the legal proceedings of the Van Dam affair ended at this point, although Van Dam subsequently attempted to bring a common law

10. For the legal and constitutional arguments, see [William Smith,] *Mr. Smith's Opinion Humbly Offered to the General Assembly* . . . (New York, 1734); [Joseph Murray,] *Mr. Murray's Opinion Relating to the Courts of Justice in the Colony of New-York* . . . [New York, 1734]; [Lewis Morris?] *Some Observations on the Charge Given by the Honourable James DeLancey, Esq, Justice of the Province of New-York, to the Grand Jury, the 15th Day of January, 1733* (New York, 1734). For an indication of Cosby's probable awareness of the emerging political unrest, see Morris' contention that the governor angrily refused to hear his negative views on the proposed ordinance: [Lewis Morris,] *The Opinion and Argument of the Chief Justice of the Province of New-York, concerning the Jurisdiction of the Supream Court of the said Province, to determine Causes in a Course of Equity*, reprinted in New Jersey Historical Society, *Proceedings*, LV (1937), 113–114.

11. Alexander to F. J. Paris, March 19, 1733, Rutherfurd Collection, I, 159, NYHS; Smith, *History*, II, 5–6; *New York Col. Docs.*, V, 944–945, and VI, 10–12; Colden, *History of Cosby and Clarke*, pp. 291–296, 299–301; Osgood, *Eighteenth Century*, II, 447–450.

suit against Cosby and published his complaint against the Governor.[12] Cosby wisely refrained from prosecuting his claim against Van Dam any further, but, as Cadwallader Colden suggested: "Mr. Van Dam gain'd his end by means of the popular discontents for the Governor & Judges both found it might be dangerous to their persons to proceed & he had this in excuse that so much partiality had appear'd in all the proceedings that he could not well expect indifferent Judgment & had no other Method to save himself." [13] If Van Dam came out of the affair unscathed, Morris did not. On August 21, 1733, the Chief Justice was suspended from his office and on the 23rd he was replaced by James DeLancey.[14] It was this act which precipitated a political crisis in New York which lasted more than four years, so that it is worth enquiring why Cosby punished Morris so harshly and why Morris responded so vigorously.

Shortly after the Van Dam trial, in answer to the Governor's demand to know what he had said in court, Morris defiantly published his opinion, openly challenging the authority of the Governor.[15] The Chief Justice justified his resort to the press by claiming that the Governor had snubbed him when he had offered his opinion on the proposed ordinance establishing an exchequer court; he had been told, he said, that Cosby would not see him, that he "could neither rely upon my Integrity nor depend upon my Judgment," and that he thought Morris "a Person not at all fit to be trusted with any Concerns relating to the King." [16] In response to Cosby's allegation that he had previously endorsed the use of the supreme court as a court of equity, Morris agreed that he had, but

12. Colden, *History of Cosby and Clarke*, pp. 300–301; Smith, *History*, II, 5. [James Alexander and William Smith,] *The Arguments of the Council for the Defendant, . . . Rip Van Dam . . . in the Supream Court of New-York* (New York, 1733); *The Proceedings of Rip Van Dam, Esq; in order for obtaining Equal Justice of His Excellency William Cosby, Esq.* (New York, 1733).

13. Colden, *History of Cosby and Clarke*, pp. 302–303.

14. *Cal. Coun. Min.*, p. 319; *New York Col. Docs.*, V, 955. See also, *New York Gazette*, October 28–November 4, 1734, and *New-York Weekly Journal*, November 11, 1734.

15. See above, n. 11.

16. New Jersey Historical Society, *Proceedings*, LV (1937), p. 114.

explained that Smith and Alexander's plea to the jurisdiction of the court had "put him upon makeing a more strict Enquiry, by which he found it neither had, nor could have such a Jurisdiction." No exchequer court could be established in New York, "not founded on an Act of the Legislature." His displacement, the Chief Justice said elsewhere, laid the issues bare, for his successors would never dare to declare "what they take to be the Law, where the Governour or the King's concerned," and one could well imagine "how secure the People are in their Liberties and Properties, under Judges who must be entirely at the Disposal of a Governour." [17] For, above all, "The reasons for displacing a Judge should . . . be not only in themselves very good, but very evident; nothing being more distastfull than the arbitary removal of Judges, because every man that has anything he calls his own must naturally think the enjoyment of it very precarious under such an administration, and our Governour's conduct has been such as fully to perswade those under his Governt that he thinks himself above the restraint of any Rules but those of his own will." [18]

Cosby must have had some inkling of the furor which Morris' suspension would create, for he deliberately refrained from asking the advice of the council once he saw how delicate the issue was. He had unsuccessfully attempted to gain Councillor Colden's cooperation by showering him with kindness, and when he abruptly announced the suspension, the astonished Colden inquired if the council was merely being informed of the act, "to which he answer'd yes & I replied It is what I could not have advise & He very briskly return'd to it I do not ask your advice. This put his having

17. [Lewis Morris?] *Some Observations*, pp. 17-18; [Lewis Morris,] *The Opinion and Argument*, p. 113. Morris' opinion of the jurisdiction of courts of exchequer might well have disturbed even a more able governor than Cosby. On July 10, 1735, Governor Gabriel Johnston of North Carolina complained to the board of trade that "several of our people have begun very modestly to question whether H.M. has a power to erect a Court of Exchequer here without an act of their Assembly, their arguments are borrowed from a book publish'd by Mr. Morris late Chief Justice of New York." *Cal. State Papers, Col., Am.*, XLII (1735-1736), p. 9.
18. Lewis Morris to Lords of Trade, August 27, 1733, *New York Col. Docs.*, V, 952.

the Consent of the Council out of the Question & defeated the whole Design he had been put upon of Cajoling me." [19]

Cosby suspended Morris without explanation, but his case against the Chief Justice was clearly stated in a long and vitriolic letter he sent Secretary Newcastle at the conclusion of the trial. The Governor charged Morris with partiality, delay of justice, and oppression of the people "by giving them a great deal of trouble and putting them to a fruitless expence, both of time and money, in their attendance on the Courts." Cosby recounted Morris' insulting behavior when he first arrived in America: he had gone to Amboy to receive the seals of New Jersey from Morris, the president of the New Jersey council, and had been kept waiting in an anteroom for an unconscionable period of time. All in all, the Judge's behavior threatened the royal prerogative in New York, for it was based upon "Boston principles" which might contaminate royal government elsewhere in America.[20]

II

The Van Dam affair produced a considerable literature on the merits of exchequer courts, the constitutional basis of courts in New York, and the extent of the royal prerogative in America, but Cadwallader Colden sensed its immediate importance when he called it "the chief handle laid hold of to incite the People against the administration." [21] The case was never concluded and the jurisdiction of the supreme court was never definitively agreed upon, though henceforth it ceased to sit in equity. The exchequer court had, after all, existed prior to Cosby's arrival. What inflamed the situation was how the Governor used the court, and against whom. The conflict

19. Colden, *History of Cosby and Clarke*, p. 299.
20. Cosby to Newcastle, May 3, 1733, *New York Col. Docs.*, V, 943, 948, 949. Cosby concluded by saying (p. 949) that "I must either displace Morris or suffer myself to be affronted," language anticipating James DeLancey's when he disbarred James Alexander and William Smith in the Zenger trial: "*either* we must go from the bench, or you from the bar." Katz, ed., *Brief Narrative*, p. 53.
21. Colden, *History of Cosby and Clarke*, p. 303.

of governor and chief justice did not significantly affect the constitutional arrangements of the colony, but it swiftly led to the disruption of New York politics. The process began in the autumn 1733 Westchester elections, when Lewis Morris was chosen county representative to the assembly. Morris' supporters marched to the polling place in Eastchester bearing a banner inscribed with the anti-Walpole slogan "Liberty and Law," only to find that all their Quaker allies had been denied the franchise by a newly-appointed Cosbyite sheriff who insisted upon their taking the oath before voting. Morris won the poll handily, nevertheless, and sailed down the Hudson after the election for a triumphal feast in New York City at the Black Horse Tavern, which was to become the headquarters of his faction in their struggle against Governor Cosby.[22]

It soon became obvious that Morris' suspension had polarized New York political life. Advocates of DeLancey and Philipse appeared in opposition to Morris at Eastchester, proclaiming the Walpolean "No Land Tax," and on May 28, 1734, the Governor's staunchest friends held a banquet in his honor, publicly memorializing him for his contributions to the safety and welfare of the colony. Administration supporters in the city also formed the "Hum-Drum-Club" (or "Governor's Club"), counting among their number some of the principal English merchants of the town. Even by late 1733, a contemporary historian concluded that, "all the province was already divided into two parties."[23]

The friends of Rip Van Dam and Lewis Morris were hard at work in New York City, where their strength was greatest among Van Dam's countrymen and the artisan population. Their appeal was based upon constitutionalism, as opposed to Cosby's alleged lawless "tyranny," as well as upon their criticism of the economic stag-

22. Smith, *History*, II, 7; Osgood, *Eighteenth Century*, II, 452; Nicholas Varga, "Election Procedures and Practices in Colonial New York," *New York History*, XLI (1960), pp. 265–267; *New-York Weekly Journal*, [November] 5, 1733.
23. *New-York Weekly Journal*, [November] 5, 1733; *New York Gazette*, May 27–June 3, 1734, January 28–February 4, 1734; George W. Edwards, "New York City Politics before the American Revolution," *Political Science Quarterly*, XXXVI (1921), pp. 587–592; Smith, *History*, II, 7.

nation of the colony. In the September 1734 aldermanic elections the Morrisite municipal slate (with a sole exception) was swept into office. Their opponents, so far as the Morrisites were concerned, were the representatives of privilege and corruption: "there voted against [the Morrisites in the South Ward] a considerable Merchant who was an inhabitant of another Ward, and about 15 of the Soldiers of His Majestie's Garrison, besides the Recorder of the City [Francis Harison] and his interest." [24] Cosby blamed the debacle on the Morrises and James Alexander: "a mislead populace in this City had . . . elected their annual Majistrates and chosen their Aldermen and Common Councel, out of such as were followers of the leaders above named." [25] The Governor's analysis was surely correct, but he failed to note that it was largely his own lack of political tact that had plunged New York back into the factional confusion from which Governor Hunter had so painstakingly retrieved it. It is only fair to remark, however, that this public chaos was largely due to the character and peculiarly vulnerable position of Lewis Morris, who had been the leading figure in New York politics since Hunter's arrival in 1710.

III

Fiercely independent public conduct ran in Morris' family, for he was the son and nephew of Welsh parliamentarian soldiers who had abandoned their homeland for the West Indies upon the restoration of the Stuart monarchy. His father, Richard Morris, married an heiress in the sugar islands and settled on an estate of five hundred acres near New York City, at "Bronck's Land," north of the Harlem River. It was there that Lewis Morris was born on October 15, 1671, only a year before his parents died. His uncle, Lewis Morris, a Cromwellian colonel, assumed responsibility for the property

24. *New-York Weekly Journal,* October 7, 1734; Edwards, "New York City Politics," pp. 587–589; *Minutes of the Common Council of the City of New York, 1675–1776* (New York, 1905), IV, 217, 228. (Hereafter, *Min. Comm. Coun.*)

25. Cosby to Lords of Trade, December 6, 1734, *New York Col. Docs.,* VI, 23.

and the youngster after the pacification of 1674, and his shrewd management added some 3,540 acres of East New Jersey land to the estate. Colonel Morris was a councillor in New Jersey, the colony in which his nephew began his political career, but throughout the eighteenth century the Morris family maintained interests and estates in both New York and New Jersey.[26]

Lewis Morris assumed control of the family lands after his uncle's death in 1690, and in 1691 he succeeded him as councillor and as judge of East New Jersey's unique court of common right. Then, in an incident which Governor Cosby would have done well to study, newly-appointed Governor Jeremiah Basse removed Morris from both the council and the bench in 1698. Morris' immediate response was to deny that the court of common right derived properly from royal authority, and, in a personal confrontation, the twenty-seven-year-old Morris "gave the Governour very saucy Language," for which he was briefly imprisoned.[27] The strength of his views did not, however, prevent Morris from resuming the very offices he had condemned as unconstitutional when Basse was succeeded by a more sympathetic governor, Andrew Hamilton, in 1700.

By the turn of the century it was clear that proprietary governors could no longer successfully govern New Jersey. Morris was prominent among the Quaker anti-proprietary party, although he himself was a staunch Anglican, and in 1701 he crossed to England to negotiate the surrender of proprietary governmental rights. He expected his friend Hamilton to be chosen the first royal governor

26. This biographical sketch is based upon "Introductory Memoir," *Governor Lewis Morris Papers*, 1–31; Robert Bolton, Jr., *A History of the County of Westchester* (New York, 1848), II, 285–311; "Correspondence Relating to the Morris Family," New Jersey Historical Society, *Proceedings*, new series, VII (1922), pp. 41–48; *DAB*, XII, 213–214 (John A. Krout); Smith, *History*, I, 179–180; John E. Stillwell, comp., *Historical and Genealogical Miscellany: Early Settlers of New Jersey and Their Descendants* (New York, 1903–1932), IV, 25–33.

27. Preston W. Edsall, *Journal of the Courts of Common Right and Chancery of East New Jersey, 1683–1702* (Philadelphia, 1937), pp. 31–34. For another intemperate performance which resulted in Morris' imprisonment, see John E. Pomfret, *The Province of East New Jersey, 1609–1702: The Rebellious Proprietary* (Princeton, 1962), pp. 331–333.

of New Jersey, however, and was angered when the post fell to Queen Anne's notorious kinsman, the governor of New York, Lord Cornbury. Morris protested as vehemently against the Cornbury administration as he had against that of Basse, and he found himself suspended once more. In 1706 he continued his opposition from the assembly, just as he was to do in New York in 1733.[28]

During the first third of the eighteenth century Morris shifted the base of his political operations to New York, although he continued to be one of the leaders of New Jersey politics. His interest in New York was the result of the favor shown him by Governor Robert Hunter, who employed Morris as his chief political adviser. Morris, whose Westchester lands had been dubbed the Manor of Morrisania by Governor Benjamin Fletcher, was elected to the New York assembly in 1710 from the borough of Westchester, and he remained in office until 1728, serving as legislative leader for Hunter and Burnet. The rewards he sought were those of political power and prestige, for as Hunter noted in recommending his appointment as chief justice of New York in 1715, Morris was well "able to live without a salary." [29] He was a remarkable figure: landlord, proprietor of iron mines, legislator, and judge in two colonies. All this, so far as one can tell, was without any formal education, and yet, as the lawyer and historian William Smith remarked, "no man in the colony equalled him in the knowledge of the law and the arts of intrigue." [30] Combined with his native shrewdness was the politician's basic instinct, the will to survive.

Although Lewis Morris was often associated with a popular constitutional outlook, when his career is taken as a whole it seems clear that he did not consistently adhere to any ideological point of view. The Livingstons of New York once complained that the Morrises "sett their witts to work to gain a party," only when their personal interests were "touched," and the genealogist John Stillwell has asserted that Lewis Morris "possessed no lofty sense of recti-

28. Osgood, *Eighteenth Century*, I, 391–397, II, 85–94. For Morris' trip to England, see Pomfret, *East New Jersey*, pp. 356–361.
29. Hunter to Lords of Trade, March 28, 1715, *New York Col. Docs.*, V, 400.
30. Smith, *History*, II, 180.

tude, but did possess a selfish ambition allied closely to the principle of rule or ruin." [31] Or, as the aging Morris himself described it, "I think I have acted rightly, but if my Masters think other ways I must endeavor to trim my sailes according to the wind." [32]

Throughout the administrations of Hunter and his successor, William Burnet, Lewis Morris remained at the center of New York public life, aided by his son whom Hunter appointed a councillor in 1721. Morris' standing in the assembly began to wane, however, as early as 1725, when Adolph Philipse was elected speaker. Then, when the assembly chosen in 1716 was finally dissolved in 1726, the new legislators once more elected Philipse speaker. Morris, in the meantime, antagonized the assembly by his collaboration in Governor Burnet's ill-considered attempt to prevent Stephen DeLancey from taking his seat on the ground that he was an alien. The family fortunes declined sharply in 1728, however, with the arrival of Governor Montgomerie, who turned to George Clarke for guidance and dismissed Lewis Morris, Jr., from the council. Philipse consolidated his control over the legislature during the Montgomerie administration, thereby depriving Morris of a sorely needed resource in his future political activity.[33]

Thus by 1732 the chief justiceship was the last vestige of Morris hegemony in New York, and Governor Cosby's dismissal of Morris from the bench was a near-mortal thrust. Quite aside from this aspect, Morris had a very immediate concern in the disposition of the Van Dam case, for he was the president of the New Jersey council and had governed the colony in the period between Montgomerie's death and Cosby's arrival. Cosby managed to secure an additional instruction, dated February 9, 1733, that required Pres-

31. John Livingston to Robert Livingston, August 28, 1750, Livingston-Redmond MSS., F.D.R. Lib.; Stillwell, *Miscellany*, IV, 32.

32. Lewis Morris to Francis Gasherie, May 27, 1739, *Governor Lewis Morris Papers*, p. 58. Even Colden observed that the Morris family tended to "exhaust the subject they treat on" by insisting on "small arguments when the Strong or Great are Sufficient." Colden to Alexander, July 13, 1729, Rutherfurd Collection, I, 125, NYHS.

33. For these developments in the assembly, see Osgood, *Eighteenth Century*, II, 416–426; Beverly McAnear, "Politics in Provincial New York, 1689–1761" (unpub. Ph.D. diss., Stanford, 1935), pp. 351–352, 564.

ident Morris to surrender half his salary. Coming as it did when the Van Dam affair was well along, this must have aggravated an already festering wound.[34] The moment had clearly come when those aggrieved by Governor Cosby would have to organize their discontent.

IV

Englishmen of the early eighteenth century, even colonial Englishmen, were sensitive to the newly emerging power of the press, and the first instinct of Lewis Morris and his friends was to commit their case to print. Van Dam published his complaint against Governor Cosby and Morris had his opinion in the salary case set in type even before he submitted it to the Governor. Both men gave their custom to New York's new printer, John Peter Zenger, rather than to his former master William Bradford. Bradford was the publicly-employed provincial printer whose weekly newspaper, the *New York Gazette*, paid careful respect to the governor and to the assembly, so that during the Van Dam affair there was no alternative periodical for the expression of discontent. James Alexander stated the dilemma of his friends neatly: "We estreamly want a good and nimble printer which if we had he [Cosby] would Soon appear from the press in his proper Colours, but Such as our press is it will be kept employed."[35] The obvious solution was to publish a second New York newspaper to state the case against the Governor.

Thus the *New-York Weekly Journal*, printed by young Zenger, began to appear on November 5, 1733.[36] It was a weekly

34. Leonard W. Labaree, ed., *Royal Instructions to the British Colonial Governors, 1670–1776* (New York, 1935), I, 286–287; Additional instructions to Cosby for dividing Morris' salary as the president of the New Jersey Council, February 9, 1733, Clinton MSS., I, C.L. Cosby later charged that Morris had been in collusion with Van Dam's counsel and, though no proof exists, it is true that they had remarkably similar interests. *New York Col. Docs.*, VI, 11.

35. Alexander to Robert Hunter, November 8, 1733, *New Jersey Archives*, V, 360.

36. For the most recent discussion of the *New-York Weekly Journal*, see Katz, ed., *Brief Narrative*, pp. 7–17.

designed "Chiefly to Expose him [Cosby] & those ridiculous flatteries with which Mr. Harrison loads our other Newspaper: which our governour Claims & has the privilege of Suffering nothing to be in but what he and Mr. Harrison approve of." [37] The *Journal*, although it has acquired a reputation for espousing the freedom of the press, was not in fact dedicated to publicizing both points of view in the developing controversy. It was used to promote the interests of Cosby's detractors, and it was written by James Alexander, with the help of both Morrises, William Smith, and Cadwallader Colden.

> The Writers in that paper exposed the Actions of Governors party in the worst light they could place them & among other well wrote papers published several that could not be justified & of which perhaps the Authors upon more cool reflexion are now ashamed for in some of them they raked into mens private Weaknesses & secrets of Families which had no Relation to the publick.[38]

The description is Colden's, and if a contributor could sketch such a severe portrait of the paper, one can well understand Cosby's complaint to the board of trade about Lewis Morris' "open and implacable malice against me [which] has appeared weekly in false and scandalous libels printed in Zengers Journal." [39]

In December 1733 the Governor assured Newcastle that Van Dam's hopes rested upon nothing more substantial than "popular clamour" and that the Councillor had found "all those appeals to the people ineffectual to provoke me to enter into a paper warr to justifye the proceedings of the Court, my own conduct, and his Majestys authority, which ought not to be prostituted to the censure of the mob." [40] By January 1734, however, Cosby's noncha-

37. Alexander to Robert Hunter, November 8, 1733, *New Jersey Archives*, V, 360; Colden, *History of Cosby and Clarke*, p. 318. Harison was the recorder of New York City, a member of the provincial council, and Cosby's publicist. For an incident revealing the baseness of his character and the Morrisites' contempt for him, see Osgood, *Eighteenth Century*, II, 455–456, and Colden, *History of Cosby and Clarke*, pp. 312–318.
38. Colden, *History of Cosby and Clarke*, pp. 318–319.
39. Cosby to Lords of Trade, June 19, 1734, *New York Col. Docs.*, VI, 5.
40. Cosby to Newcastle, December 17, 1733, *ibid.*, V, 974.

lance had given way and Francis Harison began to unleash a series of attacks against the rapidly solidifying opposition. The "paper warr" was joined, *Gazette* versus *Journal*, but the *Gazette*'s hackneyed case for authority was "generally thought no match to the other side." [41]

The *Journal*'s color, vitriol, and constitutional appeal evoked a powerful response in New York City and goaded Governor Cosby to his famous and ill-fated series of attempts to destroy the paper.[42] Chief Justice DeLancey began the process when he charged the New York County grand jury on the subject of libel in January and again in October 1734, but the jurors were reluctant to act against Zenger. The Governor then changed tactics and asked the assembly to order several issues of the *Journal* burned. The legislators, however, refused. It was therefore left to the governor's council, on November 2, to declare the papers seditious and to require the attorney general to undertake legal action against the printer and authors. Zenger was imprisoned on the council's warrant on November 17, and on the 23rd four issues of the newspaper were publicly destroyed, although, since the New York County court of quarter sessions refused to allow the public hangman to burn them, the penalty had to be carried out by the sheriff's Negro servant before the vindictive Francis Harison and a few officers of the New York garrison.

In January 1735, just as the *Gazette* was beginning its counterattack on the *Journal*, Attorney General Bradley filed the information charging Zenger with seditious libel which was to be the legal basis for his prosecution. In April the printer's lawyers, William Smith and James Alexander, initiated the legal proceedings by objecting to the commissions held by supreme court justices DeLancey and Philipse, a tactic not unlike the one they had employed against the exchequer court in behalf of Van Dam.[43] This time,

41. Colden, *History of Cosby and Clarke*, p. 319.
42. For an account of the trial see Katz, ed., *Brief Narrative*, pp. 17–26. Alexander's pamphlet and supporting documents will be found *ibid.*, pp. 41–151.
43. The advocacy of a very "strict" interpretation of the structure and jurisdiction of the courts was one of the most important aspects of the Mor-

however, the chief justice was no longer Lewis Morris, and on the 18th of April DeLancey peremptorily disbarred the two lawyers. John Chambers was appointed Zenger's lawyer by the court, and although apparently a governor's man, he managed to circumvent an attempt to pack the jury. When the case actually came to trial on August 4, however, the eminent Philadelphian, Andrew Hamilton, was on hand to defend Zenger.[44]

Hamilton's brilliant argument for Zenger's right to print true statements was couched in learned legal and constitutional terms. Basing his argument on a brief prepared by his friend James Alexander, Hamilton touched upon many of the points already raised in the pages of the *Journal* and secured the remarkable fame of the Zenger trial. To the participants, however, the issues were not constitutional and had little to do with the rights of Peter Zenger; the central point was the right of the newly-formed opposition to political existence. The spectators in the City Hall courtroom were nearly unanimous in their sympathies; they cheered Hamilton's strong points and the jury's hastily arrived at verdict of "not guilty" —"upon the pronouncing of which the numerous audience expressed their joy in three loud Huzzas & scarcely one person except the officers of the Court were observ'd not to join in this noisy exclamation."[45] Their hero was Hamilton rather than Zenger, however, and the victor was the Morrisite faction for whom they had voted in 1734 rather than the *Journal*. The crowd carried Hamilton to a feast at the Black Horse Tavern while the neglected Zenger spent a final night in jail.

---

risite constitutional program. Alexander also objected to Cosby's exercise of the equitable jurisdiction of the chancellor during the controversy over the Oblong grant. See below, pp. 80–81, and Colden, *History of Cosby and Clarke*, pp. 309–311.

44. For a detailed discussion of the disbarment, see [James Alexander and William Smith,] *The Complaint of James Alexander and William Smith to the Committee of the General Assembly of the Colony of New York, etc.* (New York, [1736]). Chambers was one of the Cosbyite candidates defeated in the September 1734 New York City elections. *New-York Weekly Journal,* October 7, 1734, reprinted in Katz, ed., *Brief Narrative,* p. 131.

45. Colden, *History of Cosby and Clarke,* p. 339.

V

The Morrisites would not have cheered so lustily on that August day had they known that the Zenger trial would mark the high-water point of their opposition to the Governor. The forces ranged against them were simply too strong. The Governor's constitutional prerogatives and the resourcefulness of those he placed in high office enabled him to retain control of the province.

An early eighteenth-century commentator on colonial government remarked that governors frequently provoked the creation of opposing factions "by making use of, and encouraging some one particular Sort or Sett of Men, and rejecting all others," and Cosby fit the pattern.[46] "I make the right use of Mr. Clarke he is my first minister," he boasted to Newcastle, thus perpetuating Montgomerie's exclusion of Lewis Morris and disappointing the pretensions of Surveyor General Cadwallader Colden, who had solicited the place through his English connections.[47] George Clarke, the provincial secretary and a long-time councillor who was recommended to Cosby by Horatio Walpole, had filled a similar role under Governor Montgomerie, conducting himself so as to arouse Colden's cynical wrath: "He [Montgomerie] was much in debt and wanted to recover his fortune by the profits of his government with as little trouble to himself as possible. Mr. Clark served him well for these purposes."[48] Clarke's personal ambition is manifest, but so was his political wisdom, and the same may be said for James DeLancey, who was an increasingly important member of the Cosby camp. Indeed, Lewis Morris later suggested that Mrs. Cosby, "who had the Intire management of that weak madman her husband," had entered into an agreement with DeLancey to suspend Clarke in his favor as

46. Wright, ed., *An Essay upon the government of the English plantations*, p. 36.

47. Cosby to Newcastle, October 26, 1732, *New York Col. Docs.*, V, 937. For Clarke, see below, Chap. 6. For Colden's efforts, see Alexander Colden to Colden, August 5, 1732, NYHS, *Colls.*, 1918, p. 73; Alured Popple to Colden, November 1, 1734, *ibid.*, p. 115.

48. Cadwallader Colden, "Letters on Smith's History of New York," [1759], NYHS, *Colls.*, 1868, p. 220; Cosby to Van Dam, January 27 and February 23, 1732, Rutherfurd Collection, IV, 33, 37, NYHS.

informal head of the government. "Some suspected the truth of this; most agreed she was capable of it; few men were willing to acquit Mr. Clark Intirely of being concern'd in the direction of his measures, and many believed they were both more concerned than they should have been." [49]

Morris' account seems implausible, but unquestionably Clarke and DeLancey were the leading figures in the Cosby administration. Other members of the Governor's coterie were imperial placemen of long standing, such as Richard Bradley (attorney general) and Archibald Kennedy (receiver general, collector of the port of New York, and councillor); or close associates whom the Governor was able to reward with jobs and favors, such as Francis Harison (examiner of the chancery court, judge of admiralty, and councillor), Daniel Horsmanden (councillor) and Joseph Warrell (a lawyer). The assembly's leader, Adolph Philipse, also stood by Cosby.[50] Many others aided the Governor and most were repaid for their troubles, because his powers of appointment of county judges and sheriffs and of the officials of Albany and New York City enabled him to extend his power throughout the province.[51]

The Morrisite opposition, on the other hand, was born in resentment and nourished by little more than fond hope. Governor Cosby assured Newcastle that Morris and his "adherents" were "so few that they amount to no more than two or three Scotchmen and I am very sorry to say that hold Employments under the King." [52] Quite clearly the three Scots were James Alexander, Cadwallader

49. Lewis Morris to Sir Charles Wager, October 12, 1739, *Governor Lewis Morris Papers*, p. 67. See also, Lewis Morris to Wager, May 10, 1739, *ibid.*, p. 44.

50. For a conveniently indexed guide to New York officialdom, see Edgar A. Werner, comp., *Civil List and Constitutional History of the Colony and State of New York* (Albany, 1884). See also, S. C. Hutchins, comp., *Civil List and Forms of Government of the Colony and State of New York* (Albany, 1869) and Edmund B. O'Callaghan, comp., *Calendar of New York Colonial Commissions* (New York, 1929). On Philipse see Colden to Alexander, December 27, 1735, Rutherfurd Collection, II, 149, NYHS.

51. For an example of Cosby's ruthless manipulation of county patronage, one which drove Vincent Matthews of Orange County into the Morrisite camp, see Katz, ed., *Brief Narrative*, pp. 129–131, 223n25.

52. Cosby to Newcastle, June 19, 1734, Add. MSS. 32689, foll. 278–279, B.M.

79

Colden, and Philip Livingston, the lord of Livingston Manor, who led the opposition in the northern Hudson Valley. Alexander and Livingston were so open in their defiance of the Governor that they were afraid they might be seriously compromised by their correspondence, which Alexander claimed was being intercepted.[53] Two other outstanding members of the Morrisite group were William Smith and Lewis Morris, Jr. Smith and Alexander formed the legal staff of the group and were punished by their disbarment in the Zenger trial; William Smith, Jr., noted sadly that his father "in Cosby's Time had suffered by being two years silenced the loss of about £2000, and the Pique & malice of Several principal gentlemen in this Province." [54] Young Morris was recognized by Cosby as the opposition's leader in the New York assembly: "he endeavoured to stirr up contentions and create misunderstandings between me the Council and Assembly." [55]

The Morrisite leaders felt themselves personally aggrieved by the Governor on a number of different counts, but they also shared at least one significant material interest—the "Oblong"—which exemplified the subtle combination of principle and self-interest in their opposition. The Oblong, a huge tract of land ceded by Connecticut to New York in resolution of a boundary controversy, was the most desirable ungranted land in the province at the time, and shortly after its transferral Francis Harison, Colden, Alexander, William Smith, and the Morrises formed a company to seek title to it in New York. Harison soon decided that he was not being treated fairly in the matter, however, and induced the Duke of Chandos and a group of his English associates to apply for a royal patent to the lands, which was granted in May 1731. Meanwhile Governor Montgomerie granted a patent to the local company in June, thus creating a direct conflict of title.[56]

Inevitably, the legal contest became political. Harison induced

53. Philip Livingston to Alexander, January 7, 1735; Lewis Morris to Alexander, February 24, 1735, Rutherfurd, *Family Record*, pp. 17–18.

54. William Smith, Jr., MSS Historical Memoirs of the Province of New York, II, 372, NYPL.

55. Cosby to Newcastle, May 3, 1733, *New York Col. Docs.*, V, 946.

56. For the Oblong controversy, see Colden, *History of Cosby and Clarke*, pp. 305–312; Smith, *History*, II, 23–24; McAnear, "Politics in Provincial New

his new-found patron, Governor Cosby, to come into the English company. The remaining New York patentees were those very men who had come to be most opposed to the Governor for other reasons. Harison brought a suit in chancery to vacate Montgomerie's grant to the New Yorkers in 1735, and Chancellor Cosby took jurisdiction with a ruthless disregard for the arguments of the respondents. As it happened, the Governor died before the case could be concluded, but his readiness to vacate the Oblong title and his announced suspicion of the validity of Long Island land titles disturbed New Yorkers of all political persuasions, for New York land grants were notoriously imprecise: "No man could [have] had any security for his Estate if they became defeasible at the will of a Governor." [57] Therefore, when Smith and Alexander attacked the Governor's chancery proceedings before the assembly's committee on grievances in October 1735, the legislators resolved that "a Court of Chancery within this Colony, in the Hands, or under the Exercise of a Governor, without Consent in General Assembly, is contrary to Law, unwarrantable, and of dangerous Consequence to the Liberties and Properties of the People." [58] Thus a particular grievance was urged on the highest constitutional level, as in the Zenger and Van Dam trials, and it was pursued not only from "the general opinion of his [Cosby's] avaricious ill principles but out of Interest which generally works with the greatest force on mens passions." [59]

Next to his manipulation of the provincial court system, Cosby's land policies aroused the greatest indignation among his opponents. The Morrisite councillors, of course, no longer shared the grants that were the most tangible reward of their office, and Morris complained to the board of trade that Cosby refused to grant any lands "unless he comes in for one third of them." [60] Cosby

---

York," I, 406–409; Andrews, *Colonial Period*, II, 230–232; C. H. Collins Baker and Muriel I. Baker, *The Life and Circumstances of James Brydges, First Duke of Chandos; Patron of the Liberal Arts* (Oxford, 1949), pp. 349–353.

57. Colden, *History of Cosby and Clarke*, p. 306.
58. *Assemb. Jour.*, I, 687.
59. Colden, *History of Cosby and Clarke*, p. 305.
60. Lewis Morris to Lords of Trade, August 27, 1733, *New York Col. Docs.*, V, 953. On November 12, 1734, for instance, Cosby and the council granted a license to purchase Indian lands to his two sons, Henry and William, Jr. *Cal. Coun. Min.*, p. 323. In the first two years of his administration, Cosby

antagonized residents of Albany in September 1733 when he was party to the destruction of a deed that the Mohawk Indians had given to the city corporation for some nearby lands, the "Mohawk Flats." [61] The Governor claimed that the Indians had been duped by the corporation into thinking that their action would preserve the lands for them in the future, and that if he had not torn up the deed the Mohawks would have shifted their allegiance to the French.[62] Colden thought otherwise: "This land is worth at least £5000 New York money & Coll Cosby being told of it & of the Defects of the Albany Title resolv'd to have it to himself." [63] Although Cosby never did grant the lands to himself, perhaps because of the indignation his destruction of the "Albany deed" had caused, the episode became a focal point for serious criticism throughout his administration. "However Coll Cosbys Interest was so great as to prevent any publick inquisition into this affair he & his friends could not avoid the Impression it made on peoples minds that he would stop at no Injustice in order to fill his pockets." [64]

Further Morrisite complaints, which once again touched them practically as well as in principle, concerned the Governor's conduct in the council, for he had ceased summoning those councillors who opposed him and he insisted upon sitting and voting at legislative sessions. Cosby was also criticized for his selection of unqualified local officials (the Morrisites had in mind the behavior of the Westchester sheriff in the Eastchester election) and for his acceptance of the assembly gift of £1,000 in 1732. They even accused him

asked 48,000 acres of New York land for himself. Alice Mapelsden Keys, *Cadwallader Colden* (New York, 1906), p. 51. For a discussion of Cosby's dealings in land, see Edith M. Fox, *Land Speculation in the Mohawk Country* (Ithaca, 1949), pp. 19–20 and for land policy generally, see Ruth L. Higgins, *Expansion in New York, With Especial Reference to the Eighteenth Century* (Columbus, O., 1931).

61. For the Albany Deed incident, see Smith, *History*, II, 24; Colden, *History of Cosby and Clarke*, pp. 304–305; Fox, *Land Speculation*, pp. 20–33; Cosby to Lords of Trade, December 15, 1733, *New York Col. Docs.*, V, 960–962; Lewis Morris to Lords of Trade, August 29, 1733, *ibid.*, 957–958.

62. Cosby to Lords of Trade, June 19, 1734, *New York Col. Docs.*, VI, 6.

63. Colden, *History of Cosby and Clarke*, p. 304.

64. *Ibid.*, p. 305.

of treachery in allowing the French sloop *Le Caesar* to put into the harbor at New York in 1733. The Morrisites communicated these criticisms within New York in the pages of the *Journal* and without in letters to the Duke of Newcastle and the board of trade, taking care to base them on constitutional grounds: the impartial administration of justice, the independence of the three branches of the provincial government, the appointment of qualified public officials, and the protection of private property.[65]

VI

The line that divided Cosbyites from Morrisites in New York is not easily drawn. To a certain extent the divisions were a self-conscious reflection of contemporary English politics, as is apparent in the London polemics reprinted in the *Gazette* and the *Journal*, the governor's men comparing themselves to the Walpole ministry and the Morrisites to the Bolingbroke-Pulteneyite opposition. The *Gazette* ran an English piece characterizing the opposition to Walpole as "not national, but personal": "The contention is not, now, between the government and the people, or between the King and the nation, nor between the ministry and the people; but between the gentlemen in power, and certain gentlemen out of power." [66] The New York administration, like Walpole's, contended that its opponents were united only in the lust for office, and denied that legitimate differences of principle were at issue. The effect of opposition, then, was merely to provoke "*tumults* and *sedition*, to the *disturbance* of the *public peace*, and to the endangering of all *order* and *government*." [67] Cosby ascribed the disruptive

65. For a typical list of the opposition complaints, see "Heads of Articles of Complaint . . . by Rip Van Dam" (December 17, 1733), *New York Col. Docs.*, V, 975–978.
66. *New York Gazette*, March 3–March 11, 1735. Perhaps a better statement of this phenomenon is the one attributed to Jonathan Swift in 1712: "The true genuine cause of animosity [is] that those who are out of place would fain be in." *Some Reasons to Prove* . . . , pp. 9–10, as quoted in Foord, *His Majesty's Opposition*, p. 42.
67. *New York Gazette*, October 14–October 21, 1734.

effect of the Morrisites to "the example and spirit of the Boston people" or, even less plausibly, to the theory that his difficulties were "spirited up from home by Mr. Pulteney and that faction." [68]

In choosing William Pulteney's slogan "King George, Liberty and Law" the Morrisites, far from denying the identification, invited comparison with the English opposition. They especially imitated Bolingbroke's appeal to "patriotism" and his faction's evocation of seventeenth-century constitutionalist heroes such as Eliot, Pym, Hampden, and Sydney. Likewise, their numerous proposals for reform were derived from a few constitutional principles and their appeal was based upon the argument that Cosby, like Walpole, ruled in a corrupt and tyrannical manner which only a return to limited government could prevent. In both instances, however, the constitutional program must be viewed with a mixture of respect and cynicism. The Morrisites had suffered numerous political losses and they lived under continual threat to their lands, offices, profits, and professions, so that it seems fair to conclude, as did Archibald Foord of the English opposition, that they made "their political expediency a virtue." [69] Motives are difficult to document and the constitutional tradition to which the New Yorkers referred is significant for the intellectual history of the colonies, but one ought to remember Philip Livingston's confession at the conclusion of the Cosby era: "we Change Sides as Serves our Interest best not ye Countries." [70]

The Morrisites must have appealed to a number of elements within the heterogeneous society of provincial New York. Many of their adherents were Dutch, sympathizing with Van Dam and the Albany corporation. Others were Long Islanders, since Cosby seemed determined to single them out for a test of their land titles,

---

68. Cosby to Newcastle, October 26, 1732, *New York Col. Docs.*, V, 937; Cosby to Newcastle, January 24, 1734, *Cal. State Papers, Col., Am.*, 1733, p. 25.

69. Foord, *His Majesty's Opposition*, p. 154. For a brilliant account of the English opposition during this period, which sheds great light on the forms available to Americans, see *ibid.*, pp. 161–216.

70. Philip Livingston to Jacob Wendell, July 23, 1737, Museum of the City of New York, New York, N.Y.

in what Smith called "his design against the people of Long Island."[71] Then, of course, Cosby's spoilsman's approach to local offices alienated most of those turned out of their places, such as the estimable Vincent Matthews of Orange County.[72] Landholders generally were aroused by Cosby's resort to the chancery court, and many New Yorkers responded to the Morrisite contention that the Governor was responsible for the economic ills of the day.[73] The opposition appealed, more generally, to the constitutionally-minded and the "industrious" poor for whom the *Journal* made a play.[74] Despite this wide basis of attraction, however, the Morrisites made little headway against the administration, for mere numbers (whatever they may have been) counted for little in the political scheme of early eighteenth-century New York.

VII

Morrisite tactics in the New York assembly demonstrate this point. Unfortunately, division lists were not recorded in this period, so that the behavior of individual members cannot be accurately assessed, but certain general patterns are clear. Insofar as the assembly could be said to be led, its leader was Speaker Adolph Philipse, father of the Cosbyite supreme court justice Frederick Philipse (himself a Westchester representative). The Philipse family had wrested the leadership of the house from the Morrises and thus could not be expected to cooperate with them, especially after Lewis Morris' treatment of Frederick Philipse in the Van Dam case. Another bad situation for the Morrises was the composition of the important New York County delegation, which included Speaker Philipse, Stephen DeLancey, Anthony Rutgers, and Garret Van Horne. DeLancey, the new Chief Justice's father, had nearly been

71. Smith, *History*, II, 25. For a list of 297 New Yorkers who supported Lewis Morris' 1735–1736 mission to England and were doubtless of the Morris political faction, see Rutherfurd Collection, II, 75, NYHS.
72. See above, n. 51.
73. See *New-York Weekly Journal*, April 8, 1734, reprinted in Katz, ed., *Brief Narrative*, pp. 134–135.
74. See *ibid.*, p. 225n33.

excluded from the assembly as an alien in 1725 at the behest of Burnet and Morris, and Rutgers was one of the administration candidates in New York City defeated by the Morrisites in 1734. Thus even though Van Horne almost certainly voted with them, the Morrisites were outnumbered three to one among the members from their strongest constituency, doubtless because the assembly which served under Cosby was elected in 1728 and dissolved only after his death.[75]

Amidst the burst of good feelings that attended his arrival in New York, the assembly voted Governor Cosby the customary five-year salary grant, thereby surrendering its greatest potential weapon against him. Henceforth, the assembly remained quite unsympathetic to Lewis Morris, Jr.'s, repeated efforts to enlist its support in the campaign against the Governor. Cosby accused young Morris of trying to delay the revenue bill in 1733 as part of an attempt to subvert the assembly's loyalty to the administration and the crown —an early example of what Smith called "the anti-Cosbyan doctrine of annual supplies." Morris failed, but bore watching, for "he had an eye to the Boston Assembly, whose spirit begins to difuse itself too much amongst the other provinces." [76]

Thwarted in his opposition to basic measures, Morris sponsored a number of bills that he hoped would damage Cosby's prestige. On May 27, 1734, he attempted to introduce a bill setting the fees of officers of the government and lawyers, and he encouraged the efforts made to question the basis of the exchequer court. In June, Cosby angrily reported to the board of trade Morris' "bold and presumptuous attempts in the Assembly against his Majesty's authority to establish Courts." [77] As if in response, the Westchester member asked leave on June 8 to bring in a bill "to prevent clandes-

75. For a list of the assemblymen for the period, see Werner, *Civil List*, pp. 305–310. For the Burnet-DeLancey episode, see Osgood, *Eighteenth Century*, II, 425–426. For Rutgers' election defeat, see *New-York Weekly Journal*, October 7, 1734, reprinted in Katz, ed., *Brief Narrative*, pp. 131–132.

76. Smith, *History*, II, 131; Cosby to Newcastle, May 3, 1733, *New York Col. Docs.*, V, 946.

77. *Assemb. Jour.*, I, 661. See also, *ibid.*, I, 660, 662. The matter had previously been considered in August 1732. (*Ibid.*, I, 637.) Cosby to Lords of Trade, June 19, 1734, *New York Col. Docs.*, VI, 5.

tine Marriages," a tactless reference to the secret wedding of the Governor's daughter to Lord Augustus Fitzroy in March.[78] Later in June, Morris brought in a bill for appointing an agent "at the Court of Great Britain independent of the Governor" and one demanding that the sheriffs of the province be "Persons of good and sufficient Security, for the due discharge of their offices." [79] The latter publicized the Morrisite complaint that Cosby had appointed indigent strangers to be sheriffs and reminded New Yorkers of the actions of Cosby's sheriff in Lewis Morris' 1733 Westchester election. It was also a slap at the Governor's son, who had been sheriff at Amboy. As was the case with most of Morris' bills and resolutions, it got nowhere in the assembly. The Morrisites' sole success was the November 1735 resolution condemning Cosby's use of the chancery court, and they succeeded only because it was the one issue they pressed that touched meaningfully on a common grievance of the province.[80] The assembly thus stood aloof from the Morris-Cosby contest, tacitly strengthening the Governor's hand by refusing to add its weight to that of the opposition.

VIII

The Morrisites were stronger in the provincial council than anywhere else, but the governor's traditional control over the upper house effectively neutralized their numbers. Eleven men held places in the New York council in 1732: Rip Van Dam, George Clarke, Francis Harison, Cadwallader Colden, James Alexander, Abraham Van Horne, William Provoost, Archibald Kennedy, Philip Livingston, James DeLancey, and Philip Cortlandt.[81] At least five of the councillors (Van Dam, Colden, Alexander, Van Horne, and Livingston) quickly swung into outright opposition and others (such as Kennedy and Alexander's kinsman by marriage, Provoost) may

78. *Assemb. Jour.*, I, 663, 667; Smith, *History*, II, 26. For a contemporary satirical ballad, see Misc. Papers (Lord Augustus Fitzroy), NYPL.

79. *Assemb. Jour.*, I, 669, 673–674.

80. *Ibid.*, I, 687. See above, p. 81.

81. Councillors for this period are listed in Werner, *Civil List*, p. 270. See also Hutchins, *Civil List*, pp. 21–23.

have wavered, so that there were times at the beginning of his administration when Cosby may have had difficulty in securing a majority (as for instance at the August 23, 1733, meeting when DeLancey replaced Morris as chief justice).[82]

Ordinarily, however, Cosby did not need six votes for a majority. Livingston lived in Albany and Colden at his Ulster County estate, and neither one came regularly to New York City for the sessions.[83] By his own admission, Colden never summoned Alexander to a council meeting after October 1732, and thus, as Alexander charged, Cosby was sometimes able to carry the council with but three votes, since only five councillors were necessary for a quorum.[84] Cosby did not long require parliamentary devices to retain the support of the council, however, for he was able to suspend his enemies and replace them with friends. Strictly speaking, the nomination of councillors was the prerogative of the board of trade, but in fact the board almost always chose councillors from among those nominated by the governor, and the replacements during the Cosby administration were uniformly men of his choosing.[85]

In April 1732 the board notified the king of a vacancy in the New York council and recommended that the newly-appointed Cosby "should have an opportunity upon his arrival of transmitting

82. Van Horne was one of those who offered to stand surety for Zenger's bail. Zenger's affidavit, November 23, 1734, James Alexander Papers, 1733-1734, no. 21, NYPL. In March 1735 Morris considered Colden, Livingston, Alexander, and Van Dam reliable supporters. He judged Van Horne slightly uncertain and thought Kennedy was "willing" but "dare[d] not" join the Morrisites. Morris to Alexander, March 31, 1735, Rutherfurd Collection, II, 115, NYHS.

83. *Journal of the Legislative Council of the Colony of New York*, 1691-1775 (Albany, 1861), I, passim. (Hereafter, *Jour. Legis. Coun.*) Livingston attended only in October and early November 1734.

84. Cosby to Newcastle, December 17, 1733, *New York Col. Docs.*, V, 974; Alexander to Alderman [Micajah] Perry, December 4, 1733, extract, *New Jersey Archives*, V, 363*n*.

85. C.O. 324:48 [IV], foll. 14b-15, PRO. For the *Journal's* view of Cosby's council appointments, see the issue of December 17, 1733, reprinted in Katz, ed., *Brief Narrative*, pp. 119-120.

a list of persons proper to supply vacancies . . . before a New Councillor is named." [86] Cosby urged that the existing New York vacancies be filled quickly, complaining that many councillors "live very remote and some very old, [so that] 'tis with some difficulty I gett a council to attend." He recommended his protégé Joseph Warrell as a replacement for James Alexander, who had "clog'd and perplexed every thing with difficulty's that related to the Crown." At the same time he proposed replacing Provoost, who would be transferred to the council of New Jersey, where he resided, by Daniel Horsmanden and Robert Walters, deceased, by Henry Lane.[87] Both Horsmanden, a recently arrived English barrister who frequently assisted Attorney General Bradley, and Lane, a New York City merchant, were reliable partisans of the administration, and their appointments were approved by the privy council in May 1733.[88]

Determined to rid himself of his principal antagonists, the Governor recommended the removal of Alexander and Van Dam in June 1734 and in December he asked that Morris be removed from his councillorship in New Jersey.[89] He renewed his attack on Van Dam in June 1735 when he assured the board of trade that "a majority of the Council have declared that they could not sit at the Board with Mr. Vandam after the open and scandalous aspersions he had thrown upon them in printed libels and papers industriously dispersed in the Province." He suggested as replacements the sole

86. Lords of Trade to the king, April 28, 1732, *New York Col. Docs.*, V, 934–935.

87. Cosby to Lords of Trade, December 18, 1732, *ibid.*, V, 939; *Board of Trade Journal, 1729–1734*, p. 347.

88. Horsmanden was admitted to the Middle Temple and came to New York before 1731. He was the son of the rector of Purleigh, whose sister was William Byrd's mother. Byrd and Horsmanden spent a great deal of time together during Byrd's 1717–1721 trips to London. William Byrd, *The London Diary [1717–1721] and Other Writings*, ed. Louis B. Wright and Marion Tinling (New York, 1958), p. 55n28. Cosby recommended Capt. William Dick of one of the independent companies stationed in New York to fill James Alexander's proposed vacancy. *New York Col. Docs.*, V, 939.

89. Cosby to Lords of Trade, June 19 and December 6, 1734, *New York Col. Docs.*, VI, 6–7, 23.

Cosbyite in the common council of New York City, John Moore, and his own son-in-law, Thomas Freeman.[90] Van Dam was suspended by the Governor on his own authority in November 1735, but no replacement for him was chosen in England. Finally, on August 28, 1735, the board of trade fully supported Cosby by recommending the removal of Van Dam, Alexander, and Morris, but the privy council took no action.[91] Clearly, however, through the loyalty of some councillors, the manipulation of attendance at council sessions, and the board of trade's support, Cosby retained consistent control of the council. Far from discomfitting the Governor on his own ground, the Morrisite councillors were thrown on the defensive and had to fight to retain their places.

The Morrisites thus had little to show for two full years of opposition to Governor Cosby. A single assembly seat and control of the common council of New York City could not outweigh the neutrality of the assembly and Cosby's constitutional powers in the struggle for control of the colony. The only remaining alternative was to attempt to have the Governor removed, for if Cosby could not be ousted from within New York, he might be undermined in London. Where provincial politics did not work, imperial politics might. With this in mind, Lewis Morris slipped out of New York in late November 1734, just after Zenger's imprisonment, and set sail for England, intent upon carrying the contest for the administration of New York into the arena of English politics.

90. Cosby to Lords of Trade, June 10, 1735, and June 19, 1735, *ibid.*, VI, 31–32.
91. Hutchins, *Civil List*, p. 22; *Governor Lewis Morris Papers*, p. 25; *Board of Trade Journal, 1735–1741*, pp. 56, 60–61; *Acts, Privy Coun., Col.*, III, 479–480.

5
The Morris Mission to London,
1735-1736

Ye gods, be kind unto the worthy Chief;
Conduct him safely soon to get Relief;
Where Great Augustus Reigns; there may he find
An easie Access, and the Sov'reign kind.[1]

ON NOVEMBER *19, 1734*, THE NEW YORK ASSEM-
bly gave Lewis Morris leave "to go home, being indisposed," and
the former Chief Justice hastened to his estate in New Jersey in

1. *New-York Weekly Journal*, December 30, 1734.

order to embark on a ship bound for London. The *Journal* proudly announced his departure; the *Gazette* cynically observed that Morris' indisposition seemed to be a "politick Shin" and that his "home" seemed to be Westminster rather than Westchester.[2] Accompanied by his younger son, Robert Hunter Morris, Morris undertook the arduous and expensive role of advocate for the newly-formed opposition to Cosby in a last ditch attempt to outflank the Governor. Morris and his friends were without important English connections, however, and they were forced to rely upon hard work and constitutional arguments, seldom successful techniques in the conduct of Anglo-American politics.

The objectives of Morris' quest were carefully selected prior to his departure. Lewis Morris, Jr., and William Smith submitted suggestions to James Alexander, who drew up a set of instructions, dated November 19, 1734, setting forth eight points to guide the New Yorker's conduct in London.[3] First, Morris was to secure the favor of his own friends until "further proofs and materials" should arrive from America. Second, he was to analyze all the evidence compiled against Cosby and, with the advice of counsel, to prepare articles of complaint against the Governor. Third, "Things thus prepared, with some of your friends wait on the Duke of Newcastle & other friends of Coll Cosbys with them, & give them the perusal of the whole and insist that they forthwith consent amicably to remove him from the government to some other or to some other office, otherwise threaten that you'll apply to the King and Council or Parliament for redress and to the press to Expose him & his sup-

2. *Assemb. Jour.*, I, 677; *New-York Weekly Journal*, November 25, 1734.
3. Lewis Morris, Jr.'s, proposals are endorsed "Proposals of what Col. Morris shall go home for" in his own hand and "Lewis Morris Junr his proposal of instructions to his father" in Alexander's hand, Rutherfurd Collection, II, 71, NYHS. William Smith's proposals are in his own hand, with marginal comments in Alexander's hand, along with a note to Alexander: "These are all the considerations further that have occurred to me which I submit to your judgment." Rutherfurd Collection, II, 73, NYHS. The draft of the complete instructions, in Alexander's hand, and endorsed "Instructions proposed for Coll Morris . . ." is in the Rutherfurd Collection, II, 75. There is also a single page endorsed "Coppy Instructions to . . . Coll Morris for his Cond[uct] in England" which is a neater transcription of the last part of Alexander's draft. Rutherfurd Collection, II, 75.

porters to all Brittain." Fourth, "if you either find that his [Cosby's] friends are not probably to be overcome, or that the Contention may last too long, then give ear to a compromise which we think . . . they'll soon offer to you." Fifth, Morris was instructed to lay before parliament and the ministry proposals for encouraging hemp growing and the cast iron industry in New York, and for "Encouraging any other manufacture that may be of benefite to it & not interfere with the manufactures of Great Britain." Sixth, he was to make sure that nothing prejudicial to the interest of New York be undertaken in parliament and that, upon his departure, he should employ an agent to protect the province "in parliament or Elsewhere, till the assembly shall appoint one." Seventh, in case Cosby should be removed, Morris was to inform his successor about the state of the province and "endeavour his consent to all those things which its insisted that Mr. Cosby should do." Eighth, "we have reason to believe those instructions would be agreeable to above nine tenths of the people of this Colony, but think it improper to require many hands to them because such secresy as the case requires would not be therewith kept and conclude, recommending you and this cause to the care of the Almighty."

Morris' instructions contained a substantial list of articles to be insisted upon in "the treaty of compromise." First, Morris' own restoration as chief justice on good behavior. Second, royal orders ending the present New York assembly and calling a new one at such time as the council advised. Third, the removal of Francis Harison from the council and his other offices, and of Daniel Horsmanden from the council. Fourth, the appointment of William Smith and Peter Schuyler as councillors. This article went on to comment that ideally several other councillors deserved to be stripped of office, especially George Clarke and James DeLancey, but observed that Clarke would probably be protected by Horatio Walpole and that DeLancey was so young and of such "good natural sense" that he could be expected to "forsake of his errors." Fifth, a letter from Newcastle and Cosby's other supporters requesting the Governor to pass the laws of the proposed new assembly for "Establishing Courts of Judicature," for the specification of qualifications of sheriffs and coroners, and for regulating the selection of councillors and assemblymen and their legislative procedures. Sixth, permission for the council to sit independently of the governor when acting in its legislative capacity. Seventh, a guarantee that Cosby appear to the suit of Van Dam and "to the suit of any subject, and to make up his past differences by compromise or arbitration forthwith." Eighth, the granting of new charters upon request to the cities of New York and Albany, specifying the annual election of municipal officials. Ninth, "That upon his failure of performance of any of these things he is to forfeit all protection from the subscribers of the letter or their interest."

The bulk of the instructions concerned terms for a possible Morrisite compromise with Governor Cosby, and it seems likely that such a solution would have pleased James Alexander, if not the entire group. At the end of December 1734 Alexander assured Morris that, "tho' he has given me personal ill useage, yet if more can be got from him for the benefit of the Country and cheaper than from a new governour I am clearly of opinion a composition ought to be fallen in with, which may tye him & all future Governours according to the instructions." [4] In January 1735 he urged one of the English merchants allied with the Morrisites to work for a compromise, providing him with three reasons for so doing: "the Compromise proposed is in Substance what Englishmen are intitled to by the original Constitution of their mother country"; New Yorkers have been restrained from rising up against Cosby's tyranny only by the hope of redress at home, but they will be content to have Cosby remain governor so long as he governs justly; an annual assembly is the most important New York demand, and it is no more than the other American colonies enjoy as a basic constitutional guarantee. [5] And as late as November 6, 1735, Alexander wrote Morris that he still thought "your own restoration independent of the Govr & a

4. Alexander to Morris, draft, December 30, 1734, Rutherfurd Collection, II, 95, NYHS.
5. Alexander to Roderigo Pacheco, draft, January 6, 1735, Rutherfurd Collection, II, 95, NYHS.

new assembly would be a compromise not to be slighted if you have not sure grounds to believe you can remove him." [6] One suspects that Lewis Morris himself was the most belligerent of the opposition. At any rate, the group drafting the instructions agreed to support him on the condition that, once a compromise had been arrived at, Morris would respect Cosby's authority and would refrain from obstructing the Governor in "receiveing the usual salary, perquisites, & emoluments of the government as other Govs used to have before him." [7]

The surviving copy of Morris' instructions is unsigned, but it seems likely that Alexander, Smith, Van Dam, Lewis Morris, Sr., and Lewis Morris, Jr., were the parties to them. The boast of widespread support in the eighth instruction takes on added plausibility, however, in a list of 297 names drawn up by William Smith and endorsed by Robert Hunter Morris: "The names of those that signed to my father's c[harge]." Included on the list were such prominent New Yorkers as Abraham De Peyster, Stephen Bayard, John Walter, Peter Bayard, William Beekman, John Cruger, Abraham Gouverneur, William Smith, Nicholas Bayard, Rip Van Dam, James Alexander, Abraham Van Horne, Oliver Schuyler, Peter Schuyler, Robert Livingston, Henry Beekman, Jr., and John Peter Zenger. Many of these men, perhaps all of them, subscribed to a fund for the support of Morris' expedition. Alexander and Van Dam each pledged £200, William Smith offered £50, and John Spratt promised 20 pistoles. [8] Morris was also pledged the credit of his two English sons-in-law in London, and the *Journal* boasted that although

6. Alexander to Morris, draft, November 6, 1735, Rutherfurd Collection, II, 143, NYHS. For the terms of compromise that Lewis Morris proposed to Sir Charles Wager on November 4, 1735, see R. H. Morris, "Diary," pp. 384–385.

7. Draft instructions to Lewis Morris, Rutherfurd Collection, II, 75, NYHS.

8. The list of names is in the Rutherfurd Collection, II, 75, NYHS. The handwriting appears to be that of William Smith, and his name is the only one which is a signature. A note on the amounts pledged by Van Dam, Alexander, Smith, and Spratt is appended to the draft instructions, Rutherfurd Collection, II, 75, NYHS.

he had personally borne the expense of his 1701–1702 journey to England in behalf of New Jersey interests, he would not have to bear the cost this time.[9]

Americans always complained of the terrific expense of English solicitations, however, and even this well-backed enterprise ran into difficulty. Several of those who had pledged their support, apparently including Smith and Van Dam, were forced to default in whole or in part because it was hard to raise funds in economically-depressed New York.[10] Morris soon discovered that living costs, the fees of attorneys and royal officials, and the cost of printing pushed his expenses beyond his means. "An universall avarice and corruption Predominates," he complained in August 1735, and in a few months he concluded that "the expense of soliciting for relief here is so great as no *one* can bear, and hardly all together." [11] The hardships of the trip were severe, but Morris persevered in his mission for eighteen months, so determined were he and his friends to regain their former eminence and to return New York government to a constitutional footing.

The necessity for Morris to travel to England was made clear by the failure of friends and a professional agent there to procure any official action against Cosby in 1733 or 1734. The agent, Ferdinand John Paris, was one of the most experienced colonial representatives in London.[12] He was then acting in behalf of the East

---

9. *New-York Weekly Journal*, December 9, 1734; Lewis Morris, Jr., to James Alexander, n.d., in Rutherfurd, *Family Record*, p. 15; R. H. Morris, "Diary," p. 209 (July 7, 1735); Alexander to Paris, March 19, 1733, Rutherfurd Collection, I, 159, NYHS.

10. Lewis Morris, Jr., to Alexander, November 18, 1735; Lewis Morris, Jr., to Alexander, n.d.; Lewis Morris, Jr., to Alexander, November 11, 1735; Alexander to [Colden?], draft, August 26, 1736, Rutherfurd Collection, II, 91, 121, 145, 185, NYHS; Lewis Morris to ?, draft, December 18, 1739, Lewis Morris Letterbook, p. 39, NJHS.

11. Morris to Alexander, August 25, 1735, Rutherfurd Collection, II, 129, NYHS; Morris to Alexander, January 11, 1736, *Governor Lewis Morris Papers*, pp. 26–27. Morris complained to Newcastle on March 21, 1736: "I have been a long time on this side of the water . . . at a greater expence than I am well able to beare." *Cal. State Papers, Col., Am.*, XLII, 184.

12. Lilly, *Colonial Agents of New York*, pp. 176, 209; Beverly W. Bond, Jr., "The Colonial Agent as a Popular Representative," *Political Science Quarterly*, XXXV (1920), p. 374; Edwin P. Tanner, "Colonial Agencies in

New Jersey proprietors, and, having become acquainted with Morris and Alexander in the course of their New Jersey activities, by early 1733 he began to warn Alexander against Governor Cosby. Alexander, who needed little prompting, asked Paris to represent Lewis Morris, who feared suspension from his post, so that Morris might "be heard to Such things as may be objected to him." Paris was also engaged to "lay Mr. Van Dams Complaints before the King in the very best Manner," and soon Alexander personally felt compelled to ask the agent to defend him against "private attempts to remove me in England." [13]

Another potential solicitor on behalf of Morrisite interests was Peter Van Brugh Livingston, son of Philip Livingston, who traveled to England on business in 1733. Morris entrusted him with the task of substantiating Morrisite accusations that Governor Cosby had treacherously permitted a French sloop to provision in New York harbor, but so far as one can tell from the *Journals* of the board of trade, Livingston was never called upon to testify.[14] Captains Vincent Pearse and Matthew Norris, Morris' sons-in-law, were more active, however. Alexander advised Paris that the two naval

England during the Eighteenth Century," *ibid.*, XVI (1901), p. 48; Mabel Pauline Wolff, *The Colonial Agency of Pennsylvania, 1712–1757* (Philadelphia, 1933), pp. 39–42. Paris had appeared before the board of trade and the privy council for the Penns, the New Jersey proprietors, several New York citizens, and the colonies of Rhode Island, New Hampshire, Georgia, St. Christopher, Antigua, Virginia, and Barbados. *Board of Trade Journal*, 1729–1734 and 1735–1741, passim; *Acts, Privy Coun., Col.*, III, passim. For Paris' involvement in the contemporaneous Penn–Baltimore dispute, see Nicholas B. Wainwright, "Tale of a Runaway Cape: The Penn–Baltimore Agreement of 1732," *The Pennsylvania Magazine of History and Biography*, LXXXVII (1963), pp. 251–293. In 1757 Paris' high fees were derided as "Ferdinando Parisian accounts." Joseph H. Smith, *Appeals to the Privy Council from the American Plantations* (New York, 1950), p. 321n312.

13. Alexander to Paris, March 19, 1733, *New Jersey Archives*, V, 329–331; *Board of Trade Journal*, 1729–1734, p. 34; Alexander to [Micajah] Perry, December 4, 1733, extract, *New Jersey Archives*, V, 363n. Alexander first engaged Paris in 1730 in defense of his council seat under Montgomerie's administration. Paris to Alexander, August 6, 1730, Rutherfurd Collection, Small Scrapbook, no. 39, NYIIS.

14. Lewis Morris to Lords of Trade, December 15, 1733, *New York Col. Docs.*, V, 958.

officers would reimburse him for his expenses and would "Join with you in advising what further Steps may be proper." [15] In January 1734, Captain Norris wrote a long letter describing the efforts of Morris' English associates and instructing the New Yorker how to proceed. Norris felt that Paris would need assistance after he had left for sea and recommended the employment of the agent for the Leeward Islands and Barbados, John Yeamans, "the ablest man in England in managing Complaints against Governours." He regretfully reported that he had failed to hire the talented West Indian agent, John Sharpe, whom Cosby had foresightedly "generally retained" before leaving for New York, but assured Morris that Sharpe had promised to be, "since he can't be our Friend, a very fair Adversary." [16] In addition to agents, however, qualified counsels had to present cases before the privy council and Norris had engaged the Attorney General and Solicitor General for the task.

Norris cautioned his father-in-law to proceed carefully in managing his case against the Governor, adhering to legal forms of complaint and demonstrating his accusations by solid "Vive Voce" evidence in England or authenticated testimony in New York. Strong proof of the Governor's misbehavior was necessary, for "tho you have told us these matters at Length, you have not enabled us to prove one of them . . . I believe we shall find Evidence sufficient to these points on this Side of the Water, and altho it is too true my Friends have not a power equal to their inclination to serve you, I make no doubt of the almighty favours our Continuance on this

15. Alexander to Paris, March 19, 1733, *New Jersey Archives*, V, 329–331.
16. Matthew Norris to Lewis Morris, January 28, 1734, Morris MSS., Box 1, R.U.L. Norris was at Bath at this time, recovering his health. Sharpe, the brother of the Maryland governor Horatio Sharpe, was one of the leading colonial agents in London. A solicitor to the treasury and a frequent correspondent of Newcastle, he was at various times the agent for Barbados, Jamaica (both of them in 1735), and other islands in the West Indies. Lillian Margery Penson, *The Colonial Agents of the British West Indies* (London, 1924), pp. 167, 250–252. He appeared before the board of trade countless times in colonial matters. Yeamans was also extremely active before the board and he, like Sharpe, was especially concerned with West Indian affairs. *Ibid.*, pp. 251, 253. For Morris' retention of Yeamans, see R. H. Morris, "Diary," pp. 375, 398.

Earth, to see you triumph over your Enemies." [17] Norris' letter suggests the difficulty of undertaking a formal complaint against a governor. The imperial administration was bureaucratic and formalistic to an extreme, so that colonial complainants required experienced agents and barristers to represent them and strict legal evidence to buttress their endless petitions and remonstrances. The administration was hard to move if it chose to stand its ground, however, and evidence was increasing that it was not going to purge Cosby unless it had to.

Very little progress had been made before Morris arrived in London in spite of the best efforts of Ferdinand Paris. The board of trade first heard of Morris' removal on November 28, when they received a letter from him and a copy of his opinion in the Van Dam case; on the 29th they read an extract of a letter from the Governor giving his version of the affair. Paris brought the privy council into the controversy on the 29th when he presented a petition from Morris asking Cosby's reasons for dismissing him and demanding restoration and compensation. Morris' first legal victory (or such it seemed at the time) was a January 8, 1734, order of the committee of the privy council calling for Cosby's reasons for removing the Chief Justice.[18] The case moved along very slowly, however, in the first part of 1734. In June Cosby wrote privately to Newcastle warning against the acceptance of Morris' petition, since if the Chief Justice should be reinstated, "it would put this province to the greatest Consternation as well as to the utmost confusion; The people in General being very much from his own reports afraid of his being restored being a very tyrant when in that post." [19] Finally, on August 21 another of Cosby's agents, Maynard Guerin, delivered to the board of trade the Governor's reasons for removing Morris—although Paris could not even secure a copy of the document until the privy council ordered it delivered to him on Novem-

17. Norris to Morris, January 28, 1734, Morris MSS., Box 1, R.U.L.
18. *Board of Trade Journal,* 1729–1734, pp. 363, 364; P.C. 2:92, foll. 267, 285, PRO; *Acts, Privy Coun., Col.,* III, 397.
19. Cosby to Newcastle, June 19, 1734, Add. MSS. 32689, foll. 278–279, B.M.

ber 1.[20] The contest between Cosby and the opposition had thus been joined in England, and it remained to be seen whether Lewis Morris' personal efforts to bring the machinery of empire to bear against the Governor could succeed in the face of Cosby's personal interest and official position.

I

Lewis Morris and his son presented their objections against Cosby as a complaint to the privy council. On the surface, the story of their mission to England is one of stylized legal moves and counter-moves within the imperial administrative bureaucracy, for their case took shape according to systematic procedures for colonial appeals which had been worked out since the Restoration. A printed "case" stating the nature of their complaint had to be prepared according to established standards, and the affair had to be handled by qualified counsel. Testimony had to be given before the privy council and a verdict rendered. Accordingly, a formal statement of the complaint was printed for Lewis Morris. Paris and Yeamans were engaged as agents for the Morrises, Sharpe and Guerin for the Governor. The Morrises also hired distinguished counsel for the actual hearing: in addition to the Attorney and Solicitor Generals, they obtained William Murray, the future Lord Mansfield.[21] Eventually a confrontation took place in the presence of the privy council, although it was clear to both sides that the

20. *Board of Trade Journal*, 1729–1734, pp. 406–407, 408 (August 8, 15, 21, 1734); "Reasons of Governor Cosby for Removing Chief Justice Morris," *New York Col. Docs.*, VI, 8–14; P.C. 2:93, fol. 29, PRO; *Acts, Privy Coun., Col.*, III, 397–398. Guerin's only appearances before the board of trade between 1729 and 1741 were on behalf of Cosby, though the *Journal* twice incorrectly identifies him as the agent of the province of New York. *Board of Trade Journal*, 1729–1734, pp. 335, 393–394, 408; *ibid.*, 1735–1741, pp. 32, 34, 44, 136. For the incorrect identifications, see *ibid.*, 1735–1741, pp. 34, 44.
21. R. H. Morris, "Diary," pp. 382–383; Alexander to Colden, n.d., NYHS, *Colls.*, 1918, p. 24; R. H. Morris, "Diary," p. 179 and n. 7. For a detailed discussion of procedures in privy council appeals, see J. H. Smith, *Appeals to the Privy Council*, pp. 289–296.

dispute would actually be resolved in terms of their personal connections to powerful officials.

Successful Anglo-American politics required the exploration of informal channels of access to the interests and sympathies of the leading imperial administrators. All colonials began at a disadvantage in such a quest, but none so severely as the American who sought to discipline a royal governor, for the crown was naturally jealous of its prerogative. The worst crime a governor could commit, Lewis Morris soon concluded, was not so bad "as the crime of complaining of it—the last is an arraigning of the Ministry that advised the sending of him." [22] The critical colonist had therefore to make clear that he did not want to undermine royal authority but only to secure proper government. He had to state his objections in terms of policy and principle, but even when his arguments were substantial the odds were against him. Morris remarked of Cosby's misgovernment that: "It is not the injustice of the thing that affects those concerned in recommending of him, provided it can be kept a secret and the people not clamor; and when they do, if they meet with relief, it is not so much in pity to them, as in fear of the reflection it will be upon themselves for advising the sending such a man, the sole intent of which was to make a purse." [23] Morris feared that the Governor's friends would protect him even though his ineptitude and weakness of character were widely recognized. Only if Cosby's reputation could be damaged to such an extent that it threatened the welfare of his English connections did the opposition stand a chance of unseating him.[24] Those who had made a governor could undo him, however, and the Morrises set about to acquire an English interest that could challenge Cosby's.

Since the Morris family had emigrated in the mid-seventeenth

22. Lewis Morris to Alexander, March 31, 1735, extract, *Governor Lewis Morris Papers*, pp. 24–25.

23. *Ibid.*

24. Lewis Morris was told that Cosby's best friends knew his character "better than I" and were ashamed of him, while Robert Hunter Morris claimed that George II personally hated the governor. Lewis Morris to John Morris, February 9, 1735, Morris MSS. (John Morris Papers), R.U.L.; Lewis Morris, Jr., to R. H. Morris, July 26, 1735, Morris MSS., Box 2, R.U.L.

century and maintained no important commercial ties to the mother country, they had few contacts with English political life. "It requires more time than you are aware of before a man can . . . know which way to come at the great folks and have any tolerable acquaintance with them & tho I have had more advantage that way than perhaps any body that could have come from America yet to tell you the truth I am as it were but walking in trammells yet and have not got my paces to perfection but come gayly on." [25] When Robert Hunter Morris and his father settled in London during the early months of 1735 they had to seek out allies, building on their meager connections, and their progress was slow. When, for instance, Lewis Morris presumed upon Colden's relationship with the Marquis of Lothian, the Scotsman begged off on the ground that "he had not interest enough" to help Morris, "but must go as the duke of Argyle went be which way it would." [26] On the other hand, chance acquaintances could be fruitful. Robert Hunter Morris befriended a brother of Anne Vane, the mistress of the Prince of Wales and a relative of Newcastle's, and Mrs. Vane was apparently well disposed toward the New Yorkers.[27] As did most Americans, however, the Morrises fell back upon their English relatives, in this case the Norrises and Pearses.

Two of Lewis Morris' numerous daughters married English naval officers, Vincent Pearse and Matthew Norris. Pearse's brother Thomas was a commissioner of the navy in 1735, having previously been an M.P. from George Bubb Dodington's borough of Weymouth. He was probably a minor protégé of Robert Walpole's, and it is clear that he went out of his way to be friendly to his in-laws while they were in London.[28] Matthew Norris' connection was

25. Morris to Alexander, March 31, 1735, Rutherfurd Collection, II, 115, NYHS.
26. Lewis Morris to Colden, April 11, 1735, NYHS, *Colls.*, 1918, p. 136; Lewis Morris to Lothian, March 26, 1735, *ibid.*, pp. 126–127.
27. R. H. Morris, "Diary," p. 380; *DNB*, XX, 112; *Burke's Peerage*, 1959, p. 155; Romney Sedgwick, ed., *Lord Hervey's Memoirs* (London, 1952), pp. 137–147, 18–19; Lower, *Pelham Family*, pp. 44–54.
28. Charnock, *Biographia*, IV, 58; *DNB*, XV, 595. Charnock (*Biographia*, I) lists seven Pearses in the navy of Charles II and one in the time of George

more impressive, for he was the son of Sir John Norris, admiral of the white and commander in chief of the British navy. Unfortunately for himself and the New Yorkers, however, the elder Norris was more talented in seamanship than in politics. He had been a member of parliament since 1708 (on the admiralty interest) and had served as a commissioner of the admiralty from 1718 until May 1730 when he had been dismissed on political grounds. Clearly on the outs with Walpole, Norris was nevertheless a figure to reckon with. He was a close friend of the most powerful Scots politician, the Duke of Argyle, he was designated to command the navy in 1735, and he held the highest office in the senior service.[29] Thus, although he left for Portugal to command the fleet in June 1735 and was out of the country during the crucial months of the Morris solicitation, the knowledge of his association with the Morrises gave added weight to their claims.

Captain Matthew Norris did his best to prepare the way for the Morrises before his departure to command the naval station ship in New York, and his many naval friends shared his warm feelings for them. Like Norris himself, however, they were of little political consequence. "I wish it was as much in the power, as I have reason to believe, tis their inclinations, but you know, Sir, in what light they stand, nor do I see a possibility of their having more influence,

---

II, Vincent Pearse (*ibid.*, VI, 90–91). Namier, *Structure of Politics*, p. 145; *DNB*, V, 1071; Thomas Pearse to Robert Walpole, November 29, 1733, Cholmondeley-Houghton MSS., Correspondence, no. 2086, C.U.L.; J. H. Plumb, *Sir Robert Walpole* (London, 1956–1960), II, 294; R. H. Morris, "Diary," pp. 211–213. Vincent Pearse may also have known Sir Charles Wager, for he visited him on Morris' behalf in December 1737. Lewis Morris to R. H. Morris, December 14, 1737, Morris MSS., Box 2, R.U.L.

29. *DNB*, XIV, 579–581; Sir Oswyn A. R. Murray, "The Admiralty," *The Mariner's Mirror*, XXIV (1938), pp. 214–215; Add. MSS. 28132, passim (especially foll. 181–183), B.M.; Burke, *Peerage* (1959), p. 123; Add. MSS. 28143, fol. 4, B.M.; Wager to Robert Walpole, September 7, 1733, Cholmondeley-Houghton MSS., Correspondence, no. 2040, C.U.L.; D. D. Aldridge, "Admiral Sir John Norris, 1670 (or 1671)–1749: His Birth and Early Service, His Marriage and His Death," *The Mariner's Mirror*, LI (1965), 173–183; Namier, *Structure of Politics*, pp. 30n2, 140, 141, 137; Add. MSS. 28145, fol. 233; Add. MSS. 28133, foll. 124–125, B.M.; Charnock, *Biographia*, II, 356.

but by a very great change of men in higher power." [30] Morris
recognized the dilemma and, although grateful for his kind recep-
tion by his daughters' relatives, lamented that they were not of "the
first rank." "I am not," he reported back to New York, "Yet
acquainted with none of the nobility." [31] As it turned out, however,
it was not a nobleman but another admiral, Sir Charles Wager, who
provided Morris' only effective voice within the ministry.

Wager was the foremost naval politician in Walpole's ministry
and one of the few commoners in the privy council in 1735. "He is a
man of great probity," reported Jonathan Belcher, and "is every day
he lives (if he pleases) in the K--g's and in Sr R's closet," so that his
advice may be depended upon "as his Majesty's and Sr R's sentiments." [32] Wager's career at sea had reached its climax in 1707
when he won a fortune by defeating the Spanish treasure fleet off
Cartagena. He soon turned his talents to administration, serving as
the comptroller of the navy and lord of the admiralty, the first lord
from 1733 to 1742. He sat in admiralty or treasury parliamentary
seats almost constantly from 1710 to 1743. His political success was
due to his patron, Sir Robert Walpole, with whom he lost his posts
in 1742. While the Morrises were in England, however, he was an
admiral of the white, the first lord of the admiralty, a member of
parliament for Westminster, and a privy councillor, altogether a
man whose acquaintance was well worth cultivating.[33]

30. Matthew Norris to Lewis Morris, November 6, 1735, Morris MSS.,
Box 1, R.U.L. For Matthew Norris, see Charnock, *Biographia*, IV, 136.
31. Lewis Morris to John Morris, February 9, 1735, Morris MSS. (John
Morris Papers), R.U.L.
32. Belcher to Richard Waldron, March 24, 1735, "The Belcher Papers,"
Massachusetts Historical Society, *Collections*, 6th ser., VII (Boston, 1894), p.
196.
33. Historical Manuscripts Commission, *Fifteenth Report, Appendix, Part
IV, The Manuscripts of His Grace the Duke of Portland* (London, 1897), IV,
501, 504; *DNB*, XX, 428–430; Sir George Jackson and Sir G. F. Duckett,
Naval Commissioners: From 12 Charles II to 1 George III, 1660–1760 ([Lon-
don?], 1889), pp. 132–134. For Horace Walpole's admiration of Wager ("one
of the bravest and best men I ever knew"), see Mrs. Paget Toynbee, ed., *The
Letters of Horace Walpole, Fourth Earl of Orford* (Oxford, 1903–1925),
I, 351, IV, 399, XII, 342. For Norris' estimate of Wager's relationship to Wal-

The Morris Mission to London, 1735–1736

How the Morrises were introduced to Wager is something of a mystery, although there are several likely possibilities. Either Thomas Pearse or Sir John Norris, who knew him well, might have brought them together. The immediate go-between, however, was probably Wager's private secretary, Francis Gashery. Gashery was apparently in line for a reported vacancy in the secretaryship of New York in mid-1735. His interest in the colony was further evident in 1739, when Lewis Morris attempted to obtain the agency for him.[34] In any case, his later correspondence with Lewis Morris confirms that his dealings with the New York politicians were extremely cordial, and his friendship was valuable, as an anonymous contemporary comment indicates: "Great Complaints are made of the Mismanagement at the Adm--ty Office the first Comm--r [Wager] being much advanced in years. Depends wholly upon the advice of his Secretary who Prime M--r like transacts business frequently, without applying to his Mar [Master?] . . . it's Said the Sec--ry must be disbanded or the Admirall resign." [35]

The Morrises were also connected to Wager through one of

pole, see Norris Journals, May 2, 1740, Add. MSS. 28132, fol. 183, B.M.

For Wager's political activities in the 1730's, see Wager to R. Walpole, July 12, 1731, Correspondence, no. 1852; Wager to Walpole, December 8, 1732, no. 1932; Wager to Walpole, September 7, 1733, no. 2040; Thomas Lewis to Walpole, September 22, 1733, no. 2044, all in Cholmondeley-Houghton MSS., C.U.L. See also, Add. MSS. 19030, foll. 170–171; Walpole to Newcastle, July 12, 1736, Add. MSS. 32791 fol. 335, B.M.

34. Euphemia Norris to R. H. Morris, December 9, 1734; Lewis Morris, Jr., to R. H. Morris, July 26, 1735, Morris MSS., Box 2, R.U.L.; Lewis Morris to Gashery, May 27, 1739, *Governor Lewis Morris Papers*, pp. 56–57; Lilly, *Colonial Agents*, pp. 99, 101, 104. Gashery never obtained the New York agency, but he did become the agent for Governor Edward Trelawny of Jamaica. Namier and Brooke, *History of Parliament*, II, 492. See also, Alexander and Richard Ashfield to Roderigo Pacheco, December 22, 1741, Rutherfurd Collection, Small Scrapbook, no. 85, NYHS.

35. "For the Rt. Honorable Sir Charles Wager," July 22, 1740, Add. MSS. 32694, fol. 362, B.M. See Lewis Morris to Gashery, December 8, 1739, *Governor Lewis Morris Papers*, p. 72. Gashery, who became a member of parliament in 1741, held a series of increasingly lucrative jobs: inspector of the captains' journals, commissioner for sick and hurt seamen (1737), assistant secretary to the admiralty (1738), commissioner of the navy (1741–1747), comptroller of victualling accounts (1744–1747), director of the South Sea

James Alexander's commercial correspondents, Peter Collinson, the brilliant Quaker merchant and scientist who came to know the Admiral through their common botanical interests. Alexander had written to Collinson on December 9, 1734, to request his aid for the Morrises, but for some strange reason Robert Hunter Morris did not deliver the letter to him until October 31, 1735. Collinson immediately rushed out to seek Wager's support, confiding to Alexander his feeling of obligation to "the Gentlemen of the plantations to do what lies in my small power to serve them but more especially in this affair which was so flagrant an instance of tyranny & oppression."[36] Morris' delay in contacting Collinson was no doubt partly because he had already been able to win over Wager, but it seems odd that he neglected to seek out such a promising ally.

Even without the intervention of Gashery and Collinson, however, Wager's long-standing interest in colonial patronage might have piqued his interest in the New York squabble. As early as 1722 Wager had solicited Walpole in favor of seekers to colonial office, although without any apparent consistency. A vain man, he may have derived satisfaction merely from the power to distribute colonial posts, just as Newcastle did, for otherwise it is hard to see what interest he had either in those he helped or the places they sought.[37]

Osgood states that Wager was the adopted son of a Rhode Island sea captain, and, if so, his American background may have

---

Company (1749 to his death), and treasurer and paymaster of the ordnance (1751 to his death). Namier and Brooke, *History of Parliament*, II, 492.

36. Collinson to Alexander, November 8, 1735, Collinson to Alexander, February 27, 1736, Collinson to Alexander, May 3, 1732, Rutherfurd Collection, II, 145, IV, 55, NYHS; Norman G. Brett-James, *The Life of Peter Collinson* (London, [1926]), pp. 19–40, 119–169. Another English merchant associate of Alexander's who was an important contact for Morris was Roderigo Pacheco, as appears in several letters in the Rutherfurd Collection, NYHS—see for instance, Morris to Alexander, August 25, 1735, II, 129.

37. Wager to R. Walpole, March 31, 1722, Correspondence, no. 944; Wager to Delafaye, November 30, 1733, Add. MSS. 32783, fol. 291, B.M.; Wager to R. Walpole, June 13, 1734, Correspondence, no. 2214; Wager to R. Walpole, January 12, 1731, Correspondence, nos. 1807, 1784, 1786, Cholmondeley-Houghton MSS., C.U.L.; Wager to Newcastle, December 2, 1738, Add. MSS. 32691, foll. 284–287, B.M.; "Belcher Papers," VII, 220; Haffenden, "Colonial Appointments and Patronage," p. 431.

caused him to sympathize with the New Yorkers.[38] Also, although he had abandoned the faith, Wager had formerly been a Quaker and was still, according to Jonathan Belcher, a staunch friend of the Friends, and he must have been well disposed to Morris' New Jersey and Pennsylvania connection.[39] What is certain, however, is that the Morrises saw Wager frequently and came to think of him as their English champion. In future years Lewis Morris would correspond with the Admiral and do him what favors he could, and when he received word in 1742 that "Sir Charles is quite laid aside and retired to Parsons Green," Morris and his family recognized that their English interest had collapsed.[40] During the tense months of 1735 and 1736, however, the Morrises boasted of "talking freely" with Wager (who "has the King's Ear") and hoped that he would "come into those measures that will best conduce to the happiness of the people" of New York.[41] In Wager the Morrises had finally secured an English connection of some importance.

II

The diary that Robert Hunter Morris kept during the greater part of his trip to London provides a vivid and detailed picture of the Morrisite solicitation.[42] Arriving in the first week of January 1735, the Morrises doubtless spent the first months discussing their difficulties with their agents, Paris and Yeamans, and contacting whomever they thought might help them. Their prospects must

---

38. Osgood, *Eighteenth Century*, III, 243n1.

39. J. Belcher to Richard Partridge, April 19, 1734, "Belcher Papers," VII, 33. See also, *ibid.*, VII, 479, and VI, 401–402; Historical Manuscripts Commission, *Eleventh Report, Appendix, Part IV, The Manuscripts of the Marquess Townshend* (London, 1887), pp. 285, 288–290.

40. Euphemia Norris to Lewis Morris, June 15, 1742, Morris MSS., Box 1, R.U.L.; Lewis Morris to Wager, May 10, 1739, *Governor Lewis Morris Papers*, p. 45; Lewis Morris to R. H. Morris, December 14, 1737, Morris MSS., Box 2, R.U.L.

41. Lewis Morris, Jr., to R. H. Morris, December 3, 1735, Morris MSS., Box 2, R.U.L.

42. The diary was kept from April 17, 1735, to January 4, 1736, and on December 16–19, 1749.

have seemed dim, however, for as early as February 9, Lewis Morris complained to his son, John, "if it had been your fortune to have made this troublesome Voyage with us I believe you would have Joyn'd with Robin [Robert Hunter] and I in Opinion that the meanest cottage in America with peace is preferable to anything here would to God we were with you and free from Cosbys Rule in any station of Life not slaves oh happy Americans too happy if you know your own blest state." [43] Nevertheless the same letter reveals that Morris was hard at work on a document answering Cosby's reasons for suspending him, having been assured by Wager and Sir John Norris that his chances of winning over the ministry were good. From April through June the Morrises continued their efforts, producing the printed statement of their case for the privy council and a "Memoriall" concerning the government of New York.[44]

Committing their views to paper, it soon became evident, was more readily accomplished than placing them before the ministry. As early as April 22 Morris began to chafe at the privy council's delay in hearing his case and feared that "they would put him off from time to time and by Delay Confirm his removal." [45] His suspicions soon began to seem well founded. The privy council had ruled on March 7 that it would hear the New York case after that of Lord Baltimore against Pennsylvania, but when the Penn-Baltimore case was heard on May 10, the Morrises were told that theirs would not come up until after the "Guernsey Cause" during the succeeding term.[46] They were similarly put off from day to day during the early part of July, until the 10th, when the clerk of the council informed them that their hearing would not be until the first meeting

43. Lewis Morris to John Morris, February 9, 1735, Morris MSS. (John Morris Papers), R.U.L.

44. A copy of the *Case of Lewis Morris, Esq.* . . . survives in the Rutherfurd Collection, II, 77, NYHS. See R. H. Morris, "Diary," pp. 180, 204–205, 207–208.

45. *Ibid.*, p. 181. For Morris' ambiguous situation in March, see Morris to Alexander, March 31, 1735, Rutherfurd Collection, II, 115; see also, Morris to Alexander, February 24, 1735, Rutherfurd Collection, II, 113, NYHS.

46. *Acts, Privy Coun., Col.*, III, 397–398; P.C. 2:93, foll. 115–119, PRO; R. H. Morris, "Diary," pp. 194–195, 198.

of the following term, on October 23. The New Yorkers' reaction was understandable: "Being much Disappointed at this unexpected and unnecessary delay, we came down Wish'd ourselves in our Country far from the Deceits of a court, and went to bed, but Slept little." [47] Perhaps, however, they were heartened by the visit of Sir Charles Wager to their lodgings on the 6th of August, when they were assured that the council would hear their case after the vacation. Wager had spoken to the president of the council, Lord Wilmington, who "said they Had rather let it Alone, but hear it they would," and the Admiral urged Morris to make a direct application to the king.[48] Three days after Wager's visit Morris reported to Alexander that he had no doubt that he would eventually be restored to the chief justiceship, but hastened to assure his friend that he would not accept the post upon terms of "being dependant upon a governour . . . but if I can make it independant tho I enjoy it but a small time I do a usefull service to my country by rendring the officer on whom the people have the most dependance of that use to them the law intended it should be." [49] At the end of August he passed along the intriguing rumor that Van Dam's complaint against Cosby had contributed to a recent parliamentary decision to "make some inquiry into the government of the Plantations & to regulate it." [50] Apparently, however, the hoped-for compromise with Cosby's friends had not yet materialized and Morris would have no choice but to press on with his formal complaint against the Governor.

Meanwhile, the Morrisites in New York, cheered by Zenger's acquittal, were in high spirits. They held another of their feasts at the Black Horse Tavern on October 11, this time in honor of the captains of the two royal navy ships in New York harbor, one of them Matthew Norris. Still trading on the election successes of a year earlier, Zenger proudly described the guests as "the elected Magistrates with a considerable number of Merchants and Gentle-

---

47. R. H. Morris, "Diary," pp. 204–205, 210.
48. *Ibid.*, pp. 365–366.
49. Morris to Alexander, August 9, 1735, Rutherfurd Collection, II, 127.
50. Morris to Alexander, August 25, 1735, Rutherfurd Collection, II, 129.

men, not Dependent on ———." While the guns of Norris' *Tartar* boomed in salute, a toast was drunk to the Captain's father-in-law: "Success to Coll. Morris, in his Undertakings." [51]

As if in response, events moved swiftly toward a hearing in London. Lewis Morris conferred with Wilmington on October 27th, and the same evening the committee of council moved to hear the case on November 1st.[52] Last preparations were made. Morris conferred with the master of the rolls, Sir Joseph Jekyll, who had been recommended as "an Honest man" who could tell him "what he was to Expect." [53] Robert Hunter Morris and Paris made last minute rounds of their official solicitors, paying fees to the Solicitor General and Murray, whom they "let . . . into the State of the Case." The Attorney General, whom they had also hoped to see, was in the country and could not be found. Paris himself was paid twenty guineas for "Councills fees." [54] The Morrises also attempted to deliver their memorial to the king: "if the King or his council read I think I have no reason to doubt carrying anything against a man of so established vile a character as the present governor." They discovered, however, that he had not yet returned to England. Morris felt somewhat encouraged by Mrs. Vane's report that she had shown his printed case to the Prince of Wales, who could help him. He was more experienced and a bit cynical in the fall of 1735, however, and hoped for only "as much assistance as [the Prince] can fairly give," realizing that "this is the Land of promises." [55] When the privy council hearing began in November, the Morrises had

51. *New-York Weekly Journal*, October 20, 1735. Matthew Norris became one of the leading members of the Morrisite faction soon after his arrival in New York in 1735. He is identified by Smith as the leader of the raucous celebrants at the conclusion of the Zenger trial (Smith, *History*, II, 22–23) and Andrew Hamilton requested him to revise his Zenger trial notes for style before the publication of the *Brief Narrative*. Hamilton to James Alexander, March 10, 1736, in Livingston Rutherfurd, *John Peter Zenger* (New York, 1904), facing p. 128.

52. *Acts, Privy Coun., Col.*, III, 398; P.C. 2:93, foll. 233–239, PRO.

53. R. H. Morris, "Diary," pp. 213–214.

54. *Ibid.*, p. 382.

55. *Ibid.*, p. 383; Lewis Morris to Alexander, October 24, 1735, in Rutherfurd, *Family Record*, p. 22.

done all that vigorous, intelligent, and ill-connected colonials could do to ensure that their cause would receive a favorable hearing.

Since Governor Cosby was not in London to defend himself he relied upon agents and lengthy letters to the ministry to state his case, but his best guarantees of success were his strong interest in the English political world and the extent to which disapproval of his conduct implied criticism of the ministry. Most "governor's men" in New York did not feel sufficiently threatened by the disturbance to intercede in London, but James DeLancey was an important exception, since his right to the chief justiceship was at the heart of the dispute.

In marrying Caleb Heathcote's daughter, DeLancey had acquired a valuable English political connection as well as the manor of Scarsdale. The family's leading politician in the mid-1730's was Sir John Heathcote, Bt., a member of parliament and one of Walpole's political managers for the county of Rutland. It was this relative upon whom DeLancey depended for help at several crucial stages of his career.[56] Only ten days after his accession to the chief justiceship DeLancey wrote his cousin that Morris was attempting to regain the post through the efforts of Matthew Norris in London, but said that Cosby was doing his best to have his English friends confirm the appointment. "If it should not be done before this comes to your hands, I would intreat you to speak in my behalf to such of your friends as can get the thing done." [57] On June 19, 1734, DeLancey reminded Heathcote of his earlier letter and reported that Morris had succeeded in having the privy council order Cosby to produce his reasons for the suspension. DeLancey hoped Cosby's reasons would be found sufficient, but entreated the Eng-

56. For a detailed account of the Heathcote-DeLancey relationship, see Katz, "An Easie Access," pp. 233–241. For Sir John Heathcote's political standing, see R. Walpole to Sir G. Heathcote, March 22, 1722, 3 ANC IX: 1:2; Duke of Rutland to J. Heathcote, October 14, 1733, 3 ANC IX:1:4; Duke of Rutland to J. Heathcote, October 17, 1733, 3 ANC XIII:B:2s, L.A.C.; Duke of Rutland to R. Walpole, October 18, 1733, Cholmondeley-Houghton MSS., Correspondence, no. 2067, C.U.L.

57. J. DeLancey to Sir John Heathcote, September 3, 1733, 1 ANC XI:B:4q, L.A.C.

lishman to intercede in his behalf: "I am persuaded the recommendation of a gentleman of your Interest and influence will have great weight more especially as your application in this case will be for one who has the honor of being allied to your family." [58]

Lewis Morris' departure elicited a third letter, in December 1734. DeLancey excoriated the Morrisite faction as being comparable to the opponents of the English ministry. He hoped that Walpole would "discountenance the man who in imitation of his brethren the Craftsman has introduced" the slogan "Liberty and Law" in New York. DeLancey noted that Lewis Morris had sailed for England to solicit his restoration, but DeLancey seemed confident of his own position. "Had he gone to England immediately upon his removal, he might have had more merit to plead on his own behalf, than he can now: but after having played the Craftsman here and endeavored to stir the people to tumults and seditions, he surely must labor under some disadvantages, which he would not have done, had he been quick and carried himself with moderation and temper . . . His Majesty's Ministers will undoubtedly discourage all seditious practices." [59] DeLancey concluded by saying that he relied "wholly" on Heathcote's "friendship and assistance." In February Heathcote assured the New Yorker of his willingness to help and DeLancey, in reply, restated his view that Heathcote's intercession on behalf of a relative would certainly move the ministry. He supposed, in this July letter, that Morris would have already "brought his affair upon the stage," and hoped to know the outcome before the year was over. [60]

No letters from Heathcote survive from this period, but it is clear that the Baronet was keeping an eye, albeit somewhat distantly, on the proceedings in London. At the beginning of November he received a frantic letter from Samuel Baker, a wealthy

58. J. DeLancey to Sir John Heathcote, June 19, 1734, 1 ANC XI:B:4r, L.A.C.

59. J. DeLancey to Sir John Heathcote, December 9, 1734, 1 ANC XI:B:4s, L.A.C.

60. J. DeLancey to Sir John Heathcote, July 7, 1735, 1 ANC XI:B:4v, L.A.C.

London mercantile associate of the DeLancey family. This letter apparently contained a copy of the case that Morris had prepared for the privy council and that Heathcote had asked Baker to show him shortly before the council hearing. Baker had just learned that the hearing would take place on November 5. "Where hope you'll please to be present and in the Interim speak to as many Lords as you can, and Mr. Sharp[e] the Solicitor in the affair would fain speak with you before the Day of Hearing if you will please to let him know when and where; his Directions is at the Botom of his Inclosed Letter to me a Good Deale depends on your being present and therefore I hope it will so happen." [61] In the event, Heathcote either did not hear of the meeting in time or did not trouble himself to come into London. Baker's letter gives some indication that the activity on the Cosby-DeLancey side was as fevered as the preparation of the Morrises. When the hearing of the case took place on November 5, the formal deliberations of the council represented only the public aspects of the conflict.

III

The privy council committee was well attended when it met in its accustomed place, the Cockpit, on Guy Fawkes Day, 1735, to hear the case of the alleged unconstitutional suspension of Lewis Morris by Governor William Cosby. Ten councillors were on hand: Lord Wilmington (the president), the Earls of Ilay and of Halifax, Earl Fitzwalter, Lord Hardwicke, Arthur Onslow, Sir Joseph Jekyll, Henry Pelham, Newcastle, and Sir Charles Wager.[62] Of the ten, three were outright partisans: Halifax (his father-in-law) and Newcastle (his patron) on Cosby's side and Wager on Morris'. Among the others, Cosby clearly held the stronger hand.

61. Samuel Baker to Sir John Heathcote, November [2 or 3], 1735, I ANC XI:B:2s, L.A.C. The "inclosed letter" which Baker refers to has disappeared. For an account of the Baker-DeLancey connection, see Katz, "An Easie Access," pp. 228–232.
62. P.C. 2:93, foll. 240–241, PRO.

Even though Jekyll, the master of the rolls, was an adviser of the Morrises and Ilay was the Duke of Argyll's brother (although a staunch Walpolean), several of the councillors were closely connected to Newcastle. Fitzwalter was Newcastle's choice as first lord of the board of trade, Hardwicke was his political adviser and ally, and, of course, Henry Pelham was his brother. No private comments by councillors have survived, so it is impossible to know to what degree personal sympathies affected the result. It was the eminent lawyer Hardwicke, however, who laid down the maxim that "good pleading is nothing else but good logic," and his handling of the hearing reveals at least his own determination to see that the merits of the opposing viewpoints be put on trial.[63]

The issue was the sufficiency of Cosby's reasons for dismissing Morris. Morris' counsel opened the hearing but were interrupted by Hardwicke who declared that Morris was innocent until proved guilty "and therefore it was not their Place to begin." Cosby's counsel then took the floor and read the Governor's reasons for the suspension, first laying "it down as a rule that it would be Exceeding Hard upon Governours to Prove Everything they Say'd," and then enlarging upon Cosby's reasons. They advanced some new arguments and offered to prove them, beginning with the affidavit of Charles Gerritsen, the sheriff of Richmond County in New York. Hardwicke intervened once more to declare that "no Ex'Party [*ex parte*] Evidence taken before a Private majestrate was Legal Evidence" before the privy council and to offer his opinion that "governours were as much obliged to Prove what they asserted as other men." He continued on the subject of "Commissions for Examination of witness," but Robert Morris could not remember what Hardwicke had said when he sat down to write in his diary

63. Philip Chesney Yorke, *The Life and Correspondence of Philip York, earl of Hardwicke, lord high chancellor of England* (Cambridge, Eng., 1913), I, 119. For an intriguing interpretation of political impartiality in the eighteenth century, see J. Steven Watson, "Arthur Onslow and Party Politics," in H. R. Trevor-Roper, ed., *Essays in British History Presented to Sir Keith Feiling* (New York, 1965), pp. 139–171. In early 1735 Morris heard that Wilmington and Newcastle were at odds, but there is no independent evidence of a feud. Morris to Alexander, February 24, 1735, Rutherfurd Collection, II, 113, NYHS.

that night. Cosby's representatives then replied that they had no proof other than that which would come under Hardwicke's objection and had no more to say about the Governor's reasons for the dismissal. However they "Spoke pretty fully to the Printing, which they said was of Dangerous Consequence," which means that they attacked Morris' publication of his opinion and his letter to the Governor concerning Van Dam's case.[64]

During the course of the hearing, Lewis Morris and Newcastle had an altercation over Cosby's additional instruction for the half-salary. Morris contended that this move had been unprecedented, there "not being an instance to be given of such an instruction in any of the Plantations . . . The Duke took this to Himself and spoke to it pretty warmly and Had the governours Generall instruction read, but first said it was almost in the same words with the Generall instruction, but upon reading it, was found as Different as the Different Circumstances required, the one making no Provision in the case of Death and the other is Very Particular in reciting the Death of Montgomery."[65] After the arguments had been concluded, the committee ordered both parties to withdraw and kept them some time before announcing that the hearing would be continued in two days' time. The Morrises and Ferdinand Paris spent the intervening day copying down additional evidence at the Plantation Office and giving additional instructions to their counselors, the Solicitor General, Sir Dudley Ryder, and Murray. Apparently their prospective third solicitor, Sir John Willes, the attorney general, never did return from the country for the hearing.

The final session of the hearing began at five o'clock on November 7. The committee's composition had changed somewhat for this meeting: Wilmington, Halifax, Wager, Onslow, Jekyll, and a newcomer, the Earl of Scarborough, were present.[66] Newcastle was absent and there is no reason to think that Scarborough was a partisan to the cause, but Wager and Halifax were on hand to defend

---

64. R. H. Morris, "Diary," p. 385; *Acts, Privy Coun., Col.*, III, 398. Gerritsen was one of the Cosby appointees as county sheriff whom the Morrisites criticized so bitterly.

65. R. H. Morris, "Diary," p. 386.

66. *Acts, Privy Coun., Col.*, III, 398; P.C. 2:93, fol. 252, PRO.

their friends. The younger Morris was impressed by the audience that evening. "The Attendance on this Hearing was Very numerous; most of the merchants trading to that Part of the world were at it, the People that Had been to New York and many others. There never was Known so full an Auditory." [67] Morris' counsel began this session. The Solicitor General "took the governours reasons to Piece's one by one" and Murray "spoke in an Elligant manner, but confined Himself Chiefly to the Printing and Publishing the Letter [to the Governor] and opinion. He made several "Pertinent Quotations from History." Then the audience was asked to withdraw and waited two hours, "when the Solicitor Generall came out and told Mr. Parris they Had agreed to report in our favor that the reasons were insufficient after a warm debate." [68] The Morrises had triumphed. On November 26 the king signed the committee of council's order (of the 7th) that "the Reasons so transmitted [by Cosby] were not sufficient for removing the Petitioner from His office of Chief Justice of New York." The board of trade prepared a copy of this order on December 5 for transmittal to New York.[69]

Three contemporary comments on the November hearing survive. On November 8 Samuel Baker wrote once more to Sir John Heathcote, this time enclosing the letter previously mentioned, for the first letter had missed Heathcote, and Heathcote had missed the hearing. Baker reported that Cosby "has had the worst of it whereby fear your relation James DeLancey Esqr must resign the Chief Justiceship which am much concerned at, could you have been here to make interest for him I always flattered my Self we could have carried the Point, in fine wee must submitt to what wee can't Remedy." This letter was directed to Sir John Heathcote in care of Sir Robert Walpole at Houghton, and adds that "the Duke of Newcastle who is now with you, was present at the Hearing and can no Doubt tell you pretty near how the Report will be to his Majesty

67. R. H. Morris, "Diary," p. 388.
68. *Ibid.*
69. *New York Col. Docs.*, VI, 37; *Acts, Privy Coun., Col.*, III, 398; *Board of Trade Journal*, 1735–1741, p. 77.

and ca." [70] Thus the letter explains Newcastle's absence from the November 7 hearing, for he was in Norfolk, and it suggests that the council's decision may have been arrived at before the second day of the hearing.

On the same day, November 8, Peter Collinson dispatched a confident letter to James Alexander. He said that "Col. Morris to the great Joy of His Friends Triumphed over his Adversary, after a fair and impartial Hearing . . . So it is left to the King whether to restore him or in what manner to provide for him, he is a Gentleman well beloved so I doubt not will have some regard shown him." The Governor had not been able to prove even one of his charges, and his only evidence had been his own word. "The only thing that was proved in evidence was the Col. writing his own Case and appealing to the Country, this entre nous was not well taken and looked on as a very wrong Step to print against a Gov. in a Province where he resides, it was the only thing the Col. was looked on to be blameworthy in." According to Collinson, Newcastle ("a strenuous friend in the Gov's interest") and Halifax (a "relation of the Gov.") had supported Cosby, "but the Gov.'s Spleen, Pike [pique] and Prejudice were so notoriously seen through the whole charge that there was no supporting it." Colonel Morris' conduct of the trial was not criticized, for the authority of the court as then constituted was allowed to be disputable. The matter of the half-salary was not finally determined. [71]

On November 21, Paris sent a letter to Alexander on the same subject. He said that, "notwithstanding the strongest efforts here of the governor's great friends," the committee had declared Cosby's reasons for removing Morris insufficient. "There was nothing stuck with any of the lords of the Council in Col. Morris's affair, but the printing and publishing of his opinion, which was endeavored by some persons to be magnified as tending to sedition." Paris noted that the Law Lords had declared that Cosby's letters were no proof

70. Samuel Baker to Sir John Heathcote, November 8, 1735, 1 ANC XI:B:2s, L.A.C.

71. Peter Collinson to James Alexander, [November] 8, 1735, Rutherfurd, *Family Record*, pp. 24–25. The letter is dated March 8, 1735, as printed, but see the original in the Rutherfurd Collection, II, 145, NYHS.

"but he must prove his complaint in the same legal manner as any other person." He was very optimistic about Morris' chances: "I am inclinable to think his Excellency [Cosby] shakes." [72]

Both Baker and Collinson pointed out that the resolution of the controversy depended upon the king's actions after receiving the report, and Collinson and Paris agreed that the only damning evidence against Morris had been his publications attacking the Governor after the Van Dam trial. These publications were, in Paris' phrase, "tending to sedition." We may be sure that Sir John Heathcote brought DeLancey's comparison of the Morrises and the English opposition to the attention of Walpole and Newcastle at Houghton. It is likely that after Walpole's defeat on the Excise Bill, he would not have felt much sympathy for an American opposition faction that threatened to upset the colonial tranquillity on which he depended, especially when the faction's newspaper modeled itself on *The Craftsman*.[73]

The truly significant aspect of the hearing is what the committee of council did *not* do. It did not make any recommendation for a change of personnel or policy in New York. The report of the committee provided Morris with nothing more tangible than moral vindication; it did not restore him to his post or remove Cosby. In December, through Gashery and Pearse, Robert Hunter Morris had heard the Earl of Ilay's statement that the committee "intended to continue Him governor, since there was nothing appear'd against Him." [74] Perhaps the ostensibly favorable decision of the council

72. Paris to Alexander, November 21, 1735, *Governor Lewis Morris Papers*, p. 26*n*, and the original in the Rutherfurd Collection, Small Scrapbook, no. 67, NYHS.

73. *The Craftsman* was published in London from December 5, 1726, through April 17, 1736, as the vehicle for newspaper opposition to the administration of the "craftsman," Sir Robert Walpole, whose "Robinocracy" provided a target for Henry St. John, Viscount Bolingbroke, and William Pulteney. The *New-York Weekly Journal* equated Governor Cosby's habits of government with the alleged tyranny of Walpole in England. For the role of *The Craftsman* in English politics, see Foord, *His Majesty's Opposition*, pp. 168–170; Jeffrey Hart, *Viscount Bolingbroke: Tory Humanist* (London, 1965), pp. 60–82; David H. Stevens, *Party Politics and English Journalism, 1702–1742* ([Chicago,] 1916), pp. 125–129.

74. R. H. Morris, "Diary," pp. 395–396 (December 19, 1735).

was due to Hardwicke's passion for legal precision and Walpole's desire to quiet the province, rather than to Wager's influence in behalf of Morris.

The Morrises' joy on November 7 was, therefore, premature. The council's order was in fact perfectly acceptable to Newcastle. It enabled him to claim that justice had been done without obliging him to come to terms with the New York opposition. Whether the council intended it or not, the hearing was a victory for Governor Cosby. Toward the end of 1735 the Morrises began to understand the political significance of the council proceedings, and they attempted to find some better weapon against the Governor. They intensified their defense of the right of Morrisites to sit in the New York council, while pressing the claims of the corporation of Albany and other New Yorkers against Cosby, and continuing their efforts to encourage new applicants for the governorship.

IV

While they tried to unseat Cosby, it was still necessary for the Morrises to defend as vigorously as possible the few important places their faction retained in New York. In letters of December 6 and 7, 1734, Governor Cosby had requested the board of trade to remove James Alexander and Rip Van Dam from the New York council, and Lewis Morris from the council of New Jersey. The board received these letters on January 22, 1735, but considered them only after a singularly long delay, on August 14, 1735. A routine letter from Cosby received on the same day was read by the board on June 26.[75] On the 14th, however, the board came to life and decided to support the Governor, ordering that a representation to the regent, Queen Caroline, be prepared, calling for two new councillors in New York and one in New Jersey in place of the three Morrisites. This document, which recited Cosby's complaints against the

75. *New York Col. Docs.*, VI, 20–26. The letter read on June 26 was also written on December 6, 1734. It contained a brief statement of the economic situation in New York and was of little importance.

opposition faction in New York, was signed on August 28, but not referred to the council until October 13.[76]

Why was no action taken on Cosby's request for nearly seven months? Lewis Morris attributed the delay to the presidency of Lord Westmoreland, who "thought it unreasonable to make any representations to the Council purely on the credit of Cosby." On May 16, 1735, however, Westmoreland was replaced by Benjamin Mildmay, Earl Fitzwalter, and since then the board of trade "notwithstanding the caveats were entered in all the offices against removing us without hearing, did by the particular instance of the duke of Newcastle represent against, even against their own inclination in such a manner as appears to be solely on the credit of Cosby."[77] Robert Hunter Morris concurred in his father's interpretation of the delay, and contended that two board members, Martin Bladen and Paul Docminique, had joined Westmoreland in his opposition to Newcastle's demand for removal of the councillors without a hearing. After Fitzwalter's replacement of Westmoreland and Docminique's death, however, the board "were fond of obliging the secretary of state and so got a report in favor of Mr. Cosby."[78] The Morrises' explanation appears to be sound. It is quite likely that Paul Docminique would have been sympathetic to Morris, for both he and his son, Charles, were London correspondents of the West Jersey Society with which the Morrises were associated. It is even more certain that the appointments of Fitzwalter and Richard Plumer, who replaced Docminique, strengthened Newcastle's hand

76. *Board of Trade Journal*, 1735–1741, pp. 56, 60–61; *Acts, Privy Coun., Col.*, III, 479; *New York Col. Docs.*, VI, 34–35. The representation was signed by James Brudenell, Richard Plumer, Earl Fitzwalter, and Thomas Pelham, all (save Brudenell) safely Newcastle's men.

77. Lewis Morris to Alexander, October 24, 1735, in Rutherfurd, *Family Record*, pp. 21–23. For similar accounts, see Paris to Alexander, November 21, 1735, Rutherfurd Collection, Small Scrapbook, no. 67, and R. H. Morris to Captain Norris, October 16, 1735, Rutherfurd Collection, IV, 43, NYHS.

78. R. H. Morris to Alexander, October 16, 1735, *New Jersey Archives*, V, 432–433. Fitzwalter's commission was read and he was seated on May 23, 1735. *Board of Trade Journal*, 1735–1741, pp. 16–17. The last meeting attended by Docminique was on March 12. *Ibid.*, p. 10. He was replaced by Richard Plumer on May 23, 1735. *Ibid.*, pp. 16–17. Morris writes "Blagdon," but obviously means Bladen.

at the board of trade in a period when the board had seldom been credited with independent initiative.[79] The board's August action represented the victory of politics over scruple, for the New Yorkers at least deserved to be heard in their own defense.

The Morrises received word of the board of trade representation on October 7 when a merchant warned Robert Hunter "of some alterations making in the Councill of New York." Young Morris and Paris then spent several days in feverish search of reliable information and finally learned that the representation had been referred to the committee of council, where it would be first on the agenda after the king's return.[80] Meanwhile, on October 11, Lewis Morris petitioned Lord President Wilmington not to be "condemn'd unheard, nor suppos'd guilty of anything we are accus'd of by Collo Cosby basely upon his saying so." [81] In November, Paris successfully petitioned the council for a copy of Cosby's charges against Alexander, Van Dam, and Morris and unsuccessfully requested copies of the Governor's evidence against the three councillors from the board of trade. The board's refusal was based on the assertion that the council office had made their representation of August 28 available to Paris, and that this was based upon Cosby's

79. R. H. Morris, "Diary," p. 359 and n. 93; Morris to Alexander, March 31, 1735, Rutherfurd Collection, II, 115; Charles Docminique to Lewis Morris, March 23, 1720, Morris MSS., Box 1, R.U.L. Paul Docminique was a merchant with landed connections in Surrey who served on the board from 1705 until his death in 1735. Owen Manning and William Bray, *The History and Antiquities of the County of Surrey* (London, 1809), II, 234, 237. Richard Plumer was the youngest son of a parliament-oriented Hertfordshire family and brother-in-law of the Earl of Abercorn. When not a member of the administration, he was quite independent in his voting habits. Owen, *Pelhams*, p. 49n4; John and John Bernard Burke, *A Genealogical and Heraldic History of the Extinct and Dormant Baronetcies of England, Ireland and Scotland* (2nd ed., London, 1841), p. 417. Fitzwalter was from an old Essex family. He subsequently served as lord lieutenant of the county and as treasurer of the Household. Thomas Wright, *The History and Topography of the County of Essex* (London, 1831), I, 89–90; C. F. J. Hankinson, ed., *Debrett's Peerage, Baronetage, Knightage, and Companionage* (London, 1959), p. 480.

80. R. H. Morris, "Diary," pp. 379–380; R. H. Morris to Alexander, October 16, 1735, *New Jersey Archives*, V, 431–432.

81. Lewis Morris to Lord Wilmington, October 11, 1735, in H.M.C., *Townshend MSS.*, p. 297.

reasons for desiring the suspensions. Undaunted by the refusal, Robert Hunter Morris bribed one of the board of trade clerks with half a guinea and looked over the papers he wanted to see.[82]

The Morrises were successful in these moves of self-defense, for although Cosby acted independently to suspend Van Dam from the New York council in November 1735, the privy council never acted to approve the more extensive changes recommended by the Governor and the board of trade.[83] The episode illustrates the value of Newcastle's control of the board to his friends and it justifies the Morrisite faith in the impartiality of the privy council. Governor Jonathan Belcher of Massachusetts had stated the problem bluntly a year earlier: "I had rather on all occasions have recourse to the King in Council than have any thing of mine decided before the Board of Trade, and when they don't find things go just as they wou'd have 'em they will act with more caution and justice."[84] The Morrisites had scored another triumph before the king's council, but if they were to retrieve their political power in America, they required some more positive action in their favor.

Lewis Morris' second line of attack against Governor Cosby took the form of a series of petitions to the privy council criticizing Cosby's alleged destruction of the Albany Deed and reiterating the Morrisite charges of misgovernment in New York. The treatment of these accusations, it soon became apparent, was identical to that of Morris' complaint about his suspension; whether out of its well-known procedural cautiousness or an unacknowledged favoritism toward Cosby, the council hesitated to discipline the Governor.

As a freeholder of Albany and as the agent of the other freeholders, Lewis Morris petitioned the king on November 12, 1735,

82. *Acts, Privy Coun., Col.,* III, 479; R.H. Morris, "Diary," pp. 388–389; *Board of Trade Journal,* 1735–1741, pp. 74–75.
83. R. H. Morris to Lewis Morris, Jr., February 13, 1736, Morris MSS., Box 2, R.U.L. Van Dam began petitioning for his restoration to the New York council in January 1736. This, however, came to naught.
84. J. Belcher to J. Belcher, Jr., November 4, 1734, "Belcher Papers," VII, 144. Belcher felt that Martin Bladen of the board of trade was unalterably opposed to him, and railed against the board throughout the early 1730's. See also, *ibid.,* VI, 126, and VII, 106.

against Cosby's destruction of the deed to property rightfully belonging to the corporation of Albany.[85] The committee of council took up the matter on December 15. The issue was the Albany complaint about Cosby's handling of the deed to the Mohawk Flats. Morris supplemented this petition with one of his own containing recently discovered evidence designed to prove that Cosby had intended the deed to be destroyed by the Indians from the beginning. Robert Hunter Morris had gotten this evidence by making one of the clerks of the Plantation Office drunk in order to see Cosby's letter to the board of trade describing his conduct at Albany. Morris' petition requested the committee of council to send for the board's books to examine the truth of his allegations, but instead the committee ordered that a copy of the petition be sent to Cosby for his answer.[86] On February 5, 1736, another petition of several members of the corporation of Albany was referred to the committee "praying that for the future their deeds be not destroyed or set aside by the law of the land." On April 21 this too was sent to Cosby for his answer.[87]

The council's failure to act in favor of the Albany petitioners can hardly have pleased the Morrises, who felt sure that the letter which Robert Hunter Morris had seen would be sufficient to bring about a council investigation of the whole affair. Before the new evidence had come to hand, they had heard that Wilmington did not believe the story of the destruction of the deed, and had been annoyed by imperfections in the form of the petition. On the other hand, they had also heard that the king, upon reading the petition,

85. *Acts, Privy Coun., Col.,* III, 486; R. H. Morris, "Diary," pp. 388–389. The petition had come to Morris from Albany on August 1 along with a letter requesting him to deliver it to the king. Although he unsuccessfully attempted to give it to Wilmington on November 5, the petition was referred to the committee of council by November 15. *Ibid.,* 360, 385. The appeal to the king was based on the fact that the Albanians could not proceed against the governor at common law.

86. R. H. Morris to Lewis Morris, Jr., February 13, 1736, Morris MSS., Box 2, R.U.L.; R. H. Morris, "Diary," pp. 394–395; *Acts, Privy Coun., Col.,* III, 486.

87. *Acts, Privy Coun., Col.,* III, 486.

"was verry angery at such an Elegall Proceeding" and had given the petition to Lord Harrington for the council to consider.[88] With the evidence of the deed's destruction and the suspicion of the king's annoyance, the Morrises must have expected some stronger action in favor of their Albany friends.

Finally, Morris attempted to petition the king for his restoration, through the Duke of Newcastle, but was never able to get hold of the Duke.[89] He then set about preparing a petition to the king complaining of Cosby's administration and setting out at some length the old Morrisite charges against the Governor. He tried to present this petition to Wilmington in Sir Robert Walpole's presence. The Lord President refused to accept it, however, on the ground that he had no more right to receive such documents than any other member of the council. Lewis Morris became furious with him, and stalked off shouting that he had done all he could to inform the king and ministry of the conduct of their Governor.[90]

This petition ("complaining of several matters affecting the government of the province by Cosby") was finally presented to the council. It was referred to the committee on February 5, 1736, and considered on April 21, when the parts of Morris' petition that concerned the Governor were ordered to be sent to Cosby, who was commended to return his answer "with all convenient speed." [91] This order went unanswered, however, since, unbeknownst to the council, Governor Cosby had died on March 10, 1736.

At the same time, Morris' final tactic in conciliar politics—his attempt to be recognized as the agent for New York—also failed. Morris presented three petitions from the province to the king on February 5, 1736, asking for a royal hearing of his account of the state of the colony, since there was no New York agent in England.

88. R. H. Morris, "Diary," p. 393.
89. *Ibid.*, pp. 393–394, 398 (December 9 and 31, 1735). On March 21, 1736, Morris succeeded in transmitting a letter to Newcastle, asking for his restoration. Lewis Morris to Newcastle, March 21, 1736, *Cal. State Papers, Col., Am.*, XLII, 184.
90. R. H. Morris to Lewis Morris, Jr., February 13, 1736, Morris MSS., Box 2, R.U.L. A précis of the memorial can be found in *Acts, Privy Coun., Col.*, VI, 617–620.
91. *Acts, Privy Coun., Col.*, III, 486.

This matter was likewise referred to committee, where it was rejected on April 21 on the grounds that "this method of applying to your majesty by way of Petition for the Appointing Agents for your Majestys Plantations is irregular and unprecedent." George II signed the committee's report on April 29, and this date marks the end of Lewis Morris' efforts to convince the imperial administration that the government of New York ought to be investigated, and that he ought to be restored.[92]

Morris' failure to achieve anything more than requests to Cosby for additional information can be attributed both to Newcastle's solicitude for his protégé and to the understandable reluctance of English officials to damage the royal prerogative by acknowledging colonial misgovernment. Metropolitan indifference to and lack of knowledge of American affairs was still another force acting to protect the Governor. And, as Ferdinand John Paris was later to observe of a New Jersey solicitation, "I fully expect, that the present Application will be lost & forgot, & nothing at all done in it. For, God knows, our Affairs at Home take up all the Time that is allowed for Business."[93] The great weakness of the case against Cosby, however, was the failure of the New York assembly to endorse it: "One petition to the King or address from [the assembly] would be of great use should other means faile whereas Petitions from others tho' a great body of the People don't appear with Such an air of the whole as from their representatives."[94] As it was, the ministry apparently considered the Morrisite complaints factional clamor which could safely be ignored. Even at the outset of his stay in England Lewis Morris sensed the predicament. "We have a parliament and ministry, some of whom, I am apt to believe, know that there are plantations and governors—but not quite so well as we do;

---

92. *Ibid.*, III, 492; P.C. 2:93, fol. 430, PRO; *New York Col. Docs.*, VI, 51–52. One petition was from the aldermen and common councillors of New York City and some of the members of the New York council. The other two were from several freeholders and inhabitants of Ulster and Queen's counties.

93. Paris to Alexander, February 10, 1746, Rutherfurd Collection, Small Scrapbook, no. 121, NYHS.

94. Lewis Morris to Colden, April 11, 1735, NYHS, *Colls.*, 1918, p. 137.

like the frogs in the fable, the mad pranks of a plantation-governor is sport for them, though death for us, and seem less concerned in our contests than we are at those between crows and kingbirds." [95] One last hope remained—that someone with greater influence and better credentials than Cosby would solicit the government of New York.

V

The news of changes of place was the talk of the town in London, especially when such posts as the governorship of New York were rumored to be available. In August 1734 an English correspondent of Cadwallader Colden's had transmitted a report that Cosby would exchange places with Lord Howe, the governor of Barbados, and, from the very outset of their trip, the Morrises hoped Cosby would be replaced by someone of greater influence. [96] Lewis Morris was both sufficiently experienced in politics and committed to the province, however, to hope for more than an indiscriminate change in the government of New York. "Changing the man is far from an adequate remedy, if the thing remains the same; and we had as well keep an ill, artless governor we know, as to change him for one equally ill with more art that we do not know." [97] Throughout 1735 and the early months of 1736 the Morrises were to be tantalized by rumors of a new administration in New York, but their hopes were consistently disappointed.

In January 1735 Morris' daughter Mary Pearse had written from Virginia to say that James Brudenell of the board of trade was to be the new governor of New York. [98] A month later Morris had

95. Lewis Morris to James Alexander, February 24, 1735, extract, *Governor Lewis Morris Papers*, p. 23.

96. Micajah Perry to Colden, August 30, 1734, NYHS, *Colls.*, 1918, p. 112. Emmanuel, Lord Viscount Howe was appointed in 1733 and died in the same year. Robert Beatson, *A Political Index* (3rd ed., London, 1806), II, 457.

97. Lewis Morris to Alexander, February 24, 1735, extract, *Governor Lewis Morris Papers*, p. 23.

98. Lewis Morris, Jr., to Colden, January 17, 1734, Bancroft Transcripts, Colden, I, 24–25, NYPL. Brudenell's name was mentioned several times. In 1735, it was suggested, in return for the government of New York, that

heard "from good hands the government is Promis'd but I can't yet learn to who but all concluded Cosby will not be long in it and I hope they Judge right."[99] In May the Morrises spoke to Thomas Orby-Hunter, the son of the New York governor for whom Robert Hunter Morris was named. Hunter was interested in the government, but was afraid he was too young for the job. Young Morris assured him that the people of New York would welcome his appointment, for "an Honest young man was preferable to an old Knave."[100] The Morrises would have been delighted with Hunter, but nothing came of his inquiry.

The most curious solicitor for the post the Morrises encountered was an obscure Colonel Smith, whom they met on July 5. They had been told that he "had a good interest and could carry it if Cosby was removed." Smith had already spoken to Wager and Walpole about the governorship. He hoped to rule New York independently of New Jersey so that the ministry could "provide for two friends instead of one," but Lewis Morris tried to discourage him about the possible profits in New York and Robert Hunter Morris worried lest the Colonel assume he had won their support.[101]

In August Smith returned to tell a tale of woe. He had spoken to the Queen only to learn that there was no vacancy in the government of New York and he had been rudely dismissed by Newcastle, who ridiculed his crippled state. Smith's retort had been that he "proposed to govern by His Head and not by his Heals," but he acknowledged to the Morrises that the ministry intended to support Cosby. He insisted that he would persist in his quest, but Lewis

---

Cosby take Brudenell's place as recorder of the town of Chichester, at a salary of £1,000 a year. See also, *Pennsylvania Gazette*, May 20–27, 1736; *New England Weekly Journal*, June 8, 1736; *New York Gazette*, May 31, 1736, quoted in *New Jersey Archives*, XI, 464, 466–467. Brudenell was extremely well connected, being the uncle of Lord Cardigan and the son-in-law of the Duke of Montague.

99. Lewis Morris to John Morris, February 9, 1735, Morris MSS. (John Morris Papers), R.U.L.

100. R. H. Morris, "Diary," p. 188 (May 4, 1735). The diary identifies him as "Mr. Hunter," but it seems likely that this is Thomas Orby-Hunter.

101. R. H. Morris, "Diary," pp. 206–207.

Morris thought that the government of New York was too big an affair for Smith, who had not "interest enough to get it." [102]

In December 1735 Sir Charles Wager told Lewis Morris that he had heard Cosby was to become governor of Barbados. He also reported that the London merchants were planning to petition the king against the move. Morris apparently attempted to encourage the transfer, but nothing came of it. [103] Similarly, in February 1736 Francis Gashery questioned young Morris about the profits of the New York government, and Robert Hunter surmised that the information was intended for Lord Granard. [104] At the same time the Morrises believed that Newcastle himself intended to remove Cosby in favor of a Colonel Hargrave, whose regiment would be given to the ex-Governor. [105] There were endless possibilities, but as we know, Cosby died in March, impervious to the efforts to dislodge him. The Morrisite attack was no more successful in England than it had been in New York.

VI

By the beginning of 1736, when it was apparent that the factional assault on Governor Cosby had failed, Lewis Morris turned once more to efforts to recover his own position in America. He had petitioned the king for restoration to the chief justiceship after approval of the council's report which found Cosby's reasons for dismissing him insufficient. Newcastle had delayed the petition a month before delivering it to court, and in early February Robert Hunter Morris was told by a clerk that nothing could be done about

102. *Ibid.*, pp. 364–365, 367 (August 5–6, 1735).
103. *Ibid.*, p. 393; Morris to Alexander, August 25, 1735, Rutherfurd Collection, II, 129, NYHS.
104. R. H. Morris to Lewis Morris, Jr., February 13, 1736, Morris MSS., Box 2, R.U.L. Granard had been the governor of the Leeward Islands in 1729, and was to have been succeeded by Cosby. Beatson, *Index*, III, 456. For the negotiations concerning Granard, who was apparently Wager's candidate for the government of New York, see P. Collinson to Alexander, August 21, 1738, Rutherfurd Collection, IV, 59, NYHS.
105. R. H. Morris to Lewis Morris, Jr., February 13, 1736, Morris MSS., Box 2, R.U.L. See also, *New-York Weekly Journal*, May 10, 1736.

the matter "till they had the Duke's Directions." [106] Newcastle had bottled up the petition, but there are indications that he was extremely sensitive to Morris' aspirations. Indeed, on the day before the council hearing the Duke had offered the New Yorker a bribe.

On November 4, 1735, Francis Gashery approached Morris with an offer from Newcastle: if Morris would drop his complaints against Cosby and put off the hearing, the Duke would join Wager in asking the government of New Jersey for him. Confident of his chances of success before the council, Morris haughtily declined on the grounds that the complaints were presented in behalf of the people of New York. They were not "in His own Brest to keep it or give it up," but were public affairs which he could not "in Honor" give up "in any terms nor would not if they gave him the government of Ireland." Morris loftily instructed Gashery to tell Newcastle that the one way to prevent the hearing was to provide for Cosby in some other way. The same evening, apparently feeling that the ministry would give in, he told Wager that he "had a Power of Compermising the Matter with Mr. Cosbies friends and would name his terms": added powers for the assembly and council, a legislative settlement of the judicial structure, and a restoration of lands to the corporation of Albany. "These things being granted, they might keep Mr. Cosby there or Send any other." [107]

Thus during the crucial days of the formal solicitation the former Chief Justice was unswerving in his devotion to public goals. But when it became clear that Cosby would not be removed or reforms made, he was free by the terms of the agreement with his friends to pursue personal ends. Wager broached the subject of a compromise again through Gashery on January 11, 1736, and asked Morris why he should not accept the government of New Jersey, "seeing it was not on Base terms and since he had done his utmost to get relief for himself and country." Morris wondered what security he would have that the place would be granted him. Wager prom-

106. R. H. Morris to Lewis Morris, Jr., February 13, 1736, Morris MSS., Box 2, R.U.L.

107. R. H. Morris, "Diary," pp. 384–385. On April 19, 1736, the *New-York Weekly Journal* reprinted a letter from Robert Hunter Morris (dated January 3, 1736) describing Newcastle's offer and Lewis Morris' refusal.

ised to confirm the arrangement with Newcastle, and soon reported that "the dukes answer was he need not be uneasy about Coll. Morris, for that he would take Care of him, that he should be restored in as full and ample a manner as he himself could wish." [108] At this time, however, Morris had yet to accept the terms upon which Newcastle and Halifax were prepared to compromise. He was still suspicious that an exchange of government of New Jersey for the surrender of all his petitions and memorials to Wilmington was designed "not so much to screen Cosby, as bigger folks." He professed to believe that his reluctance to accept the offer convinced Newcastle and his associates that he intended to lay his case before parliament, "which I believe they are affraid of; and which wont proceed quite in that dilatory way they do." [109] On February 25, 1736, Morris was told that "a select number" of the privy council which had met that day to consider his plight had decided to recommend that the king not remove Cosby yet, continuing the Governor a little longer (perhaps about three months) but reprimanding him sharply for his past conduct. Morris could not be sure whether the report was true, and decided the test of the ministry would be whether or not he was restored to the chief justiceship. If he was restored, Cosby's power was obviously at an end. If not, "I shall guess it kept up to try a compromise, or a firme resolution to support him do what he will." [110] Meanwhile, although Morris probably did not know it, Wager was assuring Newcastle that the New Jersey governorship would serve to quiet him.[111]

Lewis Morris had had some thought of being governor of New Jersey ever since 1702, when the proprietors had given up their governmental rights, and he reminded Newcastle of this disappointment in 1732.[112] By 1736 it was obvious that the administration of

108. R. H. Morris to Lewis Morris, Jr., February 13, 1736, Morris MSS., Box 2, R.U.L.

109. Morris to Alexander, January 11, 1736, Rutherfurd Collection, II, 171, NYHS.

110. Morris to Alexander, February 25, 1736, Rutherfurd Collection, II, 177, NYHS.

111. Wager to Newcastle, February 12, 1736, quoted in Kemmerer, *Path to Freedom*, p. 151 (from S.P. Dom. Naval, 22:1, PRO).

112. Lewis Morris to Newcastle, June 2, 1732, *Governor Lewis Morris Papers*, p. 18*n*.

New Jersey was better than no place in New York, and Morris could justifiably feel that he had kept his word to his New York associates by demanding the full scope of their program from the ministry. Newcastle, however, seemed in no hurry to fulfill his pledge and in December 1737 Wager ("who was wary of the Duke") applied to Sir Robert Walpole, who assured him that Morris would be appointed.[113] The board of trade was notified of the appointment in January 1738 and at long last Morris' disrupting influence was removed from New York.[114]

In 1736, though, his ambitions were still in New York. In late August of that year, Peter Collinson reported to James Alexander that "Col. Morris left us all of a sudden I believe that at last the Good man was quite tired out with Delays." [115] Morris had good reason to be disgusted with London by the summer of 1736, for in eighteen months he had achieved neither his personal objectives nor those of the Morrisite faction. The privy council had, it is true, disapproved of Cosby's manner of suspending the Chief Justice and had ignored the Governor's request to suspend the Morrisite councillors, but they had failed to remove Cosby or to make constitutional reforms in New York. Either the Morrisite constitutional arguments had not been taken seriously or the Governor's English influence was too great to be overcome by American criticism, and Morris cannot be blamed for concluding that "let [the Governor] be as wicked as he will, if the ministry joins, they both can and will support him, or anybody else." [116] When Morris learned of Cosby's

113. Lewis Morris to R. H. Morris, December 14, 1737, Morris MSS., Box 2, R.U.L. Vincent Pearse conducted this negotiation.

114. *Board of Trade Journal, 1735–1741*, p. 222; Memorandum about New York, [1737?], printed in *New Jersey Archives*, V, 511. When the decision was made to separate the government of New Jersey from that of New York in 1737, there was a spirited contest for the newly-created vacancy in New Jersey. The contenders, other than Morris, were Sir William Keith, Hamilton of New Jersey, and Thomas Smith, who may have been the crippled "Colonel Smith" who had earlier applied for the government of New York. Haffenden, "Colonial Appointments and Patronage," p. 426.

115. P. Collinson to Alexander, August 28, 1736, in Rutherfurd, *Family Record*, p. 25.

116. Lewis Morris to Alexander, February 24, 1735, in Rutherfurd, *Family Record*, pp. 18–19. The statement was made in the discouragement of the first days of the stay in England, but it is obvious that Morris was equally

death he probably set off for New York confident of a return to power, but he was wiser in the knowledge that political ability and constitutional briefs could not overcome good connections in Newcastle's empire. Indeed he may well have come round to privy councillor Lord Ilay's point of view, that "politics is a continual petty war and game, and as at all other games, we will sometimes win and sometimes lose, and he that plays best and has the best stock has the best chance." [117] In the last analysis, however, Colden may have best diagnosed the plight of the Morrisites when he observed that "no pains should be neglected to open Peoples eyes & if we cannot do it in this Country how can we expect to do it in England. If some People had taken half the pains here that they are forced to do elsewhere the Dispute had been over before now." [118]

---

depressed and cynical a year and a half later. His mood had gone full circle during the months abroad.

117. "Bute MSS." (H.M.C., *Fifth Report, Part I, Appendix* [London, 1876], p. 618), quoted in Foord, *His Majesty's Opposition*, p. 62.

118. Colden to Alexander, July 29, 1735, Rutherfurd Collection, II, 123, NYHS.

6
Lieutenant Governor Clarke,
1736-1743

NEW YORK POLITICS TOOK ON A STRANGELY
subdued air in the summer of 1735. The Governor's faction was in
control of the local situation, and the Cosbyites gained renewed
confidence from their endorsement by the imperial administration.
The calm was shattered suddenly, however, by the news of the
Governor's illness. Cosby was struck down by a severe attack of
tuberculosis in November 1735 and it was obvious that he was about
to die. Thus, the problem of succession to the executive office once
more convulsed the colony.

The Cosbyites, seeking to retain their power, were trapped in a
constitutional snare. The line of succession descended from the gov-

ernor to the lieutenant governor to the senior member of the council. There was no lieutenant governor in 1735, however, and the eldest councillor was the old Morrisite stalwart, Rip Van Dam. The board of trade had recommended Van Dam's suspension from the council in August 1735, but the privy council had not acted upon the suggestion. The Cosbyites therefore had to take matters into their own hands. The council convened at Cosby's bedside on November 24, 1735, formally to suspend Van Dam from the body, leaving the Governor's chief adviser, George Clarke, the senior member and heir apparent.[1]

Van Dam and the Morrisites sprang into action against Clarke. Van Dam, acting upon the advice of Smith and Alexander, petitioned the privy council to restore him to the council but was refused on the ground that no action could be taken until a new governor was appointed "unless new advices should arrive from New York which may make it necessary to take them into consideration." [2] Van Dam contended that his suspension had not been valid, but that even if it had been the suspension "dyed" with Cosby.[3] At the same time, the Morrisite faction in New York began to rouse itself. Zenger's *Journal* once more came to Van Dam's aid, its tone even more strident than it had been in opposition to Cosby. Morris' son-in-law, Matthew Norris, lent the prestige of the commander of the station ship of the British navy to Van Dam's cause.[4]

George Clarke, meanwhile, appealed to the imperial authorities. Promising to restore tranquillity to the province, he requested the

1. *Cal. Coun. Min.*, p. 325. For the Morrisite reaction to the suspension, see Lewis Morris, Jr., to Alexander, December 25, 173[5], Rutherfurd Collection, II, 91.

2. *Acts, Privy Coun., Col.*, III, 479–480; *Board of Trade Journal*, 1735–1741, pp. 111, 119; Lords of Trade to Lords of Council, June 18, 1736, *New York Col. Docs.*, VI, 69–70; P.C. 2:94, fol. 36, PRO; Van Dam to Smith and Alexander, and reply, March 11, 1736, Rutherfurd Collection, II, 179, NYHS.

3. Clarke to Lords of Trade, March 16, 1736, *New York Col. Docs.*, VI, 43.

4. Colden, *History of Cosby and Clarke*, p. 348. As late as April 1737 Clarke complained of Norris' intervention in behalf of the Morris faction: "Perhaps he wished to see us again in a flame." The Lieutenant Governor confidently asserted, however, that Norris "will not be able to raise another." Clarke to board of trade, April 9, 1737, *Cal. State Papers, Col., Am.*, 1737, p. 107.

board of trade to rule out the possibility of restoring Morris to the supreme court bench and to remove Van Dam and Alexander from the council: "these being the heads of the factions who openly declaim against the Kings Prerogative." [5] He explained to the board that although Van Dam had served as an adequate president after Montgomerie's death ("a time wherein no spirit of Party appeared"), in the heated aftermath of Cosby's administration he would be "but a Tool in other Hands." [6] Clarke also urged the confirmation of James DeLancey as chief justice, "so that Coll. Morris may have no hopes of being restored." [7] He set about mending his political fences in London, writing to Newcastle and Horatio Walpole in search of support—telling Newcastle that he was a friend of Walpole's and asking Walpole to recommend him to the Duke.[8]

James Alexander was Clarke's true rival in New York, since the elderly Van Dam was politically inept and Lewis Morris was still absent in London. When the council selected Clarke to act as president on the day of Cosby's death, Alexander had refused to vote. On March 24, two weeks later, Alexander posted a notice at the market and other places, and in the *Gazette*, proclaiming to the public that he had not advised or consented in any way to Clarke's taking on the administration of government in New York, or to his doing any act of government as president.[9] This action angered Clarke, who protested to the board of trade that although Alexander had not given his opinion on whether the administration devolved on Clarke, he had failed to oppose his swearing-in, and had acted with the rest of the council in drawing up the proclamation giving notice of the Governor's death and confirming all officers in their places. Clarke supposed that Alexander's subsequent action was an

5. Clarke to Lords of Trade, March 16, 1736, *New York Col. Docs.*, VI, 43.

6. *Ibid.*, VI, 44.

7. Clarke to Lords of Trade, May 3, 1736, *ibid.*, VI, 53.

8. Clarke to H. Walpole, Newcastle, March 16, 1736, *ibid.*, VI, 48, 47.

9. *Cal. Coun. Min.*, p. 325; *New York Gazette*, March 28, 1736, quoted in *New Jersey Archives*, XI, 456–457; I. N. Phelps Stokes, *The Iconography of Manhattan Island, 1498–1909* (New York, 1915–1928), VI, 546.

effort to mollify the "faction's" anger at his not having opposed Clarke's installation in office. By this time, Alexander was refusing to attend the council when summoned to meetings.[10]

Clarke was in a strong position, however, for there was little that could be done to oppose him. The assembly was adjourned, but the council firmly took his part and carried on in its regular fashion. The fragile hopes of Clarke's opponents rested in Lewis Morris' success in England, but by mid-summer 1736, reports were filtering back that Morris had not been restored. There were some reports of his success, but these were without official confirmation, and the supporters of Van Dam and Alexander became discouraged: "the people begin to suspect they have been imposed on, and prepare themselves to look for the signification of His Majestys pleasure in another manner than their Leaders promised them." [11] Clarke pressed the board of trade for his appointment as lieutenant governor as a means of ending the Morrisite hopes of capturing the government of the province, and setting "the Quiet of the Province upon a Lasting Foundation." [12]

News of Lewis Morris' arrival in Boston reached New York on September 18 and precipitated a final outburst of enthusiasm and optimism among his allies, who had already begun their attempts to take the administration away from Clarke. By the New York Charter of 1731, September 29 was the day on which the governor or commander in chief nominated the civic officials, and October 14 was the day on which they were sworn in. This occasion gave Van Dam the opportunity to exercise his pretensions to the president's

10. Clarke to Lords of Trade, April 7, 1736, *New York Col. Docs.*, VI, 50. An animosity had developed between Clarke and Alexander as early as the Hunter administration. See Alexander's draft of a memorandum to Montgomerie, August 31, 1728, Rutherfurd Collection, I, 85, NYHS.

11. Clarke to Lords of Trade, May 29, 1736, *ibid.*, VI, 64; D. Horsmanden to Colden, July 23, 1736, NYHS, *Colls.*, 1918, p. 153; *New York Gazette*, May 31, 1736, quoted in *New Jersey Archives*, XI, 468.

12. Clarke to Lords of Trade, May 29 and July 26, 1736, *New York Col. Docs.*, VI, 64, 73. He gave Newcastle another reason for desiring a commission as lieutenant governor—it would protect him against a suit by Van Dam for his salary and compensate him for the expenses of the administration. Clarke to Newcastle, May 3, 1736, *ibid.*, VI, 54.

authority, and he presented a slate of appointments in opposition to Clarke's. In the common council elections in the city, also on September 29, Van Dam's nominees won, and he thus had some hope that his executive appointments would be accepted. The aldermen and magistrates had carried out a referendum on the same day, asking who was the rightful president, and Van Dam had won this contest as well, although the exact results were challenged by Clarke. The common council feared to give its outright support to Van Dam, however, for it was aware of the council's support of Clarke and the strength of his legal and constitutional position. On October 12 the common council settled upon the device of requesting all the attorneys practicing before the mayor's court to attend its meeting on October 14 to decide the question.[13]

The situation was now quite out of hand. The Van Dam leaders, with the sympathy of the New York City government, and aided by the *Journal*'s sharpest polemics, had created an angry mob in the city. On October 1, Clarke published a proclamation warning Van Dam's officers against assuming any authority under his appointments. The council then ordered that gunpowder be purchased, and on October 5, that the garrison at Fort George be provisioned.[14] President Clarke and his family took refuge inside the fort, whence he wrote to Newcastle and the board of trade, suggesting that Alexander, William Smith, and Lewis Morris, Jr., be sent to England and tried for treason, and that Zenger be bribed with a pardon to inform against them.[15]

Morris arrived in New York on October 8, and conferred with his friends the next day. Later he addressed a huge crowd, declaring that he believed Van Dam had a right to the administration and that he was willing to act as chief justice under him. He argued that the assembly, which Clarke had adjourned, was dissolved, and intemper-

13. Smith, *History*, II, 28–30; Clarke to Lords of Trade, October 7, 1736, *New York Col. Docs.*, VI, 78–80; George W. Edwards, "New York City Politics Before the American Revolution," *Political Science Quarterly*, XXXVI (1921), 592–596; *Min. Comm. Coun.*, IV, 348.

14. *Cal. Coun. Min.*, p. 327.

15. Clarke to Newcastle, Lords of Trade, October 7, 1736, *New York Col. Docs.*, VI, 76–77, 80.

ately concluded: "If you don't hang them, they will hang you." [16] The assembly met on October 12, and Morris solemnly declared that he knew of no English orders recognizing Clarke as the president of the council. The legality of Clarke's administration was debated by the representatives, and Clarke adjourned them to the next day. Van Dam was planning to administer the oaths of office to the New York City officials he had appointed on the 14th, as the charter provided, and this direct violation of Clarke's proclamation would surely have initiated violence between the supporters of the rival claimants to the presidency.[17] New York was only a step from civil war.

At the last minute, however, early on the morning of the 13th, the brigantine *Endeavour* arrived with a royal instruction naming Clarke as the president and commander in chief of the province and justifying his claims to authority. Clarke opened the instruction in the presence of the council, and immediately displayed it to the assembly. His officers were sworn in without dispute on the 14th, and the opposition completely vanished.[18] The hope of Van Dam's legitimate succession to the administration had been the life of the opposition, and it was completely strangled by the official recognition of Clarke's position. Clarke's triumph was completed by the arrival of his commission as lieutenant governor on October 30.[19]

The province had passed overnight from the brink of war to a state of acquiescence, and Clarke was soon writing confidently to Newcastle: "the people seem perfectly contented, and the hopes of a few desperate men, are all placed in the expectation of seeing a Governor soon come from England, imagining that in that event they shall be able to revive a troublesome spirit." If he were continued in office, however, he would "be able to restore them to as much unanimity, content and happynes as they ever knew, and the

16. Smith, *History*, II, 30; Colden, *History of Cosby and Clarke*, pp. 347–348.

17. Smith, *History*, II, 30–31; *Assemb. Jour.*, I, 688.

18. Clarke to Newcastle, October 14, 1736, *New York Col. Docs.*, VI, 81; *Cal. Coun. Min.*, p. 327; *Min. Comm. Coun.*, IV, 349–352.

19. *Cal. Coun. Min.*, p. 328; *New York Col. Docs.*, VI, 71. The commission was dated July 13, 1736.

Province to a more flourishing condition than ever." [20] Colden ascribed the bellicose tactics of Morris and his friends to their "hopes to have rais'd the Peoples Spirits to that height as to have made it necessary for the Kings Ministers to have given way to their Humours by restoring Mr Van Dam & making it likewise necessary for a succeeding Governor to fall in with their Measures." [21] However, the official confirmation of Clarke's right to rule destroyed in one stroke the popular belief in Van Dam's authority and the good credit of Lewis Morris, who had urged violent action in Van Dam's behalf. Daniel Horsmanden appraised the situation at the end of 1736: "Zenger is perfectly Silent as to polliticks his Correspondents I believe heartily Crop Sick, and Old Morris retired to Hell Gate to eat his own Sapan & Milk, and says the Devil may take 'em all; But if his natural disposition will let him be at rest, I'm mistaken in the Man." [22] Horsmanden was right on all counts. The Morrisite opposition to Clarke was quieted, although Morris himself was to resume his political activities shortly. Lewis Morris' political future was in New Jersey, however, for the leadership of New York had been won decisively by George Clarke.

I

Clarke was born in Swainswick, Somersetshire, in 1676, the son of a government official and a near relation of the royal administrator, William Blathwayt.[23] Poorly educated, he was articled to an

20. Clarke to Newcastle, November 23, 1736, *ibid.*, VI, 84.

21. Colden, *History of Cosby and Clarke*, p. 350. For Colden's moderate, if self-serving, views on Morrisite strategy in 1736, see Colden to Alexander, n.d., and May 25, [1736,] Rutherfurd Collection, II, 89, 183, NYHS.

22. D. Horsmanden to Colden, December 22, 1736, NYHS, *Colls.*, 1918, p. 164.

23. E. B. O'Callaghan, ed., *Voyage of George Clarke, Esq. to America* (Albany, 1867), p. xxiv. O'Callaghan describes Blathwayt as an uncle of Lieutenant Governor Clarke; Edith Fox (*Land Speculation*, p. 1) calls them cousins, as does Gertrude A. Jacobsen (Blathwayt, p. 378). It may well be that Clarke's father was the George Clarke who served as Blathwayt's deputy as secretary of war under William III. Mark A. Thomson, *Secretaries of State*, p. 67; Osgood, *Eighteenth Century*, I, 31; S.P. 44:166, foll. 122, 244, PRO. The most reasonable surmise, however, is that he was the son of George Clarke

attorney and later practiced law in Dublin, where his career was abruptly terminated when he was accused of a nasty assault on a local merchant. Blathwayt arranged to have Clarke appointed secretary of the province of New York in 1703, perhaps to give him a fresh start, and he arrived in July of the same year to begin a career which was to last more than forty years.[24]

The newly-arrived official quickly secured a leave of absence and returned briefly to England to marry the daughter of Governor Edward Hyde of North Carolina, a distant cousin of Queen Anne. The young couple built a villa at Hempstead Plains on Long Island, at some distance from New York City, where Clarke settled into the life of a country gentleman.[25] They were almost studied in their lack of involvement in New York society, raising a family of ten children of whom not one married a New Yorker. This was understood to be a deliberate choice in an age of arranged marriages and it caused William Smith to remark that "they made no connections in the colony." [26] Clarke remained outside the ruling elite of New York, preferring to play the part of an independent royal official.

George Clarke was one of the few professional officeholders in colonial New York. He served for thirty-five years as provincial secretary and in the minor offices that pertained to the secretaryship (clerk of the council, court of appeals, and supreme court, and register of the prerogative court), managing the secretaryship through a succession of deputies: Isaac Wileman, Isaac Bobin, and Frederick Morris.[27] In 1702 Blathwayt arranged to have Clarke appointed his deputy in New York as auditor general of the plantations, a post

of Swainswick, Somersetshire. John Collinson, comp., *The History and Antiquities of the County of Somerset* (Bath, 1791), I, 154–155.
24. O'Callaghan, *Voyage of G. Clarke*, pp. v–xxxi.
25. *Ibid.*, pp. xxxiii–xxxvi; E. Fox, *Land Speculation*, p. 2; Smith, *History*, II, 68; John and John Bernard Burke, *A Genealogical and Heraldic Dictionary of the Landed Gentry of Great Britain and Ireland* (London, 1847), I, 224.
26. Smith, *History*, II, 68; O'Callaghan, *Voyage of G. Clarke*, pp. lxxiii–lxxvi. One of Clarke's daughters apparently married into the wealthy and powerful Beckford family of Jamaica, however. See Governor Hunter to Alexander, September 7, 1731, and August 18, 1732, Rutherfurd Collection, I, 147, 153, NYHS.
27. E. B. O'Callaghan, ed., *Letters of Isaac Bobin Esq., Private Secretary of Hon. George Clarke, Secretary of the Province of New York, 1718–1730*

Clarke retained after Horatio Walpole supplanted Blathwayt in the auditor generalship in 1717.[28] Governor Hunter nominated him for the New York council, in which he served from 1716 to 1736. In addition, he was a member of the 1718 committee that adjusted the border between Connecticut and New York.[29]

Clarke's involvement in New York politics was carefully calculated. Until Montgomerie's arrival in 1728 he kept well in the background, spending most of his time on Long Island. Later, he became the confidential adviser of Governors Montgomerie and Cosby,[30] but until his own administration in 1736 he remained a distant and mysterious figure. Clarke was able to assume this stance because his appointments were by royal authority and unlimited by time. He could be removed from office only by action from England, but his English position was extremely strong and he seldom had to worry about defending himself at home. His relationship to Blathwayt had given him an interest in the highest places of English administration and had gotten him his initial appointments. Governor Cornbury ruefully described Clarke as "Mr Blathwait's kinsman." He was also a friend of John Champante, the long-time agent of New York in England, and his wife's Hyde connection may have helped him.[31] His chief source of English support, however, was Horatio Walpole.

Horatio was the younger brother of Sir Robert Walpole, and

(Albany, 1872), passim; E. Fox, *Land Speculation*, p. 8. Bobin, who considered himself an expert on matters of trade, had communicated with Sir Robert Walpole prior to his arrival in New York, and it may be that Sir Robert sent him to Clarke to provide him with an employment. Isaac Bobin to Robert Walpole, December 21, 1716, Cholmondeley–Houghton MSS., Correspondence, no. 75, C.U.L.

28. Werner, *Civil List*, pp. 162–163; Jacobsen, *Blathwayt*, p. 378; Osgood, *Eighteenth Century*, II, 424–425. In New York, the auditor was entitled to 5 per cent of the revenues he audited. For an argument that Blathwayt's patronage was extremely limited, see Jacobsen, *Blathwayt*, p. 343.

29. C.O. 324:48, foll. 2b–3 [II], PRO; Lords of Trade to Hunter, March 15, 1716, *New York Col. Docs.*, V, 471; Werner, *Civil List*, pp. 270n21, 206.

30. Colden, "Letters on Smith's History of New York," NYHS, *Colls.*, 1868, p. 220; Lewis Morris to Wager, October 12, 1739, *Governor Lewis Morris Papers*, p. 67.

31. Letter to Lord Cornbury, March 9, 1709, Add. MSS. 15895, fol. 339, B.M.; F. Harison to John Champante, October 5, 1710, Rawlinson A 272, fol. 255, Bodleian Library, Oxford, Eng.

one of the most experienced English diplomats of the eighteenth century. He was a prominent Whig member of parliament, and held a long series of important and profitable posts in the government: he was an under-secretary of state, secretary of the treasury, cofferer of George II's Household, and a privy councillor. Lewis Morris claimed that when he had told Sir Robert that he had letters of recommendation to his brother, Walpole had retorted that Horatio was "a mischievious Elf and the delight he had in being mischievous might induce him to stir but by no meanes any affection for my recommender or consideration for the sufferings of the people." [32] Elfin or not, Horatio Walpole's interest in the colonies and in Clarke stemmed from his appointment as the auditor general of the plantations in 1717 and continued until his death in 1757. He became Clarke's English patron, as well as his superior in office, and their unofficial relationship was well known to New Yorkers.[33] Colden believed, for instance, that it was through Walpole's intervention that Clarke had become Governor Montgomerie's confidant. When Lieutenant Governor Clarke applied to the crown and parliament for reimbursement for the losses he had suffered in carrying out his official duties, he managed to have the matter referred to Walpole and probably succeeded through his interest. In return, Clarke pressed the Auditor General's claims upon a reluctant New York assembly.[34]

32. Morris to Alexander, March 31, 1735, Rutherfurd Collection, II, 115, NYHS; *DNB*, XX, 623–625; Werner, *Civil List*, p. 163; E. Fox, *Land Speculation*, p. 2; Namier and Brooke, *History of Parliament*, II, 595.

33. On Clarke's relationship to Walpole, see NYHS, *Colls.*, 1934, pp. 187–189; Lewis Morris to Wager, May 10, 1739, *Governor Lewis Morris Papers*, p. 45; Osgood, *Eighteenth Century*, II, 423–425; I. Bobin to Clarke, September 15, 1723, in O'Callaghan, ed., *Letters of I. Bobin*, p. 147; Smith, *History*, II, 53, 56, 63; *Board of Trade Journal*, 1742–1749, p. 220; O'Callaghan, *Voyage of G. Clarke*, p. xlii; H. Walpole to [Newcastle], June 23, 1746, Add. MSS. 32707, fol. 345.

34. *Board of Trade Journal*, 1742–1749, p. 220; O'Callaghan, *Voyage of G. Clarke*, p. xlii. Walpole also tried to arrange a pension for Clarke out of the 4.5 percent in 1746. H. Walpole to [Newcastle], June 23, 1746, Add. MSS. 32707, fol. 345, B.M. Walpole's influence was also employed in behalf of Robert Livingston, who joined Clarke in supporting the Auditor in the 1721 controversy over his New York fees and received in return a commission

Horatio Walpole brought his brother Sir Robert to Clarke's side in 1743. Clarke had petitioned the king and Newcastle for the appointment of his sons to more profitable military posts. Robert Walpole wrote to Newcastle in support of these applications and set out Clarke's case in the strongest possible terms, emphasizing his contributions to the welfare of New York and the empire. He concluded: "They and their father are at a distance, and no body here to make them known or intercede for them, and being in a Colony that is under your Graces care, and direction, they seem to have a naturall title to your graces protection, and I hope that my recommendation which proceeds purely from the want of a better sollicitor will not check your Graces goodness, and favour towards them when their pretensions are so well founded." [35] George Clarke had been in contact with Newcastle before this letter was written, having corresponded with him as lieutenant governor of New York. He had frequently asked the Duke's protection at the beginning of his administration, although he admitted that he was unknown to Newcastle. Newcastle helped George Clarke, Jr., when he went to England in 1737, however, and he seems to have responded to the Clarke petition of 1743. [36]

Thus Clarke's English connections were extremely strong. He was fortunate that he never faced a concerted attack in England on the authority or offices he held in America, but very likely this was because of the widespread knowledge of his influence at home. He was left free to pursue an independent path in New York, and he was singularly successful in maintaining his offices and reaping their profits.

---

for his son as secretary for Indian affairs in New York. Osgood, *Eighteeenth Century*, II, 423–425; I. Bobin to Clarke, September 15, 1723, in O'Callaghan, ed., *Letters of I. Bobin*, p. 147; Smith, *History*, II, 53, 56, 63; Leder, *Robert Livingston*, 262–265, 272, 275–276.

35. R. Walpole to Newcastle, March 2, 1743, Add. MSS. 32700, fol. 44; Petitions of G. Clarke, Jr., to Newcastle and the King [1742 or 1743?] Add. MSS. 33057, Foll. 87, 89; G. Clarke to Newcastle [1742 or 1743?], Add. MSS. 33057, fol. 93, B.M.

36. Clarke to Newcastle, March 16, 1736, *New York Col. Docs.*, VI, 47; Clarke to Newcastle, April 3, 1738, *ibid.*, VI, 115; Clarke to Newcastle, November 28, 1737, *Cal. State Papers, Col., Am.*, 1737, pp. 287–288.

Clarke's salaries as secretary of the province,[37] clerk of the council, deputy to the auditor general, and even lieutenant governor of New York were not sizeable, but there were a multitude of fees connected with these offices, particularly the secretaryship, and Clarke was determined to collect them in full.[38] His major concern, however, was the accumulation of grants of land, and his fortune was based on land speculation. In New York, grants of land were the prerogative of the governor acting with the council. A New Yorker seeking a land patent had to secure from them, successively, a warrant to purchase the land from the Indians, a warrant to survey the land, a warrant for the patent, and letters of exemplification.[39] In his capacity as secretary (and clerk of the council) Clarke issued these documents for a fee, and often received shares of land for his assistance.[40] The governor, or lieutenant governor, also received fees for the patents and "kick-backs" in the form of shares of the lands granted. Clarke, like others hungry for frontier lands, evaded the 2,000 acre per person per grant restriction by using trustees— granting the lands to persons who would hold them in trust and release them to him after the patent had been granted.[41] These tech-

37. The secretary's salary was £73 sterling out of the crown revenues in the province and £70 currency voted by the assembly. During 1737 and 1738, however, the assembly set the salary at £60 currency. O'Callaghan, *Voyage of G. Clarke*, p. xxxii; Werner, *Civil List*, pp. 160–161, 254; *Assemb. Jour.*, I, 699–700, 744. At a later period, a New York governor considered the secretaryship "about as lucrative as" the governorship—if the lower living expenses of the secretary were taken into account. Naylor, "Royal Prerogative in New York," NY State Hist. Assoc., *Quarterly Journal*, V (1924), 238–239.

38. O'Callaghan, ed., *Letters of I. Bobin*, passim, especially pp. 90–91, 109–113, and 134–135. Clarke retained sufficient interest in his salary to demand, when governing the province as president, that he be paid the full salary of the governor—the governor "not being intituled to any but from his arrival here." He justified his claim by Van Dam's conduct after Montgomerie's death. Clarke to Newcastle, May 3, 1736, *New York Col. Docs.*, VI, 54. For Clarke's fees, see also, E. Fox, *Land Speculation*, p. 3n10.

39. The role of land speculation in New York politics is treated at some length by E. Fox, *Land Speculation*, pp. 16–27.

40. The official fees of the secretary ranged from £3 (New York currency, or £1.15.0 sterling) per patent for grants under 1,000 acres, to £5 for those between 1,000 and 2,000 acres, and £4 per 1,000 acres for still larger grants. Banyar to Moore, April 21, 1767, C.O. 5:113, fol. 115, PRO. Clarke shared these fees with his deputy secretary.

41. E. Fox, *Land Speculation*, pp. 3, 4, 7.

niques did not escape the notice of such contemporaries as William Smith: "By his offices . . . he had every advantage of inserting his own, or the name of some other person in trust for him in the numerous grants, which he was in a condition, for near half a century, to quicken or retard; and his estate, when he left us, by the rise of his lands and the population of the colony, was estimated at one hundred thousand pounds." [42]

Colden termed the granting of lands "one of the best Perquisites which a governor of New York enjoys," and Clarke was easily the most astute land speculator in the New York of his time.[43] His conduct in the granting of the "Oblong" lands was a model of his sharp practice. Horatio Walpole had secured Clarke shares in the English company that had acquired a royal patent for the land. At the same time, Clarke and four other councillors acquired shares in the New York company that obtained a patent from Governor Montgomerie, so that Clarke had a share in whichever grant was found to be valid. When his double-dealings became known, both Walpole and the American claimants were angered with Clarke, but he was able to pacify them all while retaining a 2,000-acre share in the final grant.[44]

Clarke's deputy secretaries were his trustees as was his son Edward, who as Indian commissioner was useful to his father in discovering and purchasing Indian lands. After he was lieutenant gov-

42. Smith, *History*, II, 68. See also, Colden to Secretary Popple, December 15, 1727, *New York Col. Docs.*, V, 485; Colden to A. Kennedy [1727 or 1728?], draft, NYHS, *Colls.*, 1934, pp. 188–189.

43. Colden to Lord Halifax, August 25, 1758, Dartmouth MSS., D 1778, II, 42, William Salt Library, Staffordshire Record Office, Staffordshire, Eng. Officially, the fee due the governor was 25 shillings per 100 acres in the patent, payable when the provincial seal was affixed to the patent. Colden to Lords of Trade, October 13, 1764, C.O. 5:325, fol. 84, PRO. Clarke collected either the secretary's (£3 to £5 per 1,000 acres) or the governor's fees (£12.10.0 per 1,000 acres), or accepted a share of the lands granted in lieu of fees from 1703 to 1743. Since thousands of acres of land were patented in most years, it is clear that Clarke's accumulation of fees and lands was very large. For the calculation of profits arising from land for a similar royal official in New York, see Catherine Snell Crary, "The American Dream: John Tabor Kempe's Rise from Poverty to Riches," *William and Mary Quarterly*, 3rd ser., XIV (1957), pp. 176–195.

44. E. Fox, *Land Speculation*, pp. 17–18, 49; C. H. and M. L. Baker, *Life of Chandos*, pp. 349 ff. See above, pp. 80–81.

ernor, men whom he had appointed to local offices acted as Clarke's trustees, perhaps in gratitude for their appointments. Likewise, since the commander in chief of the colony had the authority to promote the officers in the Independent Companies stationed in New York, Clarke was able to use such military men in the same way. Clarke used trustees to acquire at least twenty-two different tracts of land containing about 102,469 acres of New York land in all, and during his administration alone (1736–1743) he obtained 55,713 acres.[45]

When Clarke began his administration he complained to Newcastle of the extraordinary expense of maintaining the dignity of the government in New York. Three years later he made the same complaint to the board of trade, claiming that he had been forced to sell "a small tho favorite estate" in order to support himself in a style suitable for the lieutenant governor.[46] After he had returned to England, he asserted that he had lost over £6,000 in the service of the crown, and petitioned Newcastle to present his case to the king. He claimed an outlay of £1,500 for raising a military company in New York for service in the 1740 West Indies expedition, £2,500 in personal effects when the fort in New York was burnt during the 1741 Negro conspiracy, and £2,000 for his capture by a French privateer upon his return voyage to England in 1745. He explained his return to England after delivering the government of New York to Admiral Clinton by his "having a numerous family and [being] unable to bear up under his great losses and sufferings, . . . hopeing to find Relief from His Majesty's Gracious Bounty." [47] Nor was he disappointed, for on March 3, 1746, a royal warrant for £4,000 was issued to him in compensation for his "several great Losses and sufferings," upon Horatio Walpole's report to the commissioners of the treasury and Robert Walpole's intercession with the Duke of Newcastle.[48]

45. E. Fox, *Land Speculation*, pp. 6–8, 49–50; *Cal. Coun. Min.*, pp. 332–334.
46. Clarke to Newcastle, November 23, 1736, *New York Col. Docs.*, VI, 84; Clarke to Lords of Trade, January 28, 1740, *ibid.*, VI, 159.
47. Petition of G. Clarke, Jr., to Newcastle, [1742–1743?], Add. MSS. 33057, fol. 93, B.M.
48. Warrant from the King to Clarke, March 3, 1746, D 1778, II, 22, Wm. Salt.

Lieutenant Governor Clarke, 1736–1743

Before we accept the story of Clarke's expenses as lieutenant governor, and his losses of 1741 and 1744, we must remember that he was one of the largest landholders in New York, that his personal fortune was estimated at £100,000, and that he lived the life of a wealthy country squire for many years after his return to Cheshire.[49] Clarke was the prototype of the self-interested official; he came to America to make a fortune and made one, whereupon he returned to England. The forty-two years he spent in New York bred in him little feeling for the province and no social attachment to it.

II

The peculiarity of George Clarke's relation to New York is reflected in his conduct as lieutenant governor from 1736 to 1743. Since he had come to America to make a fortune, he was determined to have his administration meet this end. In political terms, this meant that he had to protect himself in office and to encourage an attitude of "business as usual" in the province so that his fees and salaries would be paid and settlers would be tempted to enter his lands. He supported an aggressive frontier policy so that his Mohawk holdings would appreciate in value,[50] but his main effort was to end the bitter factionalism that had racked New York politics since 1733.

Clarke's aloofness from New York society and independence in politics both hindered and aided him in the task of reducing party warfare. He had been Cosby's political adviser, yet he escaped the criticisms of the anti-Cosby party. According to Smith, "He shared a part of the odium which fell upon Mr. Cosby, but escaped much more of it by a closer attachment than before to his rural villa on the edge of Hempstead plains, and left it to Mr. Delancey to enjoy the praise or blame of being the Sejanus of that Governor."[51]

49. Smith, *History*, II, 68. There is no reason to believe that Smith actually knew the extent of Clarke's personal fortune. What is clear, however, is that Clarke was very rich by the time he left America.
50. Fox, *Land Speculation*, p. 4.
51. Smith, *History*, II, 32–33.

Clarke's adroitness in avoiding identification with an unpopular cause worked against him as lieutenant governor, however. Those who had opposed Cosby, "Deem him [Clarke] a man of much art, but suspect his sincerity & add to their generall Jealousy of all governours a very great suspicion of him in particular . . . On the other side, the partizans of Mr. Cosby's administration, whether it was from disappointment of Mr. Clarke's not entring into their measures with so much warmth as they expected he would, or for what other reason, began seemingly or really to grow cool towards him, and after that so violent against him, as to exceed all manner of decency in the opposition they made." [52] Thus neither of the parties of the previous administration felt sure of Clarke, the Morrisites because he had been so close to Cosby, and the Cosbyites because he had refused to identify himself completely with their party. Clarke maintained an Olympian attitude, working with each group when it served his purpose to do so, and by this tactic he eventually eliminated the parties that had come into being during Cosby's administration.

In the council, Clarke began playing the part of a full-fledged Cosbyite. On May 16, 1736, he took the oath as chancellor, the very role in which Cosby had created so much ill-will. On July 24, 1736, he appointed Daniel Horsmanden, who had been recommended by Cosby as a councillor and was the publicist for the Cosbyites, judge of the court of vice-admiralty. On September 29, Clarke renominated William Cosby, Jr., as sheriff along with the other Cosby-appointed officers of New York City. Cosby was appointed again in 1737 and 1738, and land patents were granted him by the council in 1736, even though he was one of the chief targets of the party that had opposed his father. [53]

There was good reason to humor the Cosby faction in the council. Of the eight councillors in 1736, five were consistent members of that group: Archibald Kennedy, James DeLancey, Philip Cortlandt, Henry Lane, and Daniel Horsmanden. Cadwallader Col-

52. Lewis Morris to Wager, May 10, 1739, *Governor Lewis Morris Papers*, p. 44.

53. *Cal. Coun. Min.*, pp. 326-328, 332, 334; Lewis Morris to Wager, May 10, 1739, *Governor Lewis Morris Papers*, p. 44.

den, Philip Livingston, and Abraham Van Horne were the Morrisite councillors, but both Colden and Livingston lived far from New York City and seldom attended meetings. Although Alexander had never been suspended or removed from the council, he was not summoned by Clarke on the grounds that the board of trade had recommended his removal, and he did not attend. Van Horne refused to attend of his own accord, pretending, according to Clarke, that he was ill. Thus, the five members who attended regularly had all been allied to Governor Cosby during his administration. The only addition to the council in the Clarke administration was George Clarke, Jr., who was appointed in 1738.[54]

Clarke depended upon the council to aid him in his land dealings, for their consent was necessary for the various steps in grants of land, and they proved willing to aid his speculations. He failed, however, to retain the political sympathies of the council, which opposed several of the bills that the Lieutenant Governor and the assembly had approved.[55] One reason for his difficulties was a change in council procedure that had come about in response to a Morrisite criticism that Governor Cosby had been sitting with the council when it met in its legislative capacity. The board of trade, on the advice of the Attorney and Solicitor General, advised Cosby that this practice was contrary to the principle according to which the three branches of the legislature—the assembly, the legislative council, and the governor (with his legislative power, the negative voice)—ought to act separately. Cosby had died before receiving this order, but Clarke told the board of trade that he would abide by it, and he never sat with the council when it considered legislation.[56] The councillors doubtless acted more freely in Clarke's absence than if he had been present to argue his case.

More important than any procedure, however, was Clarke's

---

54. Hutchins, *Civil List*, pp. 22–23; Clarke to Lords of Trade, April 7, 1736, June 2, 1738, December 7, 1739, *New York Col. Docs.*, VI, 50, 119, 152–153; Lords of Trade to Clarke, August 9, 1738, *ibid.*, VI, 119.

55. Osgood, *Eighteenth Century*, II, 474–475; *Jour. Legis. Coun.*, I, 691, 693, 696, 698.

56. Secretary Popple to Cosby, January 23, 1736; Opinion of the Attorney and Solicitor General, January 15, 173[6]; Clarke to Secretary Popple, May 28, 1736, *New York Col. Docs.*, VI, 39–40, 41–42, 56.

lack of political and social contact with the councillors, for in choosing to go it alone Clarke refused to make political concessions to them, and the social isolation of his family left him without informal bonds to others of the ruling group in New York. His aloof attitude toward the council is illustrated in his request that the board of trade recommend the attorney general of New York rather than a prominent merchant for a seat at the council board: "I think it highly necessary that such of the King's Officers as hold the most considerable posts should be prefer'd to seats at that Board, and I have found the want of them more than once in matters that concern the Government."[57] At the same time he recommended his son, as secretary of the province, for a seat. This attitude was not calculated to win him much sympathy from the council or from New Yorkers in general, for political success in New York required a much nicer sense of local social position. Clarke's reward was the loss of leadership in the council to James DeLancey, who was much better connected in New York and much more concerned with the internal workings of the province. William Smith noted the result: "In the two late sessions, therefore, Mr. Clarke had little or no assistance from his Council, where DeLancey kept the majority cool, himself privately abetting the opposition of the Lower House."[58]

As lieutenant governor, Clarke lavished much of his attention on the assembly. Unlike Cosby, who never dissolved his complacent assembly, Clarke met three different legislatures during his administration: the holdover Cosby assembly; the assembly of June 1737 to October 1738; and the assembly which sat from March 1739 until Clinton's arrival.

The legislature which Clarke inherited from Governor Cosby had been elected in 1728. Under the leadership of the Philipse family it had cooperated with the Governor, appropriating a five-year salary grant in 1732 and resisting Lewis Morris, Jr.'s, anti-administration proposals. Interim elections and the passage of time worked changes in the composition and attitudes of the assembly, however, and Clarke found it unmanageable. A large number of the

57. Clarke to Lords of Trade, June 2, 1738, *ibid.*, VI, 119.
58. Smith, *History*, II, 65.

members continued to support the Cosbyite cause, but a determined group of fifteen upheld the right of Rip Van Dam to present his arguments for the government of New York to the assembly, and Clarke was forced to adjourn the body from March to October 1736. Neither of the factions that had arisen in the Cosby administration could muster a controlling majority and both seemed displeased with Clarke. They offered the Lieutenant Governor a meager half-salary (£780) and added extra insult by demanding the right to appropriate money for the support of the government independently of the lieutenant governor and council, and without scrutiny by the auditor general (Clarke's patron, Horatio Walpole).[59] Clarke therefore decided to call a new assembly, the first in nine years.

The decision to dissolve the old assembly was a daring one for Clarke to make, for the Morrisites had been demanding new elections for years and it was generally acknowledged that they would win the day. In any case, the next session was bound to be especially difficult, since the five-year revenue bill that Cosby had secured in 1732 had run out and Clarke was faced with the necessity of renegotiating the provincial finances. Superficially, it looked as though a new assembly dominated by Alexander and the Morrises would be even more recalcitrant than the last, but the situation had changed greatly since the fall of 1736. Colden believed that the old Morris opposition had assured Clarke that they no longer questioned his right to the government and would be ready to serve him, "& I believe he expected they would be more so to attone for what had passed." [60] Merely by issuing writs for an election Clarke had satisfied one of their most frequent complaints against Cosby. Moreover, there was a common interest binding Clarke to the Morrisites —the Mohawk Valley. The city of Albany and the Dutch in the north of the province had obligations to Alexander and Morris, and

59. Colden, *History of Cosby and Clarke,* pp. 350–351; Clarke to Lords of Trade, May 9, 1737, *New York Col. Docs.,* VI, 94–95; Lewis Morris to Wager, October 12, 1739, *Governor Lewis Morris Papers,* p. 67; Declaration of the fifteen members of the assembly, April 15, 1736, in Stokes, *Iconography,* IV, 547.
60. Colden, *History of Cosby and Clarke,* p. 351.

the latter had long supported the Burnet policy of a vigorous opposition to the French and defense of the northern frontier.

The Morrisites won a resounding victory in early 1737. They carried the city of New York, where James Alexander was elected to the assembly, and both the Morrises came in for Westchester. Lewis Morris, Jr., was elected speaker, and Peter Zenger was appointed the official printer of the province.[61] Clarke wrote confidently to the board of trade that "the majority is of those, who opposed me before I was appointed Lieutenant Governor, but if appearances dont deceive me, I have reason to hope they will make good the deficiencyes of the Revenue and give another; they will expect from me at the same time such laws for the good of the Province as I can pass, more than that, the speaker tells me, they wont insist on." [62] Lewis Morris, Jr., began the session in a belligerent fashion, proposing a bill disabling any assemblyman "who shall accept any Office of Profit after his Election." This was defeated, but in the next session of the assembly, Alexander continued the threat, proposing a bill to vacate the seat of any representative who "shall accept of any Office Gift or Grant from the Governour, or Commander in Chief." The bill was never read a second time.[63] Clarke was at work to mollify the Morrisites, however, and in October 1737 he succeeded in having Alexander and William Smith reinstated to the bar, from which they had been excluded since their defense of Zenger in 1735.[64]

The partnership finally jelled in December 1737, when Clarke agreed to a bill emitting bills of credit for financing the debt of the province, and to a revenue bill for the support of the government for one year. The revenue bill was the first ever accepted by a New

---

61. Stokes, *Iconography*, IV, 552; *Assemb. Jour.*, I, 759.
62. Clarke to Lords of Trade, June 17, 1737, *New York Col. Docs.*, VI, 96.
63. *Assemb. Jour.*, I, 697–698, 705.
64. Smith, *History*, II, 40–41; Colden, *History of Cosby and Clarke*, p. 354. Philip Livingston privately claimed credit for arranging the reinstatement of Smith and Alexander, having succeeded in reconciling "parties to quiet the minds of our People." Livingston to Jacob Wendell, September 23, 1737, Museum of the City of New York.

York governor for such a limited period. The Lieutenant Governor explained this concession by saying that he had not given up hope of securing an unlimited support or one for a period of several years, as his instructions required, but hoped to secure such a bill in the next session.[65] At the same time, Clarke agreed to the Morrisite bill for the triennial election of the legislature, and supported it enthusiastically in England through George Clarke, Jr., though this was contrary to his instructions. He agreed to an act establishing courts to try petty cases, which the Morris group had long sought, and also to one for strengthening and supporting the garrison at Oswego and regulating the Indian trade at that fort.[66] These acts were popular, and Clarke hoped that they would encourage immigration into the province, and that the Oswego act in particular would help to settle the frontier.

Things were not entirely as Clarke wished them, however. The council opposed or amended several of the bills of this session, including the triennial act.[67] Meanwhile, the New York City elections were carried by those opposed to the old aldermen (that is, the party of the Morrises and Alexander), and, in a fiercely contested by-election in New York City for a vacant assembly seat, Adolph Philipse defeated the Morris-Alexander candidate, Cornelius Van Horne.[68] Clarke must have felt his position jeopardized, for the council (and the opposition in the assembly, composed of those who

65. Clarke to Lords of Trade, February 17, 1738, *New York Col. Docs.*, VI, 111; *Assemb. Jour.*, I, 733–734.

66. Stokes, *Iconography*, IV, 555; *The Colonial Laws of New York from the Year 1664 to the Revolution* (Albany, 1894–1896), II, 951; E. B. O'Callaghan, ed., *Documentary History of the State of New York* (Albany, 1849–1851), IV, 244–256; Lords of Trade to Clarke, August 9, 1738, *New York Col. Docs.*, VI, 129. The triennial act was disallowed by the crown on November 30, 1738. A septennial act was successfully enacted in 1743.

67. Smith, *History*, II, 40–41.

68. Edwards, "New York City Politics," *Political Science Quarterly*, XXVI, 596; Colden to Mrs. Colden, September 11, 1737, NYHS, *Colls.*, 1918, p. 179. The election returns were contested in the assembly and an important quarrel took place testing the right to vote of Jews and nonresidents. See Stokes, *Iconography*, IV, 552–553; *Assemb. Jour.*, I, 710–712; 716–717; Smith, *History*, II, 37–40.

had supported Cosby and were now beginning to look to James DeLancey for leadership) had been antagonized by his dissolution of the old assembly and his assent to the recent Morrisite bills. "In this dilemma he determined to undermine the popular leaders," according to William Smith. He offered certain of the Morrisites, particularly Lewis Morris, Jr., and Simon Johnson, places of office, promising "his influence upon the council in their favour, after it had been concerted that the Board should resolutely refuse their consent." [69] The strategy succeeded, for the offices were not confirmed to the nominees, and the supporters of the Morris party were demoralized, since one of their cardinal principles had been opposition to political jobbery. Colden claimed that a similar trick had been played on Lewis, Sr. Clarke had turned out all the Cosby-appointed officers in Westchester County in favor of Morris' nominees, on the correct supposition that Morris' complicity in this jobbery would lose him all sympathy in his own party.[70] Lewis Morris' commission for the government of New Jersey arrived in the fall of 1738, and he departed for Burlington, utterly defeated in his ambitions in New York.

Clarke's sudden alienation from the leaders of the assembly was apparent in the autumn session of 1738. He urged them to provide a permanent revenue for the province, to support settlement in the Mohawk Valley, and to guard against French encroachments in the north, but they ignored his requests. Instead, they refused to provide even one year's support for the government unless Clarke would assent to legislation for the extension of bills of credit that the province had issued long before. Clarke dissolved the assembly on October 20.[71]

Elections were held once again and a new assembly, Clarke's third, met in March 1739. It immediately showed its colors: Adolph Philipse was chosen speaker to replace Lewis Morris, Jr., and William Bradford replaced Zenger as the official printer. The Morrisite representatives from New York City were completely swept out,

69. Smith, *ibid.,* II, 44–45.
70. Colden, *History of Cosby and Clarke,* p. 352.
71. *Assemb. Jour.,* I, 735, 740, 742, 745–748.

and a slate sympathetic to Philipse was returned.[72] Philip Livingston expressed the Morrisite reaction in a letter to his son:

> I am very much Surprized to hear of the Election with you that Messrs. Philipse, Moore, Clarkson, and Roome are Choisen for the City [New York] members—which I would not have Expected, tho Suppose it to be too true. I wish your uncle v. Horn and Mr. Alexander had gott in. Since it is otherwise must be Content. this assembly I suspect will be of a long Standing and may prove to be what we do not like, which cant be prevented So must do best we can.[73]

James Alexander conceded that "what was called the Country party is very weak in this assembly," but hoped that if the assemblymen considered the "interest of the country . . . Its very indifferent of what party they have been." [74] Lewis Morris claimed that the antagonism between the two parties had been dying in the 1738 session, and that the dissolution had been sudden and mysterious, ending the pacification. Most people thought, he said, that it indicated Clarke's true allegiance, and that he would throw his weight to the Cosbyites in the new assembly—else why would he have dissolved as pliable an assembly as that led by Lewis, Jr.? Moreover, the Cosbyites won the elections of 1739 by criticizing the excessive spending of the previous assembly and promising to provide no more than a half-salary for the executive. Morris believed Clarke and his new assembly to be "diffident of each other," and thought the difficulty was the lack of trust in the Lieutenant Governor, for no one was quite sure where he stood.[75]

Clarke's role in regard to the new assembly was changed in at least one respect, however, for there was no longer any organized group of Morrisites in the province. Morris himself was discredited, his son "a little in the shade for his compliances to Mr. Clarke," and Alexander excluded from the assembly.[76] The new assembly was

72. Werner, *Civil List*, p. 309.
73. Philip Livingston to Robert Livingston, Jr., March 24, 1739, Livingston-Redmond MSS., F.D.R.
74. Alexander to Colden, April 6, 1739, NYHS, *Colls.*, 1918, p. 194.
75. Lewis Morris to Wager, May 10, 1739, *Governor Lewis Morris Papers*, pp. 44–45; Lewis Morris to Wager, October 12, 1739, *ibid.*, pp. 66–69.
76. Smith, *History*, II, 65.

controlled by the old Cosby men under the leadership of Adolph Philipse and in alliance with Chief Justice DeLancey, and was suspicious of Clarke for his apparent desertion of his old allies.[77]

The new assembly asserted its independence from the very start, insisting upon practically complete control of colonial finances. In April Clarke accepted a one-year support of the government.[78] The board of trade pressed him to settle the revenue on a more permanent basis, but, in October 1739, he was finally defeated on the issue. The assembly absolutely refused appropriations for more than one year at a time, and demanded the right specifically to appropriate the funds they supplied by assigning salaries to individuals rather than to their offices or the treasury. "They remained inflexible and seemed resolved to run all risques rather than give into it they knew the Country were unanimous in the same sentiments and from thence they were assured of their elections on a new choice." [79]

Clarke prorogued the assembly for a few days, but they remained firm. They knew, he said, that "from the strong appearances of an open rupture with Spain and France, that instead of disolving them I would lay hold of their present sitting to put the province in a posture of defense." Clarke feared, besides, that new elections would renew the political animosities that had gripped the province, and, upon the advice of the council, he agreed to the assembly's terms. At least, "being thus reduced to the necessity of giving way to the Assembly, I got them to make provisions for fortifying the Province." [80] Clarke thus succeeded in securing his own salary (although the assembly had reduced it from £1,560 to £1,300) and in

77. New groupings were forming in the assembly, although many veterans of the Cosby-Morris factionalism were still on the scene. Philip Livingston observed that some of the Cosbyites ("the Court Party") went so far as to oppose the election of Adolph Philipse. Livingston to Jacob Wendell, September 23, 1737, Museum of the City of New York.

78. *Assemb. Jour.*, I, 754–755.

79. Clarke to Board of Trade, November 30, 1739, *New York Col. Docs.*, VI, 150–151.

80. Lords of Trade to Clarke, February 6, 1739; Clarke to Lords of Trade, November 30, 1739, *New York Col. Docs.*, VI, 139, 150–151; *Assemb. Jour.*, I, 766, 768, 771, 772, 775, 776.

obtaining provisions for the defense of the colony. These two projects were very nearly all he managed to extract from the recalcitrant assembly, and his defense of his failure to secure a permanent revenue became a familiar refrain in letters to the board of trade:

> Had I not passed those bills I should undoubtedly have thrown the province into as great convulsions as ever but by passing them tho it was the most irksome thing I ever did, I have got the province fortified I have secured the Senecas Country from falling in to the hands of the french, and I boldly affirm I have reduced the province to a state of greater quiet than it has known in forty years before; thus everyone here is highly pleased.[81]

That Clarke did not succeed in obtaining a permanent revenue and in providing even more adequately for a vigorous northern policy was the result of his final assembly's unwillingness to work with him. This assembly was determined to have its way, and, led by the chief justice, James DeLancey, it capitalized on Clarke's fear for his salary and his obsession with the safety of the north to force the Lieutenant Governor to compromise imperial policies. Smith thought DeLancey responsible for the obstruction of Clarke's plans, because DeLancey had been angered by Clarke's dissolution in 1737, and, "discerning the advantages of popularity, not only for the better securing his salary, for which he now became dependent upon the Assembly, but to be revenged upon the Lieutenant Governor, and to gain an influence upon his successors, and with a view perhaps to the succession itself, studied to recommend himself to the House." [82] DeLancey gained control of the lower house during the Clarke administration and retained it until his death, to the discomfort of Governor Clinton. With his first emergence as the leading

81. Clarke to Lords of Trade, June 13, 1740, *New York Col. Docs.*, VI, 160. For subsequent revenue bills, see *Assemb. Jour.*, I, 783–785, 786–788, 790–791 (1740); *ibid.*, I, 812–16, 822 (1741); *ibid.*, I, 833–834, 836 (1742). See also, John F. Burns, *Controversies Between Royal Governors and Their Assemblies in the Northern American Colonies* (Boston, 1923), pp. 322–326.
82. Smith, *History*, II, 65. DeLancey was dependent upon the assembly for his salary after 1739, when they began the practice of specific appropriations of the revenue, voting separately on each salary they were willing to pay.

local politician in the early 1740's and with the disappearance of the factions of the Cosby administration, New York politicians reoriented themselves once again.

Clarke defended his record as lieutenant governor by arguing that he had quieted the violent factionalism of the mid-1730's and had restored the province to economic well-being. In 1741 he dispatched to the board of trade a graphic description of the disastrous state of the colony at the time of his appointment. He was confronted, he claimed, by excesses of "party rage," decay of the shipbuilding industry, stagnation of real estate and trade, and by a rapidly declining population. Clarke's remedy was pacification of opposing political factions (a "steady course of moderation") in order to give "new life to trade and to people the town and Province." He felt that the job had been completed in 1741; empty houses tenanted, rents high, new houses built, shipbuilding and "Trade in General" on the rise.[83]

There was a good deal of justification for these claims. The economy undoubtedly did improve during his administration and he unquestionably did succeed in destroying the Cosby-Morris division in New York politics, just as Governor Hunter had put an end to the Leislerian antagonisms of an earlier period. On the other hand, however, Clarke fell far short of Hunter's self-sacrificing conduct of imperial business in the colony. Hunter had been willing to go without a salary for years in order to preserve the tradition of long-term grants of revenue, neglecting his personal interests in order to maintain the independence, dignity, and leadership of the royal governor. Clarke, who well could have afforded to go without his own salary for a while, quickly acquiesced in the assembly's demand for a one-year appropriation.[84] He permitted the legislature to initiate the procedure of specific designation of appropriations, a further intrusion upon executive authority, and signed bills for paper money and triennial elections of the assembly that he knew ran contrary to

83. Clarke to Lords of Trade, December 15, 1741, *New York Col. Docs.*, VI, 207; Clarke to Lords of Trade, February 17, 1738, *ibid.*, VI, 111.

84. Osgood (*Eighteenth Century*, II, 470) contends that Clarke was really unable to support the dignity of a lieutenant governor without a salary, but Mrs. Fox's investigation of his landholding seems to belie any such assertion.

English intentions. Perhaps even Hunter would have failed to carry out his instructions fully in 1740, but Clarke gave the impression of being a man who put his own prerogatives before those of his sovereign. Perhaps this was the price paid by the imperial administration for the appointment of an official who had been too long in America. At least it proves that unfamiliarity with the New York situation was not the only reason for the failure of a governor to perform his duty adequately.

III

The conclusion of George Clarke's political career typified his relation to the colony in which he had made his fortune: he departed for England as soon as his successor had arrived in New York. Of course most royal governors left America after they had been replaced in their posts, but most Americans who were given executive responsibility in the colonies remained. Clarke was the only New York executive appointed while living in the colony who did not stay. While not born or bred in America, Clarke had lived on Long Island for forty years and his decision to retire to the life of an English country gentleman exemplifies the lack of sentiment and cool calculation that marked his entire public life.

The first intimation of Clarke's intention to quit New York for England came to light in late 1734, when a report circulated that "George Clarke is going home in the spring never to return." [85] Apparently Clarke had received permission from Whitehall to leave New York, and in the early summer of 1735 it became known that he had sold his household effects.[86] Why he remained is uncertain, since he never mentions the affair in his surviving correspondence, but it seems reasonable to assume that the news of Governor Cosby's illness and his own prospects for governing New York must have held him in America.

85. E. Norris to R. H. Morris, December 9, 1734, Morris MSS., Box 2, R.U.L.

86. Lewis Morris, Jr., to R. H. Morris, July 26, 1735, Morris MSS., Box 2, R.U.L.

Once appointed lieutenant governor, Clarke lived in fear that he would be supplanted by a governor sent over from England. This was a real threat to a professional placeman, for the lieutenant governor did not receive a salary except when he acted as commander in chief. Besides, a new governor might attempt to recover half of the salary already paid the lieutenant governor, as Cosby had done to Van Dam and Morris. Clarke pressed Newcastle and the board of trade to continue him in command of New York at least until the profits of the office should compensate him for his expenses.[87]

Even before Clarke's commission as lieutenant governor arrived, American newspapers were rumoring the appointment of a new governor for New York—the Marquis of Carnarvan in May 1736, and Ralph Jennison (M.P. for Northumberland) in September.[88] The blow actually fell in June 1737, when the board of trade notified Clarke that Lord De la Warr had been appointed governor of New York and New Jersey, and that "he will with all convenient speed set out for his Government."[89] De la Warr's appointment had been rumored in May and definitely confirmed by August 22, 1737, and Clarke acknowledged it on October 14.[90]

De la Warr, as we know, remained an absentee governor, but his appointment and a series of conflicting reports of his intentions stimulated Clarke to frenzied efforts to protect his post. In August 1737 De la Warr was made colonel of the first troop of Horse Guards and there were rumors that he had resigned the government of New York. In November the *Pennsylvania Gazette* printed a dispatch from London alleging that De la Warr would be replaced by

87. Clarke to Newcastle, March 16, 1736, and May 3, 1736; Clarke to Lords of Trade, May 29, 1736, *New York Col. Docs.*, VI, 47, 54, 64.

88. *Boston Weekly News-Letter*, April 29–May 6, 1736, quoted in *New Jersey Archives*, XI, 463; *New York Gazette*, September 20, 1736, quoted *ibid.*, XI, 478–479.

89. Lords of Trade to Clarke, June 22, 1737, *New York Col. Docs.*, VI, 97.

90. *New England Weekly Journal*, August 30, 1737, quoted in *New Jersey Archives*, XI, 511; *Boston Weekly News-Letter*, May 25–June 1, 1738, quoted *ibid.*, XI, 533; Clarke to Lords of Trade, October 14, 1737, *New York Col. Docs,.* VI, 110.

Major General James Tyrell, the governor of Pendennis Castle. In December, however, the *New York Gazette* announced that De la Warr would continue in the government and would arrive in the spring. In March the *Gazette* said that his personal effects had been loaded onto a ship bound for New York.[91]

In the face of this confusion, Clarke attempted to dissuade De la Warr from taking up the New York governorship and at the same time tried to buy the job from him. Smith, taking his usual jaundiced view, insinuated that Clarke had attempted to frighten De la Warr out of coming to New York. "His Lordship declared, that Mr. Clarke's letters concerning the Colony were perplexed and discouraging."[92] The hard evidence, however, is merely that Clarke emphasized the less glamorous aspects of American government in order to persuade the governor to sell him the post. George Clarke, Jr., wrote to De la Warr in June 1740, offering to purchase the government from him on behalf of his father. He offered 1,000 guineas, "to idemnify Your Lordship from any loss, or expence occasioned thereby, which is all that the Government there under its present circumstances allows me to offer." Clarke had found, his son said, that the unruly spirit of the people could be checked only by the authority of a fully-commissioned governor, and that "the weight and Authority of a Lieutenant Governour, though managed in the best manner, would not be able to subdue it." Horatio Walpole agreed in this analysis, and Clarke asked De la Warr to intercede with Newcastle to have his father succeed him as governor of New York: "This will greatly facilitate his Majestys affairs, and . . . it will be some advantage to my father."[93]

91. Beatson, *Index*, II, 179; *New York Gazette*, November 7 and November 28, December 27, 1737, March 4 and 7, 1738, quoted in Stokes, *Iconography*, IV, 554, 555, 556; *Pennsylvania Gazette*, November 17–November 24, 1737.
92. Smith, *History*, II, 33.
93. G. Clarke, Jr., to De la Warr, June 20, 1740, *New York Col. Docs.*, VI, 163–164; Werner (*Civil List*, p. 155n13) says that De la Warr resigned in September 1737. O'Callaghan (*New York Col. Docs.*, VI, 163n1) concurs. Both follow Collins (Sir Egerton Brydges, ed., *Arthur Collins's Peerage of England . . . Greatly Augmented, and Continued to the Present Time* [London, 1812], V, 25–26). De la Warr's negotiations with Clarke in 1740 and Clinton in 1741 indicate that he had not previously resigned the government

The Conduct of Politics in New York, 1732–1753

George Clarke did not have sufficient interest in England to procure the governorship at this time, perhaps because of the deterioration of Sir Robert Walpole's position, and Newcastle gave it to his relation George Clinton in mid-1741. Clarke was certain that Clinton would soon arrive to take command in New York, and told the assembly in September 1741 that it would be the last time he spoke to them.[94] Clinton was delayed for two years, however, and did not arrive until September 1743.

By this time Clarke had decided to retire from government in New York. He had already given his secretaryship to his son, George, Jr., and now refused, on account of infirmity, to be sworn into Governor Clinton's council. At the end of 1743, he told the board of trade that he would return to England on "private Business." [95] He left two soldier sons in New York, but his favorite son and namesake remained in England with him, exercising the secretaryship of New York by deputy and never bothering to qualify as a councillor of the province.[96] The Clarkes had done with New York as anything other than absentee landlords and officeholders.

George Clarke's administration was satisfactory from his own point of view, and it was even minimally successful for the ministry who, as Peter Collinson pointed out in 1738, had decided to maintain Clarke in office "at Least, till all your former Breaches are Healed." [97]

---

of New York. He had, however, resigned as governor of New Jersey so that Lewis Morris could be appointed.

94. Clarke's speech to the assembly, September 17, 1741, *Assemb. Jour.*, I, 808.

95. *Cal. Coun. Min.*, p. 343; *Board of Trade Journal*, 1742–1749, p. 99. Clarke had not given up the idea of officeholding in America, however. In 1746, after the Lieutenant Governor had returned to England, Walpole proposed (as an alternative to a pension on the 4.5 percent) that Newcastle provide for Clarke with the government of New Jersey. Lewis Morris had just died. Hardwicke was backing Belcher for the government, but Walpole stressed Clarke's superior record as an American governor. Belcher got the job. H. Walpole to [Newcastle], June 23, 1746, Add. MSS. 32707, fol. 345, B.M.

96. Actually, in January 1745 Clarke tried to have his son Hyde transferred from New York to a company in Georgia. Clinton to [?], January 3, 1745, draft, Clinton MSS., II, C.L. See also, Clinton to Newcastle, January 26, 1744, *New York Col. Docs.*, VI, 253.

97. Collinson to Alexander, September 18, 1738, Rutherfurd Collection, IV, 59, NYHS.

Imperial principles had suffered, but the province had been quieted and strengthened, and Clarke probably felt disappointment only in his failure to be appointed governor. On the other hand, Clarke was doubtless pleased to leave New York. There was little choice land left to be appropriated, the assembly was increasingly intransigent, and, above all, James DeLancey had become a formidable obstacle to the executive's freedom of action. Unfortunately for the prospects of royal government in New York, however, Clarke did not pass on this intelligence to his successor, George Clinton.

7

Governor Clinton: New York, 1743-1753

IN MID-SUMMER OF *1743*, THE PEOPLE OF NEW York waited anxiously to catch a glimpse of their new governor, knowing that his conduct would closely affect their personal fortunes. Governor Cosby had plunged the province into five years of political chaos, and few could have expected another such blow from Whitehall. Clarke's interregnum had served to dampen the political fires of the 1730's, but it had witnessed the growth of practical political power in the assembly and the emergence of a new political faction under the leadership of James DeLancey. Governor George Clinton would have to deal with the assembly on more nearly equal terms than his predecessor did and, if he was to restore New York to its pre-Cosby balance of government, he would have to be a man both of consummate political skill and strong English connections. As matters turned out, however, the Governor's powerful influence in England could not compensate for his lack of political touch.

I

The dilemma was obvious and inescapable. So long as military men devoid of administrative and American experience were appointed governors, they would have to rely upon the guidance of politically-seasoned colonists. "A governor is no sooner appointed," remarked the placeman Archibald Kennedy, "than the first Question is, Into whose Hands shall I throw myself?" The answer was not as simple as Kennedy thought, however: "Into whose but such as can best manage the Assembly." [1] The practical task for the newly-arrived governor was to size up the political situation rapidly and to make a snap judgment as to where to cast his lot. The secretary of the board of trade explained the problem to Cadwallader Colden: "A governor has at first a pretty difficult lesson to learn, and if he falls into right Hands, He may certainly pave the Way for a peaceable, and an agreeable Way of making his Fortune; But otherwise he opens the Door of Complaints, & it may be some cannot easily be wiped off." [2] Before Clinton left England, he sought and received counsel on selecting local advisers to aid him in governing New York. The two names most frequently recommended were those of George Clarke and James DeLancey. When the governor reached America, however, Clarke was represented to him as an "unpopular man, and not so fitt for my Confidence, as Chief Justice DeLancy," and he became entirely dependent upon the Chief Justice.[3]

1. Archibald Kennedy, *Essay*, p. 34.
2. A. Popple to Colden, November 1, 1734, NYHS, *Colls.*, 1918, p. 115.
3. Clinton to Newcastle, September 30, 1748, Add. MSS. 32716, fol. 400, B.M.; Statement of Case, 1746/7, Clinton MSS., C.L.

The Conduct of Politics in New York, 1732–1753

James DeLancey [4] was the son of a late seventeenth-century Huguenot immigrant to New York who had amassed a fortune in commerce, specializing in the supply of goods that Albany merchants exchanged with Montrealers for furs. The elder DeLancey had achieved a place in the Anglo-Dutch elite of the province by marrying into the Dutch landholding aristocracy, serving in public office, and joining the Church of England. From the very first James DeLancey was groomed to carry on the elevation of the family. He was sent to Corpus Christi, Cambridge, and Lincoln's Inn in the early 1720's and thus became one of the best educated men in his province and one of the bare handful of New Yorkers to gain some experience in England. He returned to America in 1725 and completed the anglicization of his family by marrying the heiress of Caleb Heathcote, the lord of Scarsdale Manor and New York's receiver general.

DeLancey was appointed to the royal council of New York in 1729, and from that moment until his death he was one of the colony's leading officeholders. He presided over the commission appointed in 1730 to frame the Montgomerie Charter of New York City, and in June 1731 he was appointed second judge of the provincial supreme court. He became chief justice of the court in August 1733 as a result of Lewis Morris' intransigence in the Van Dam salary case, and he was one of Governor Cosby's closest advisers. During Clarke's administration he used the chief justiceship as his power base and by 1737 he had begun to create a loyal following in the assembly. He maintained a strong hand in the council and thus, in 1743, lacked only executive power in his steady progress toward domination of New York government.

Governor Clinton's patronage provided DeLancey, a superb tactician, with the opportunity he sought, and in the first three years of the new administration he fortified his political position.[5]

---

4. *DAB*, V, 212–213; Edward F. DeLancey, "Memoir of James DeLancey," in E. B. O'Callaghan, ed., *Documentary History of the State of New York* (Albany, 1849–1851), IV, 1037–1059. For a more detailed account of Delancey's political career, see Katz, "An Easie Access," pp. 209–224.

5. DeLancey helped to promote his own selection by convincing Clinton that Clarke would mislead him as badly as he had Cosby. DeLancey also

On September 13, 1744, Clinton granted him the commission as chief justice during "good behavior," rather than, as in Cosby's appointment, at "pleasure." This was an unprecedented act in New York, quite contrary to the governor's instructions, and, to all intents and purposes, it gave DeLancey life tenure in the second most powerful post in the province.[6] Clinton thought so highly of DeLancey that he offered him the command of the regiment being formed in 1746 for an attack on Canada, despite his lack of experience for such a job: "For altho you have not been regularly bred up in the army yet your extensive abilitie and Fortune I am convinced will make your service highly agreeable to all Degree of men."[7] From 1743 to 1746 Clinton had absolute faith in the Chief Justice and brought his powers of patronage into play in behalf of De-Lancey's friends.

The council is a case in point. Soon after arriving in New York, Clinton recommended four men to fill the vacant places on the council: Peter Warren, Joseph Murray, John Moore, and Jeremiah Rensselaer.[8] Warren was the admiral and brother-in-law who would soon prove such a valuable connection for DeLancey in England. His appointment was approved by the privy council in 1744 and although he never did come to New York to qualify as a councillor, he occupied a place that Clinton soon wished he could control.[9] Joseph Murray, a lawyer and one of DeLancey's sturdiest sup-

frightened Clinton by telling the Governor that Clarke sought to succeed him in his government. Clinton to Newcastle, October 20, 1743, and December 13, 1744, *New York Col. Docs.*, VI, 248, 268.

6. *Cal. Coun. Min.*, p. 345. Bernhard Knollenberg (*Origin of the American Revolution: 1759–1766* [New York, 1960], p. 71) asserts that the governor was instructed to give commissions during good behavior. This is a misreading of the instruction preventing arbitrary and capricious removals of judges, which was not a directive to change the nature of the commission. British officials were always clear on this point. See the opinion of the attorney and solicitor general, 1753, *New York Col. Docs.*, VI, 792. Likewise, Lewis Morris' grant of the chief justiceship to Robert Hunter Morris in New Jersey in 1738 was a misuse of his power, rather than a legal precedent for future governors.

7. Clinton to DeLancey, August 24, 1746, draft, Clinton MSS., IV, C.L.

8. Clinton to Lords of Trade, November, 18, 1743, *New York Col. Docs.*, VI, 248.

9. Clinton to Warren, [London,] April 9, 1743, Clinton MSS., I, C.L.; C.O. 324:48, foll. 14b–15 [IV], PRO; *Acts, Privy Coun., Col.*, III, 834.

porters in the previous administration, was sworn into the council in June 1744. The New York City merchant John Moore, a friend of the Chief Justice, was appointed later in the same year, while Rensselaer was approved in 1745; Rensselaer soon died, but he was replaced, on Clinton's recommendation, by DeLancey's firm friend Stephen Bayard.[10] Thus by the end of 1745 Clinton had secured four of five vacant council seats for friends of James DeLancey, giving the Chief Justice, himself a councillor, control of the upper house by virtue of his influence over four of the remaining eight resident members: Horsmanden, Moore, Murray, and Bayard. Clinton also came to DeLancey's aid with his patronage in New York City, continuing the appointments of John Cruger and Stephen Bayard as mayors, and of Daniel Horsmanden as recorder to the common council.[11]

DeLancey further increased his power by encouraging Governor Clinton to compromise himself with the assembly. Clinton had accepted the governorship in order to improve his personal fortune, and before coming to New York he had negotiated with the imperial administration for a salary based upon royal revenues rather than the benevolence of the provincial legislature. In spite of the fact that Newcastle arranged an unprecedented additional salary of £1,200 sterling, to be paid out of the quit rent revenues,[12] Clinton was exercised over the payment of his regular salary by the assembly. He claimed that English friends had advised him not to insist upon a long-term grant of salary ("in the manner it had been formerly granted to former Governors") but to accept his salary "in such manner as was likely to please the People and make my self easy," following the advice of James DeLancey "as a person most likely to serve for this purpose." [13]

With DeLancey's help the Governor was granted a salary of

10. *Acts, Privy Coun., Col.,* III, 834, and IV, 792; *Cal. Coun. Min.,* p. 334.
11. *Cal. Coun. Min.,* pp. 346, 343; *Min. Comm. Coun.,* V, 99, 101, 129, 132, 155, 180.
12. Katz, "An Easie Access," pp. 281–283; Royal Warrants of April 27, 1742, and February 25, 1747, Clinton MSS., C.L.; William A. Shaw, comp., *Calendar of Treasury Books and Papers, 1742–1745* (London, 1903), V, 173.
13. Statement of Case, 1746/7, Clinton MSS., C.L.

Governor Clinton: New York, 1743–1753

£1,560 in November 1743, but in return Clinton accepted the assembly's demand to vote support annually and to appropriate funds to individuals rather than to offices. In short, he gave up Clarke's half-hearted fight for the long-term support of royal government which the governor's instructions required and capitulated to the assembly without a struggle. By suggesting this concession, DeLancey pleased the Governor, who got his salary, and the assembly, which retained the financial control of the province. The Chief Justice had now achieved a fusion of executive and legislative influence, since "all the officers of the Government became entirely dependent on the Chief Justice & his Faction in the Assembly both for the nomination to their offices & for their Sallaries or rewards for their services & in effect the Governor had inadvertantly put the whole executive powers into their hands." [14]

DeLancey was so emboldened by his success and confident of Clinton's support that eventually he went too far. In 1746 Clinton had introduced into the assembly a bill aimed at preventing deserters from the New York regiments and the bill had been passed over the objections of the New York City members, who were more concerned with manning their privateers than with maintaining the regiments. [15] DeLancey, however, who supported the New York merchants, secured the defeat of the legislation in council, and in doing so severely antagonized the Governor. Afterward, Clinton claimed that his power to carry a measure in the assembly without the DeLancey interest had angered the Chief Justice, and when he gave a party at the executive mansion where the drinks ran freely, a quarrel developed between the two. Clinton defended the "country members" who had supported his bill, and called the city members "scrubs." "This heightened the dispute and occasioned some harsh

14. Colden to Dr. John Mitchell, July 6, 1749, draft, NYHS, *Colls.*, 1935, pp. 20–21. Colden characterisically exaggerates the situation, but his comment is generally to the point.

15. *Assemb. Jour.*, II, 98 (February 13, 1746). Robert Livingston had led the opposition to the bill in the assembly, where it passed 12-9. Of those voting "nay," there were four members from New York City, two from Dutchess (DeLancey's uncle, Henry Beekman, was one), and one each from Livingston Manor (Robert Livingston), Ulster, and King's counties. This was a strongly mercantile, south-eastern coalition.

words on which, Mr. C. Justice left the room." Clinton sent after him to ask that the quarrel be forgotten, but found to his horror that DeLancey had spread a rumor over New York that not only revealed the quarrel but exaggerated it.[16]

This dispute provided the pretext that ended the association of the Governor and the Chief Justice, and brought DeLancey's opposition to Clinton and his schemes into the open. It does not seem possible that as shrewd a politician as DeLancey could have been forced into opposition accidentally, especially since Clinton had gone out of his way to patch things up. DeLancey had already organized an efficient opposition party, as we shall see, and must previously have decided that he would have more freedom to operate independently. His was, as Colden realized, a "pretended disgust."

Clinton was confused and embittered by this experience. He later admitted to the ministry that he had erred grievously in allowing such an opposition to form and in accepting a revenue on the assembly's terms, excusing himself by his excessive confidence in the public character of the Chief Justice, and his desire "of keeping the people easy under my administration." [17] He began to suffer severe attacks of those physical maladies (reminiscent of the elder Pitt's) that afflicted him throughout his years of government in New York. Moreover, he experienced "not only the pains of the Body but those of the mind, having the misfortune to govern a set of Bruits for men they can't be called who tho I have made it my study to do everything for the good of the province yet there are a set of 'em that are daily seeking something to perplex me but as I said nothing better can be expected from such wretches." [18] His anxiety grew out of his belated realization of how DeLancey had betrayed

16. Colden, post May 26, 1747, draft; Statement of Case, 1746/7, Clinton MSS., C.L. Similar, though less particular, interpretations of the disagreement were given by Smith (*History*, II, 83) and William Livingston ("A Review of the Military Operations in North America . . . ," Massachusetts Historical Society, *Collections*, 1st ser., VII–VIII [1801–1856], 80).

17. Statement of Case, 1746/7, Clinton MSS., C.L.

18. Clinton to Gov. Knowles, April 22, 1747, Clinton MSS., V, C.L. Clinton was afflicted with crippling headaches, poor eyesight, and the gout.

him, and he claimed that the Chief Justice, "while I confided in his advice deceitfully led me into measures with a view afterwards thereby to distress my administration in order to lure me out and to obtain this Government for himself and for this purpose headed a seditious faction composed of men of republican and levelling principles." [19] Clinton's denunciations of DeLancey after their break in 1746 were not far from the mark. The Chief Justice had in fact used his relationship to Clinton to consolidate his own power in the province, and it appears that DeLancey deliberately abandoned the Governor in the hope that he would not be able to manage the administration by himself. Unquestionably, DeLancey intended to succeed Clinton in the government of New York. He was intriguing through Sir Peter Warren to obtain a commission as lieutenant governor, so that Clinton's departure would leave him in command of the province, and for the remainder of Clinton's administration DeLancey exercised his considerable political skill in trying to discourage him from remaining in his post. Henceforth, the "Faction," as he called it, made Clinton's life miserable.

There was more than ambition behind DeLancey's defection from the administration, however, for a genuine division on policy had arisen between him and the Governor. Their disagreement concerned French Canada and the conduct of the fur trade during King George's War, the American extension of the War of the Austrian Succession which had broken out in 1744 and was to continue until 1748. Clinton, because of his martial upbringing and English sympathies, was strenuously in favor of meeting the French head-on, and he actively supported the Warren-Pepperell expedition to Cape Breton which resulted in the capture of Louisbourg. Moreover, in 1746, he found himself in command of the intercolonial forces that were assembling in northern New York for a projected expedition against Canada, on orders from the Duke of Newcastle. Clinton was encouraged in his prosecution of the war by those New Yorkers committed to the old Burnet-Colden scheme of halting the Albany-Montreal fur trade, reinforcing the frontier, and developing Indian

19. Clinton to Newcastle, October 11, 1748, draft, NYHS, *Colls.*, 1935, pp. 20–21.

alliances and trading networks in the north independent of those already established by the French.[20]

DeLancey led the opponents of the war.[21] His commercial interest was in the Indian trade and he had no enthusiasm for any war that aimed to strike down the French in Montreal and set the northern Indians on the march. He preferred to see Montrealers trading and Indians hunting so that New Yorkers could continue to market the furs procured by the Canadians, and it was probably for this reason that he refused Clinton's offer of the command of a regiment in August 1746.[22] This desire for what contemporaries called a "neutrality" between Albany and Montreal was fairly widespread in New York, especially among Albany fur dealers and New York merchants active in the Indian trade.[23] Most merchants, in fact, whether or not they were directly involved in the Indian trade, seem to have favored the neutrality. They considered land wars unremunerative, agreeing with their Whig brothers in England that profits were easier to come by at sea. American war profits came mainly from privateering and trade with outlying areas such as northern North America and the West Indies, which were badly in need of supplies, and New York merchants tended to ignore national loyalties that conflicted with rewarding ventures.[24] Thus

20. Osgood, *Eighteenth Century*, II, 418–422.

21. Clinton and Governor Shirley of Massachusetts discussed DeLancey's open opposition to the war and Clinton warned Bedford against the Chief Justice. [Clinton] to Bedford [September 24, 1749, delivered], "State of Disloyal Affairs in New York," Clinton MSS., C.L.

22. DeLancey tactfully refused the command on the grounds of inexperience and ill-health, since he was asthmatic. DeLancey to Clinton, August 30, 1746, Clinton MSS., IV, C.L.

23. There is a large bibliography on the subject of the neutrality between Albany and Montreal. See, for instance, Charles H. McIlwain, ed., *Peter Wraxall's Abridgment of the Indian Affairs* (Cambridge, Mass., 1915), pp. lxxxiv–lxxxv; Flick, ed., *History of the State of New York*, II, 215–219, 225–227; Jean Lunn, "The Illegal Fur Trade Out of New France, 1713–1760," Canadian Historical Association, *Report*, 1939, p. 76; Osgood, *Eighteenth Century*, III, 363–377, 391–395. For the history of the fur trade in New York politics and DeLancey's involvement see, Katz, "An Easic Access," pp. 218–223.

24. See Richard Pares, *War and Trade in the West Indies, 1739–1763* (London, 1936); Dorothy Burne Goebel, "The 'New England Trade' and the French West Indies, 1763–1774: A Study in Trade Policies," *William and*

DeLancey's obstruction of the war effort evoked a favorable popular response. It appealed not only to the merchants, but also to the farmers, who did not want to lose labor during harvest times, and to the inhabitants in general, who did not want to be taxed for a war that did not seem to further their interests.

After 1746, therefore, James DeLancey headed a well-organized group that attempted to drive Governor Clinton from New York. Growing as it did out of the conflict over war policy as well as from DeLancey's intense political ambition, the opposition was based mainly on the support of the New York merchants with whom his family and business connected him. Clinton, on the other hand, regarded the merchants as his particular enemies: he complained that his opponents consisted "chiefly in merchants, and would subside, if it were not supported by them." He accused the merchants of manipulating the assembly against the administration and of an "utter disregard of the Laws of Trade." [25] Unhappily for Clinton, mercantile opposition placed the governor at a special disadvantage, for the New York merchants' English correspondents could be brought into action at home to oppose anything that threatened to disrupt trade,[26] as Burnet had found to his dismay. Most of the large landholders of New York were also allies of the DeLanceyites, whom Clinton characterized as "Men of very considerable estates & family interest." [27] They were well represented in the assembly, especially through the manor representatives. Nevertheless, the landed gentry were politically independent, just as they were in England, and DeLancey could never count on them as part of his coalition.

The council was DeLancey's chief base of operations, as Clinton learned in the fall of 1746. When the Governor requested the

---

Mary Quarterly, 3rd ser., XX (1963), 331–372. For the commercial potentiality of land war, see Theodore Thayer, "The Army Contractors for the Niagara Campaign, 1755-1756," *ibid.*, XIV (1957), pp. 31–46.

25. Clinton to Lords of Trade, October 4, 1752, *New York Col. Docs.*, VI, 765.

26. Clinton to H. Clinton, October 22, 1752, Clinton MSS., C.L.

27. Clinton to Lords of Trade, June 22, 1747, *New York Col. Docs.*, VI, 356.

council to draw up his messages to the assembly in preparation for the proposed military expedition to Canada, he discovered that DeLancey, Murray, and Horsmanden "woud be silent, 'till one after another, instead of taking the plain and obvious meaning of what I said would carp at particular Expressions and perplex me and the rest of the council." [28] Clinton contended that the opposition in the council was highly organized, with Horsmanden acting as publicist ("the Secretary and writer"), Murray as the legal expert ("the Councillor and Sollicitor"), and Stephen Bayard the popular spokesman ("the common Cryer").[29] Their procedural technique was to secure referral of all important matters to a committee chaired by Daniel Horsmanden and meeting without the Governor, "by which means they got what entries they pleased made in the Council books and in words that suited all their purposes." [30]

DeLancey also came to exercise a commanding influence over the New York assembly. William Smith counted five relatives and seven "close acquaintances" of DeLancey's in the 1752 assembly. There were only twenty-seven members of the lower house at that time, and Robert Livingston was the only man of any consequence who opposed DeLancey among the remaining fifteen. According to Smith, most of the others were directly influenced by the DeLanceyites.[31] DeLancey's electoral base was in New York City, but he was also strong in Dutchess County, which was controlled by his uncle Henry Beekman, and among the mercantile community of Albany. DeLancey's growing power enabled him to sway representatives by promises of jobs and services but, most important, he sealed his control of the assembly by securing the speakership for his cohort, David Jones.[32]

The Chief Justice had a characteristically clever scheme for

28. Statement of Case, 1746/7, Clinton MSS., C.L.
29. Clinton to John Sharpe, November 30, 1747, draft, Clinton MSS., VII, C.L.
30. Colden, post May 26, 1747, draft, Clinton MSS., C.L.
31. Smith, *History*, II, 142–143.
32. *Assemb. Jour.*, II, 95–97; Charles W. Spencer, "Sectional Aspects of New York Provincial Politics," *Political Science Quarterly*, XXX (1915), 419; Colden, post May 26, 1747, draft, Clinton MSS., C.L.

integrating his power in the two houses of the legislature. Colden contended that DeLancey contrived to have a joint committee of the council and assembly appointed, "which met as often as they pleased at a Tavern where every message resolve and Bill was ready formed and brought into either house as was thought most proper with such boldness and power that all who were not in the Secret had no time allowed to consider or make opposition and this was don without this Committee's making any report of their proceedings in form to either Council or assembly but by some one or other member making some motion in the terms that had been agreed in the Committee." [33] According to Clinton, the opposition was thus able to bring "ready engrossed" bills into the assembly and, having alerted the members, rush them through without debate, "whereby many of the well disposed Country Members have been surprized into Votes without a right understanding of the Matter before them." Thus the Chief Justice controlled a "Government within a Government." [34] DeLancey's success shows clearly in the legislative history of the Clinton administration and the Governor ruefully ascribed it to "the dread most people have of the chief justice and the force of money in which he and his family abound." [35] Clinton's adherents accused DeLancey of demogogic tactics which forced the independent citizenry of New York to become "dupes to a dictator of their own creation" and stigmatized his program as consisting of "patriot" measures.[36] In the end, Clinton himself argued, the DeLanceyite opposition proceeded from "a design to overturn his Majesty's Government by wresting the Power out of the Hands of His Officers, and placing it in a popular faction." [37]

Even allowing for Clinton's tendency to self-justification, it seems clear that DeLancey's mastery over the assembly was a serious

33. Colden, post May 26, 1747, draft, Clinton MSS., C.L.
34. Clinton to Newcastle, September 30, 1748, Add. MSS. 32716, fol. 401, B.M.
35. Clinton to Newcastle, [ante December 15, 1747], Bancroft Transcripts, Colden, I, 46–47, NYPL.
36. William Livingston, "Review of Military Operations," pp. 84–85.
37. Clinton to [Newcastle?], September 27, 1745, abstract, Add. MSS. 33029, foll. 42–45, B.M.

impediment to the conduct of government in New York. A supporter of Clinton pointed out that the assembly was "the main source" of DeLancey's power and charged, with some reason, that the Chief Justice could not afford to "serve the Crown at the risk of a dissension with the house."[38] A more dispassionate servant of the crown explained how the dangerous situation had come into being. Governors, he reasoned, were forced to rely upon American politicians who could influence the assembly: "Hence Prime Ministers and Courtiers are established; and, of course, Anti-Courtiers: Hence Parties are formed . . . Is the publick Good really the Point in View? or is it to shew how dextrously the one Side can manage the Assembly for [the Governor], and the other against Him?"[39] Clinton's initial choice of DeLancey as his adviser led directly to the personal aggrandisement of the Chief Justice and indirectly to the establishment of a faction bent on pursuing a course running contrary to royal wishes. DeLancey's adroitness, position, and wealth may have rendered the outcome unavoidable. In any case, by 1746 Governor Clinton's work was cut out for him if he was to regain control of the province.

II

DeLancey's defection left Clinton without the *sine qua non* of colonial government, a trusted local adviser. The Governor realized his impotence: "I then am left intirely alone. What am I to do, I cant pretend to Govern alone and can Expect nothing from the Faction unless I give my Self up intirely to them." Clinton was determined to take up arms against the DeLancey faction rather than to submit to its demands and, if he failed, to retreat to England in disgrace.[40] His solution was to turn to the tutelage of Cadwallader Colden.

38. William Livingston, "Review of Military Operations," p. 85.
39. Archibald Kennedy, *Essay*, p. 34. Kennedy's remedy for the situation was to pay the governor's salary out of royal revenues, as in Virginia.
40. Clinton to Guerin, July 23, 1747, draft, Clinton MSS., C.L. One of the demands made by the DeLanceyites was for Clinton to make Daniel Horsmanden his private secretary.

A Scotsman, Colden[41] had studied medicine at Edinburgh before emigrating to America in the second decade of the eighteenth century. He was enticed from Pennsylvania to New York by the patronage of Governor Robert Hunter, who secured him the surveyor generalship of New York in 1720. Burnet appointed him a royal councillor, a post he held until 1776. Colden was one of Governor Burnet's chief advisers and the architect of his scheme for regulatng the northern Indian trade and closing the Canadian border to neutralist fur traders. He played an active role in the Morrisite faction, as we have seen, but he circumspectly avoided paying a price for his partisanship. Carefully gauging the temper of the times, Colden stood aloof from New York politics during the Clarke administration, living on his country estate and devoting himself to his scientific pursuits. The son of a minister, he was a tough Scots-Presbyterian moralist and, in politics, a confirmed and philosophical Tory-Royalist. Unhappily for George Clinton, however, an inflexible supporter of an extreme view of royal government was not a promising ally in a struggle with a demagogue.

As New York's senior councillor in 1746, Colden stood aside from the political in-fighting of the early Clinton administration. Although he was the father-in-law of Peter DeLancey, the Chief Justice's brother, Colden could not be placed in any existing New York faction at the time that Clinton sought his help. He later claimed that the DeLanceyites had solicited his aid in June 1746, holding out the lure of a place on the influential joint committee of the council and the assembly. Colden refused to come in with DeLancey, subsequently pleading constitutional objections to such an opposition, but he was at first also reluctant to throw his lot in with the Governor.[42] He feared, correctly, that if he joined Clinton's administration the DeLancey faction would attack him ruthlessly, hoping to destroy the Chief Justice's principal local adversary and the Governor's sole hope of aid.[43]

41. *DAB*, IV, 286–287; NYHS, *Colls.*, 1917, vii–viii. See the excellent biography by Alice M. Keys, *Cadwallader Colden* (New York, 1906).
42. Colden, post May 26, 1747, draft, Clinton MSS., C.L.
43. Colden to Clarke, November 26, 1746, NYHS, *Colls.*, 1919, p. 290; Colden's memorandum, [ca. December 8, 1746], *ibid.*, p. 307. See also, Clinton to Newcastle, September 30, 1748, Add. MSS. 32716, fol. 401, B.M.

In the face of what must have seemed a virtually suicidal opposition to the ambition of James DeLancey, why did Colden terminate his comfortable semiretirement? Above all, he was a sincere defender of the prerogatives of the crown in America, and DeLancey appeared a very real threat to royal government in New York. Also, as the author of Burnet's Indian trade policies, Colden was a firm advocate of war against the French and despised the policy of neutrality. As a speculator in land, and an official who profited by every acquisition of Indian territory, he had a stake in extending and pacifying the frontier.

Finally, DeLancey had already proved that a close association with Clinton was most profitable to a man concerned with patronage, and Colden had a very large family to provide for. Clinton's chief blandishment was the offer to recommend Colden in England for a commission as lieutenant governor of New York. As we shall see in the next chapter, Clinton did his best to obtain the commission, but failed. He also put Colden in charge of much of the distribution of local patronage in Ulster and the other Long Island counties.[44] Above all, the Governor provided for Colden's sons. Alexander Colden was appointed register of the New York admiralty court and was given the reversion to his father's post as surveyor general (which Clinton had conferred on the senior Cadwallader Colden for life). John Colden was appointed to the profitable clerkship of the peace and common pleas for Albany city and county. Other sons were given lucrative military and supply posts which Clinton controlled in his capacity as captain general of New York.[45]

44. Colden to Clinton, December 8, 1748, Clinton MSS., VIII; Colden to Catherwood, January 3, 1748, Clinton MSS., C.L.

45. Clinton to Thomas Corbett, May 23, 1747, Adm. 1:3818, PRO; Clinton to Lords of Admiralty, September 11, 1747, Clinton MSS., VI, C.L.; Clinton to Colden, April 1, 1748, Colden to Clinton, April 9, 1748, Alexander to Colden, April 17, 1748, NYHS, *Colls.*, 1920, pp. 33–34, 45, 47; Werner, *Civil List*, p. 167. Colden to [John Rutherford?], n.d. [1746?], NYHS, *Colls.*, 1919, p. 312. Colden to Clinton, April 9, 1748, Clinton to Colden, April 25, 1748, J. Colden to Collinson, November 19, 1748, *ibid.*, 1920, pp. 46, 61, 81. Colden to Clinton, February 9, 1749, Bancroft Transcripts, Colden, I, 96; Colden to Clinton, February 9, 1749, Affidavit of John Colden, March 27, 1749, NYHS, *Colls.*, 1920, pp. 94–95, 108–109.

His family thus provided for, Colden consented to become Clinton's *eminence grise,* advising the Governor and writing his speeches.

In 1746, when the Clinton-Colden alliance was formed, the Governor had few supporters. Only two councillors besides Colden had escaped the DeLancey net: Captain John Rutherford and the provincial receiver general, Archibald Kennedy. Rutherford was a recent arrival in New York, a military man who had a vested interest in the vigorous prosecution of the war. His relations with the Governor were very cool at first, but they soon became fast friends.[46] Kennedy had long been a "governor's man" in New York, supporting the existing administration while quietly accumulating the profits of his office. Clinton obliged him by promoting his son in the militia in 1749, and the reasons he gave Henry Clinton for so doing are revealing: "You must push with all your might for Young Kennedy to succeed to the first vacancy You being Sensible what Interest his Father has, that he must not be disobliged nor is it possible for me to carry any points here if I have not the liberty from home of obliging my friends."[47]

Clinton's closest New York merchant ally was Edward Holland, whose appointment to the council he procured in 1750. He also appointed him mayor of New York, a position he held until 1756, and recommended him as contractor for victualling royal navy ships in New York.[48] Clinton was also very close to Dr. John Ayscough, whom he appointed sheriff of New York in 1746, and who was soon to become his private secretary.[49]

Besides Colden, however, Clinton's only really useful ally was Peter Warren's nephew, William Johnson. The young Irishman was managing the Cosby lands on the Mohawk for his uncle, and had built up a thriving fur traffic centered on the trading fort at Oswego. His friendship with the Indians was unrivaled by any other

46. Colden, post May 26, 1747, draft, Clinton MSS., C.L.; Clinton to Newcastle, February 13, 1748, *New York Col. Docs.,* VI, 416.
47. Clinton to H. Clinton, September 20, 1749, Clinton MSS., C.L.
48. *Cal. Coun. Min.,* p. 352; Clinton to Bedford, May 23, 1751, C.O. 5:1096, fol. 340, PRO; Clinton to the Commissioners for Victualling His Majesty's Navy, November 21, 1748, Clinton MSS., VIII, C.L.
49. *Cal. Coun. Min.,* p. 352.

New Yorker, and his home was a trading post and social center for the braves of the Six Nations. Since he lived farther west and was unconnected by interest or temperament to them, Johnson was quite independent of the Dutch traders of Albany, and he was especially antagonistic to the commissioners for Indian affairs. His trade was based on direct contact with the Indians, as Burnet had hoped would be the case, and he had no use for the Montreal alliance.[50]

Immediately after his quarrel with DeLancey in 1746, Governor Clinton made a journey to Albany to confer with the Indians and secure their participation in the intended expedition against Canada. Colden accompanied him, though the rest of the council refused to go. They were confident that the neutralism of the Indian commissioners and the Albany traders would prevent an agreement, and reasoned that Clinton and Colden would be ruined by their failure to procure an Indian army. Surprisingly, however, Johnson's success in attracting large numbers of Indians to the conference and Colden's persuasiveness enabled Clinton to convince the Six Nations to march against the French. Henceforth, Johnson managed Indian affairs for Clinton, permitting the Governor to escape the crippling neutralism of the DeLanceyite commissioners for Indian affairs. Eventually, Clinton's retort to the faction was to abolish the commissioners altogether and to appoint Johnson sole commissary for Indian affairs. The Governor even managed to ward off Sir Peter Warren's attempts to bring his nephew over to DeLancey's side, and retained Johnson's allegiance throughout his administration, despite the assembly's 1752 success in reinstating the Albany-oriented commissioners.[51]

A curious footnote to the story of Governor Clinton's following

50. For the two best, however inadequate, biographies, see James T. Flexner, *Mohawk Baronet: Sir William Johnson of New York* (New York, 1959) and Arthur Pound and Richard E. Day, *Johnson of the Mohawks* (new ed., New York, 1930).
51. Werner, *Civil List*, pp. 170–171, 85; Clinton to Johnson, September 7, 1747, in Sullivan, *Johnson Papers*, I, 115; Colden to Shirley, July 25, 1749, NYHS, *Colls.*, 1920, pp. 126–127; Johnson to Warren, July 24, 1749, in Sullivan, *Johnson Papers*, I, 239–240.

concerns his treatment of Philip Livingston, the secretary for Indian affairs. Clinton waged a bitter campaign against Livingston in order to bolster Johnson's position and to end the French fur trade. In December 1746 he asked Newcastle to remove Livingston from his secretaryship and requested Henry Pelham to have the treasury stop Livingston's salary on the ground that he was weakening the allegiance of the Six Nations to England.[52]

Actually, however, Livingston was involved in the retail aspects of the Indian trade, was a proponent of the Burnet Indian scheme, and was opposed to the DeLancey neutrality policy.[53] It is unclear why Clinton should have misread him so completely and charged him with complicity in the neutrality. Perhaps the Governor simply could not understand why an Albany man should oppose the French trade. Livingston had supported the war in order to protect his property, and his son Robert, representing Livingston Manor, had remained an independent in the assembly. In the 1752 assembly, for instance, Smith noticed that, "Of the whole House, the only wealthy member, neither connected with Mr. DeLancey nor in the sphere of his influence, was Mr. Livingston." [54] Nevertheless, Clinton's persecution of the family forced Philip Livingston to acquiesce in the assembly tactics of the Chief Justice.

On Livingston's death in 1749, Clinton and his English agent defeated the attempts of his relatives to keep the secretaryship in the family.[55] Clinton thus kept control of Indian affairs, but at the expense of alienating one of the most powerful families in the province—the very family that was soon to prove such an effective countervailing force to the Chief Justice and his faction, and which could have brought a great deal of landed and merchant support to

52. Clinton to Newcastle, December 9, 1746, *New York Col. Docs.*, VI, 314.

53. McIlwain, *Wraxall's Abridgment*, p. lxviiin1; Milton M. Klein, "The *American Whig:* William Livingston of New York" (unpub. Ph.D. diss., Columbia U., 1954), pp. 244-246.

54. Smith, *History*, II, 143.

55. Ayscough to Guerin, January 30, 1749, extract, and Alexander to Catherwood, February 15, 1749, Clinton MSS., IX, C.L.; Clinton's petition to Bedford [presented April 20, 1749], Clinton to Bedford, May 23, 1751, C.O. 5:1096, foll. 104, 340, PRO.

the administration.[56] A more astute politician than Clinton (or Colden, who may well have kindled Clinton's antipathy) would have come to terms with Livingston.

Clinton had, however, succeeded in allying himself with Colden and Johnson, and in regaining control of northern policy. He promoted Colden to DeLancey's old seat at the right of the throne, but soon found that the Surveyor General had neither the political ability, connections, nor wealth necessary to head off the Chief Justice in his march to control of New York politics.

III

A brief consideration of the political history of the Clinton administration will suffice to illustrate its outstanding characteristics—the strength of the organized opposition of James DeLancey, the inability of George Clinton to provide political leadership, and the Governor's permanent loss of political initiative to the assembly. After the break between Clinton and DeLancey in 1746, the administration fell into three distinct periods: the war (1746–1748), the struggle over the support of the government (1748–1750), and the years of compromise in anticipation of a new government (1750–1753). As a whole, these seven years witnessed an attempt on the part of the royal government to reassert its full prerogative in New York, an attempt that was thwarted by a sturdy independence on the part of the assembly and James DeLancey, abetted by the helplessness of Governor Clinton.

The war years were particularly difficult for Clinton, since he had to cope with the newly-arisen opposition at the same time that he prosecuted the hostilities against the French.[57] DeLancey and the neutralists, unwilling to lend themselves to a vigorous conduct of the war, made Clinton pay a high price for the assembly's cooperation. Their first move came in the summer of 1746 when Clinton

56. Klein, "The *American Whig*," pp. 267–271; Alexander to Colden, December 5, 1751, NYHS, *Colls.*, 1920, pp. 303–304.

57. Osgood, *Eighteenth Century*, IV, 174–200; Keys, *Colden*, pp. 132–259; Smith, *History*, II, 68–160; Mrs. Martha J. Lamb, *History of the City of New York* (New York, 1877), I, 608–630.

and Colden went to Albany to enlist Indian support for the projected attack against Canada. While the Governor and his adviser treated with the Indians, DeLancey and the renegade councillors seized the opportunity to govern the province from New York. Much to Clinton's dismay, they issued formal orders to military officers and corresponded with neighboring colonies on their own authority, without informing him.[58]

With Clinton's return to New York, the battle began in earnest. One tactic of the DeLanceyites was to discredit Colden in all quarters, and they brought representations in the council and resolutions in the assembly designed to provoke him, realizing that Clinton without an adviser was a rudderless ship. "They had the more reason to expect success in this attempt, as they knew the governor had not by his former course of life been accustomed to the intrigues and artifices commonly used in popular Government, but to the punctuality of military discipline."[59] At the same time, they deliberately forced Clinton to dissolve an obstreperous assembly, and then worked for the defeat of Speaker Adolph Philipse, the leader of the country members who had passed the apportionment and deserter bills that precipitated the quarrel between DeLancey and the Governor. Philipse did indeed lose his seat for New York City, and with it the speakership. The new assembly, meanwhile, continued to provide somewhat sparingly for the prosecution of the war. It also voted an annual support of the government which Clinton felt obliged to accept on the grounds that the defeat of the French was his primary task.[60]

Clinton's counterattack was the removal of the DeLanceyites Daniel Horsmanden and Stephen Bayard from their provincial offices. In December 1746 Clinton asked Newcastle to suspend Horsmanden from the council on the grounds that he was collabo-

58. Colden, post May 26, 1747, draft; Clinton to Newcastle, July 24, 1746, draft, Clinton MSS., C.L.

59. Colden, post May 26, 1747, draft, Clinton MSS., C.L.

60. *Ibid.* For the crucial Westchester election of 1750, see Alexander to R. H. Morris, August 2, 1750, Rutherfurd Collection, Small Scrapbook, no. 148, NYHS; Clinton to R. H. Morris, August 29, 1750, R. H. Morris Papers, I, 6, NJHS.

rating with the opposition faction in their attempts to obstruct the projected expedition against Canada.[61] Not having heard from Newcastle or the board of trade on the subject, Clinton suspended Horsmanden on his own authority in September 1747. He also removed Horsmanden from his seat on the supreme court and the recordership of New York City.[62] At the same time, he suspended Stephen Bayard from the council and nominated his friend Edward Holland to replace Bayard as the mayor of New York City.

From 1746 to 1748 Clinton secured New York's participation in the war against France only at the cost of such severe financial concessions to the assembly as accepting annual support bills and specific designation of appropriations rather than long-term, undesignated support of the government. He was advised by Colden, who withstood the personal attacks of the DeLancey faction and in fact carried out most of the Governor's executive duties for him. By 1748 Clinton had begun the task of reconstructing the council with his own supporters. In the next two years, he broadened his attack to include the assembly in a vain attempt to win back for the crown the powers he had so far conceded.

Before Clinton swung into his counteroffensive, however, the assembly asserted its independence of the Governor by naming an agent in England. New York had been without an agent for some time, and early in 1748 the appointment was attached to the revenue bill that included the Governor's salary. Thus as Clinton recognized, "I was obliged either to yield to their method of appointing an Agent, or go without my own appointment." [63] The agent was to

61. Clinton to Newcastle, December 9, 1746, *New York Col. Docs.*, VI, 312.

62. For the details of Horsmanden's unsuccessful attempts to secure reinstatement in England, see Clinton to Guerin, July 23, 1747, draft, Clinton MSS., C.L.; *Cal. Coun. Min.*, pp. 366–367; Clinton to Lords of Trade, September 27, 1747, *New York Col. Docs.*, VI, 378–379; *Acts, Privy Coun., Col.*, VI, 269–272; Clinton to Lords of Trade, September 29, 1747, *New York Col. Docs.*, VI, 404; Horsmanden to Lords of Trade, September 29, 1747, *ibid.*, VI, 405; *Board of Trade Journal, 1742–1749*, pp. 263–264, 266, 276–277; *Acts, Privy Coun., Col.*, IV, 58, 792; Lords of Trade to the king, July 5, 1753, *New York Col. Docs.*, VI, 789.

63. Clinton to Newcastle, April 22, 1748, *New York Col. Docs.*, VI, 420.

act upon the advice of a committee of the assembly, independent of the governor and council. To add insult to injury, the agent named in the bill was Robert Charles, the private secretary of Sir Peter Warren, DeLancey's in-law and ally. Clinton wrote to the board of trade asking that they not accept Charles as the legal agent of New York, but was refused on the ground that the repeal of the whole revenue act, which was the only way to void the agent's appointment, "would be attended with bad consequences." [64]

Once the war had ended with the peace of Aix-la-Chapelle, Clinton was no longer obliged to accept the assembly's financial help at any cost to the prerogative of the crown. The assembly had been fond of annexing its obstructionist measures, such as Charles's appointment and the specific appropriation of salaries, to bills providing for the defense of the colony, but with the peace this lever was not so powerful.[65] Clinton decided to assert his authority, and in September 1748 he wrote Newcastle:

> I am now determined to embrace the first opportunity of letting the assembly know that I expect they should put an end to all their late innovations, and incroachments upon His Majesty's government, which have been introduc'd at the beginning of my administration: and which I acquiesced to during the war, purely to avoid obstructing his Majesty's government in some material articles then depending before them and shall insist in general upon resetting His Majesty's government in this Province upon the same foot it was upon, in the time of my predecessors.[66]

Accordingly, in October 1748 he vetoed the assembly's salary bill and, for the next two years, forfeited his own salary in hope of breaking the opposition of the faction in the assembly.[67]

64. Lords of Trade to Clinton, June 29, 1748, *ibid.*, VI, 427. For Charles, see, Nicholas Varga, "Robert Charles: New York Agent, 1748–1770," *William and Mary Quarterly*, 3rd ser., XVIII (1961), pp. 211–235. For Charles's first solicitation of the office, see Charles to P. Livingston, August 31, 1742, Rutherfurd Collection, II, 207, NYHS.

65. Clinton to Lords of Trade, October 20, 1748, *New York Col. Docs.*, VI, 456–457.

66. Clinton to Newcastle, September 30, 1748, Add. MSS. 32716, fol. 399, B.M.

67. Clinton to Lords of Trade, November 15, 1748, *New York Col. Docs.*, VI, 468.

Clinton was encouraged by Governor William Shirley of Massachusetts, whose advice to him was to "persevere" in order "to carry the essential Points of his Majesty's Service and the Reestablishment of his Government in the Colony." Shirley assured Clinton that he had "plainly the better of the Assembly in every part of the Dispute; and that every point must turn out right, and according to your Desire." [68] Meanwhile, Clinton pleaded with the ministry for support against the assembly's rebellious use of public money which was thus placed "at the private disposition of an Assembly" which could "make use of it for their Secret Services." [69]

The assembly refused to mend its ways, however, and Clinton wavered in his determination to discipline it. Both John Catherwood and Robert Hunter Morris, his agents in England at the time, advised him not to insist upon a five-year support but to accept the arrears due him and a one-year support. Catherwood, for instance, assured the Governor that in following Shirley's advice to insist upon the traditional support he was "labouring a point for another to your own prejudice." [70] By the end of 1749 Clinton had made no headway with the assembly and saw no indication of support from across the Atlantic: "He, therefore, dissolved the House, determining, if he was not supported by the ministry, to give way to the anti-Cosbyan doctrine of annual supplies, and the rather, because it was impossible for him to form a party in his favor, til the clamors of the public creditors were appeased." [71] Clinton received no word from the secretary of state or the board of trade during this period, and in December 1750, discouraged, he signed a support bill which ran for only one year.[72] He wrote to Secretary Bedford excusing himself for this compliance with the demands of the as-

68. Shirley to Clinton, November 7, 1748, Clinton MSS.; Shirley to Clinton, July 24, 1749, Clinton MSS., IX, C.L.
69. Clinton to Lords of Trade, August 7, 1749, *New York Col. Docs.*, VI, 524.
70. Catherwood to Clinton, May 2, 1750, Clinton MSS.; R. H. Morris to H. Clinton, January 13, 1750, Clinton MSS., X, C.L.
71. Smith, *History*, II, 131.
72. Clinton to Lords of Trade, December 2, 1750, *New York Col. Docs.*, VI, 598.

sembly on the grounds that there was a precedent for it in Clarke's administration and that the ministry had failed to support his stand: "the King must enforce the Authority of his own Commision, or else resolve to give up the Government of this province in to the hands of the Assembly." [73]

Clinton's surrender to the assembly ushered in the last three years of his administration, years of compromise and maneuvering for position in anticipation of a new administration. Each year, Clinton assented to annual support bills and, in return, the assembly was reasonably compliant with his wishes. This was due partly to a feeling of safety on their part, and partly to a fear of antagonizing the ministry, which was engaged in examining the state of affairs in New York with an eye to reasserting royal authority in the province.

Alarmed by the reports from Clinton and his agents in England, and by the New York–New Jersey boundary dispute, in October 1750 the privy council ordered the board of trade to prepare a "state" of New York since the beginning of Clinton's administration. This report occupied the board until April 2, 1751, and the result was, in Clinton's words, "confounded long." [74] It was little more than a tedious compilation of all the papers in the Plantation Office relating to New York between 1743 and 1751, to which a short conclusion was appended.

The board found that Clinton's administration had witnessed

73. Clinton to Bedford, December 13, 1750, *ibid.,* VI, 602–603.
74. *Board of Trade Journal,* 1750–1753, pp. 109, 140, 181; Clinton's observation, Catherwood to Clinton, March 1751, Clinton MSS., C.L. The board had ordered the preparation of such a report as early as February 7, 1749 (*Board of Trade Journal,* 1742–1749, p. 378) and the privy council had ordered a report on New York and New Jersey, then in the midst of a quarrel over their mutual boundary, on February 2, 1750 (*New York Col. Docs.,* VI, 544; *Board of Trade Journal,* 1750–1753, p. 42). The report is printed in *New York Col. Docs.,* VI, 614–703 (incorrectly called "Report of the Privy Council upon the State of New York") and is summarized in *Acts, Privy Coun. Col.,* VI, 295–310. Dickerson considers that the compiling of the report was the work of John Pownall. O. M. Dickerson, *American Colonial Government 1696–1765. A Study of the British Board of Trade in Its Relation to the American Colonies . . .* (Cleveland, 1912), p. 74.

the reduction of "the legal prerogative of the Crown," the violent wresting of the "most essencial powers of Government" from the governor's hands, the abandonment of the defense of the province and the alliance with the Six Nations in time of war, and the omission and refusal of the "whole" support of government for two years. "Every thing which the Crown has a right to demand, or the Province for their own sakes, in interest oblige to provide, has been denied merely in resentment from personal quarrels, and on account of differences between the Governor and some members of the council and assembly." [75] The board concluded that the only way of reconciling the personal feuds and recovering the lost prerogatives of the crown was to send over a new governor armed with sufficient instructions, after tempers in New York had died down. A new chief executive would be "unopposed by any set of Men upon personal dislike, capable of great influence from his Station and deserving of it from his character." Above all, he could secure a permanent revenue to provide for the expenses of the government and thus resolve the conflicting claims to authority that disturbed the province.[76] The privy council considered this report on August 6, 1751, and ordered the board of trade to prepare instructions for the governor of New York agreeable to the conclusions in the report.[77]

The assembly, meanwhile, waited anxiously to discover the contents of the report, but without much success. Their agent, Robert Charles, hounded the privy council after the report had been completed by the board of trade, but he was refused permission to see a copy. On July 29, 1751, he reported a pessimistic rumor: "Several rights and privileges claimed by the General Assemblies of your

75. *New York Col. Docs.*, VI, 636.
76. *Ibid.*, VI, 637.
77. Order in Council, August 6, 1751, *New York Col. Docs.*, VI, 727. The result of this order was the preparation of the well-known thirty-ninth article in Sir Danvers Osborn's instructions, reprinted in Labaree, *Royal Instructions*, I, 191–193. For Sir Lewis Namier's argument that Charles Townshend was responsible for the thirty-ninth article, see Namier, *Crossroads*, p. 204; Namier and Brooke, *History of Parliament*, III, 540; Sir Lewis Namier and John Brooke, *Charles Townshend* (London, 1964), p. 37.

colony, of which they have been many years in possession, are struck out; and complaints are made of *particular persons*, which I was in hopes had long ago been dropped." [78] Charles expected the report to be taken up again after the August 6 order in council, and hoped for a public hearing, but wrote on May 4, 1752, that no further consideration had taken place.[79] This uncertainty, and the suspicion that the report had recommended action unfavorable to their house, blunted the aggressiveness of the leaders of the assembly from 1750 until the arrival of Danvers Osborn in 1753. At the same time Clinton's agent, John Catherwood, interpreted the privy council's action as a vindication of the Governor's resistance to DeLancey, and Clinton himself began to act with more self-assurance.[80]

In these years Clinton was able to improve his situation in the colony by taking new advisers into his confidence and by acquiring a majority in the council. By 1750, according to William Smith, Clinton had begun to see that the heated antagonism between Cadwallader Colden and James DeLancey threatened the conduct of provincial government.[81] Abandoning his sole reliance upon Colden, the Governor therefore turned to Lewis Morris' old ally, James Alexander, who had devoted himself to his private affairs and had not sat in the council since 1737. Alexander was aided by his legal colleague of the Cosby days, the elder William Smith, although Colden's advice and pen were often called into service when he was in New York City. In 1749 Clinton also struck up an association with Robert Hunter Morris, who was then en route to England on New Jersey proprietary business. The net result of the incorporation of these Morrisite stalwarts into the Clinton administration was a more balanced view of provincial problems and reduced ill-will between the assembly and the government.[82]

The board of trade, revitalized under Halifax, finally roused itself to help Clinton regain control of the New York council in the

78. Quoted in Smith, *History*, II, 144–145.
79. *Ibid.*, II, 146.
80. Catherwood to Clinton, September 13, 1751, Clinton MSS., C.L.
81. Smith, *History*, II, 129.
82. *Ibid.*, II, 129–130.

last years of his administration. In 1750 the Governor's agent complained to the board that of the seven members of the council, one lived 200 miles from New York City, and two others (DeLancey and Murray) headed a faction against the royal government in the province.[83] The tide had already begun to turn in Clinton's favor, however, for in April 1750 his allies Edward Holland and William Johnson were appointed in place of the deceased Philip Van Cortlandt and Philip Livingston, both of whom had opposed him.[84] The board restored Alexander to the council in July, on the grounds that he had lost his seat because his name was mistakenly omitted from Clinton's instructions; he replaced the DeLanceyite John Moore, who had died. In January 1752 Clinton's placeman John Chambers was appointed in lieu of Stephen Bayard, who had moved to another province. Thus of the eleven members in 1752, six (Colden, Kennedy, Holland, Johnson, Alexander, and Chambers) were open advocates of the Governor, two (George Clarke, Jr., and Warren) were in England permanently, one (Rutherford) was visiting at home, and, of the former DeLancey majority, only the Chief Justice and Murray remained. In January 1753, William Smith replaced the deceased Sir Peter Warren.[85]

Clinton was overjoyed by the council appointments. He assured the new secretary of state, the Earl of Holdernesse, that there was a great difference in the proceedings of the council, "from what it was, when the Faction had the majority in both Council and Assembly."[86] More important, the Governor's recovery of control in the council impressed the assembly with the apparent strength of his interest in England: Smith, for instance, was appointed in the face of strong competition from Lewis Morris, Jr. (recommended by his brother, Robert Hunter Morris) and Oliver DeLancey (James's

83. Catherwood's memorial to the board of trade, [July 1750?], C.O. 5:1036, fol. 40, PRO.
84. For Peter Warren's possible intervention in behalf of the DeLanceyites, see Catherwood to William Johnson, April 2, 1750, in Sullivan, *Johnson Papers*, I, 269–270.
85. C.O. 324:48, foll. 14b–15 [IV], PRO.
86. Clinton to Rutherford, December 8, 1750, Clinton Letterbook, p. 149, C.L.; Clinton to Holdernesse, November 25, 1751, *New York Col. Docs.*, VI, 751.

brother, recommended by Sir Peter Warren and board of trade member Richard Plumer).[87]

Clinton strengthened his improving position by conscientiously placing his friends in important jobs as they came vacant. John Chambers was appointed second justice of the supreme court in July 1751.[88] William Smith was appointed attorney general in August 1751, although he quickly lost the post to Newcastle's placeman, William Kempe.[89] In these last years of his administration, Clinton was reconciled with Lewis Morris, Jr., who had been defeated in the 1750 assembly elections by the Chief Justice's brother, Peter DeLancey. The Governor restored Morris to the admiralty bench in 1752.[90] Clinton even seems to have made peace with the DeLanceyite Daniel Horsmanden, for he appointed him third justice of the supreme court in July 1753. Smith said that this happened after Horsmanden had broken with DeLancey and Clinton had fallen out with Colden.[91] The hard and fast lines of the 1746 dispute were unquestionably disappearing. The historian Thomas Jones said that in 1752 New York was in its "happiest state," for "all discord had ceased; parties were forgotten and animosities forgiven." [92]

The uncertainty created by the board of trade report, and Clin-

87. Smith, *History*, II, 147; C.O. 324:48, foll. 14b–15 [IV], PRO; Lewis Morris, Jr.'s, memorial to the board of trade, 1752, *New York Col. Docs.*, VI, 767–768.

88. *Cal. Coun. Min.*, p. 381; Clinton to R. H. Morris, August 18, 1751, R. H. Morris Papers, I, 23, NJHS.

89. Clinton to Bedford, June 28, 1749, *New York Col. Docs.*, VI, 514; Paris to Alexander, November 10, 1749, *Calendar of the Stevens Family Papers* (Newark, N.J., 1940), I, 138; Clinton to Bedford, August 31, 1751, *New York Col. Docs.*, VI, 737; Clinton to Catherwood, February 18, 1752, Clinton Letterbook, pp. 10–12, C.L.; Alexander to Colden, February 18, 1752, NYHS, *Colls.*, 1920, pp. 311–312; Clinton to R. H. Morris, February 19, 1752, R. H. Morris Papers, I, 39, NJHS; Stokes, *Iconography*, IV, 636.

90. R. H. Morris, "Diary," pp. 404–405 (December 16, 1749); Clinton to R. H. Morris, August 29, 1750, R. H. Morris Papers, I, 6, NJHS; Lewis Morris to Mrs. Norris, June 3, [1744], *Governor Lewis Morris Papers*, p. 190; *Cal. Coun. Min.*, p. 385.

91. *Cal. Coun. Min.*, p. 389; Smith, *History*, II, 115.

92. Thomas Jones, *History of New York During the Revolutionary War*, ed. Edward Floyd DeLancey (New York, 1879), I, 1–2.

ton's success in filling the council and other high offices with his allies, plus his acceptance of annual support of the government, all contributed to the relative calm in New York politics from 1750 to 1753. This calm was also due, however, to the preoccupation of the principal politicians with the arrival of a new governor. Smith contended that, "It was therefore expedient, while Mr. DeLancey's friends were negotiating in England for the gratification of his ambition, to suspend hostilities against Mr. Clinton." [93] This argument was undoubtedly true, though in his bitterness Clinton was unable to give it full weight. He ascribed the assembly's compliance more "to their fear of disobliging their constituents than any regard the members, elected by his [DeLancey's] influence, had to me, and whatever pretences Chief Justice DeLancey may make to his Friends in England of his serving of me, ought to have no weight with my Friends, because I have daily Instances of his extending his Resentment against me." [94] In 1753, as in 1746, Clinton considered DeLancey the "Primum Mobile of the Opposition." [95]

The Clinton administration constitutes an ambiguous chapter in the history of royal government in New York. Seen from the imperial point of view, it is a story of decline: perfunctory participation in King George's War, reappearance of political factionalism, continued legislative usurpation of royal financial prerogatives, and collaboration with the French in illicit fur trade. Seen from Clinton's own perspective, however, the record is not so bleak. He attempted to reassert the government's right to long-term financial support. He ultimately succeeded in quieting the worst excesses of political factionalism and he arranged for at least minimal New York participation in the French war in the face of traditional American indifference. He remained in office for ten years, the longest tenure of the eighteenth century.

In the final analysis, however, Clinton must be put down as a

93. Smith, *History*, II, 146.
94. Clinton to R.H. Morris, May 19, 1751, R.H. Morris Papers, I, 16, NJHS.
95. Johnson to Warren, July 24, 1749, in Sullivan, *Johnson Papers*, I, 239.

man who was unable to make the most of a perilous situation because of his inability to act quickly, confidently, and independently. Only a shrewd and courageous stance at the beginning of his government could have enabled him to overcome the advantages accruing to the assembly and to DeLancey from the deficiencies of Clarke's administration. As it was, his blind dependence upon James DeLancey and the remorseless pressures of his precarious financial position put him at a permanent disadvantage after his first few years in New York.

Chief Justice DeLancey, on the other hand, brilliantly exploited the opportunities presented to him, and by 1747 he controlled majorities in both houses of the legislature and dominated the supreme court. His position weakened, however, after 1750, when Clinton regained some of his lost standing by means of the careful exercise of his appointive power and the intervention of the imperial government. In response, DeLancey had to reach out for executive power. He began a concerted effort to discourage the Governor from remaining in New York at the same time that he attempted to discredit him in the eyes of the ministry, and meanwhile he sought the lieutenant governorship for himself.

After 1746 it was clear that DeLancey had triumphed in America, but in England the issue was in doubt until 1753. The events dealt with in this chapter pertain only to the domestic side of New York politics, but in the eighteenth century politics in New York were inevitably conducted with one eye on the metropolis. The English side of the Clinton-DeLancey contest proved to be decisive.

8
Governor Clinton: Negotiations in London, 1746-1752

A ROYAL GOVERNOR WHO HAD GAINED HIS post because of strong family connections had a distinct advantage in the conduct of Anglo-American politics. An American politician's local advantages of position and experience, on the other hand, were of little avail in influencing decisions made in London. Thus it was frequently the case that a governor's strength at Whitehall gave him the leverage necessary to control an independent-minded colony, since the promise of imperial intervention or the ostentatious demonstration of British approval reinforced the authority of a colonial executive. The Cosby administration conformed to the pattern, but Admiral George Clinton's governorship turned out quite differently. In Clinton's case the governor's superb English connection failed him and the imperial administration refused to come to his support, so that his American challenger was able to exercise his own considerable English influence to control the New York political scene.

I

After the first few years of his government Clinton was constantly made aware of the importance of English intervention in New York politics. Although he was closely allied to Newcastle, he was quite unsure of his support at home. For one thing, he feared DeLancey's connections, real and pretended. Such powerful figures as Sir Peter Warren and Sir William Baker constituted a serious threat to Clinton, and DeLancey's claims to interest with the ministry provided one of the firmest underpinnings for his New York faction. But even if Clinton exaggerated the dimensions of the DeLancey connection, the New York opposition could threaten him by the classical technique of creating enough dissention in the colony to destroy the ministry's faith in the governor.[1] The tactic had been unsuccessfully employed against Cosby, but the Admiral was much less confident than his predecessor had been. In any case, Clinton felt obliged to turn to England for a resolution of his political dilemma in New York.

Clinton and Colden had quite specific ideas about the sort of English support they required to head off the faction's encroachments on the royal prerogative. In 1745 Clinton suggested, even before an opposition had been formed, that only parliament could bring New Yorkers to "a more submissive behavior, or make a Governour independent." [2] Parliament could legislate a permanent

1. Clinton to Bedford, April 9, 1750, draft, Clinton MSS., X, C.L.; Colden to Catherwood, November 21, 1749, NYHS, *Colls.*, 1920, p. 160.
2. Clinton to Newcastle, November 18, 1745, *New York Col. Docs.*, VI, 284.

revenue for royal government in New York based either on quit rents or import duties.[3] In 1747 Clinton requested the admiralty to assign a warship to New York for the protection of provincial trade, claiming that the absence of such a ship caused the people of New York to turn against him.[4] The Governor also had the bright idea of suggesting that the privy council interrogate the leaders of the New York opposition, thus forcing them to confess their errors.[5]

Above all, however, Clinton and Colden hoped for a general approval of their policy by the secretary of state or the board of trade in the form of a letter or, preferably, additional instructions ordering the Governor to reassert the powers of the crown. Clinton bombarded them with pleas for help. At the outset he asked the board to consider the nature of the faction in New York, and to "advise His Majesty's Ministers as to what Instructions you shall think proper on this occasion, or other methods which you shall think necessary for supporting His Majesty's authority and security of this Province against all attempts of his Enemies." [6] In 1748, Clinton and Shirley suggested that the king disallow some of the assembly's acts, and send instructions to the Governor forbidding him to assent to such acts in the future.[7]

Clinton made the same suggestions again in 1749, and requested in addition that the king confirm the suspensions of Horsmanden and Bayard and approve Clinton's new nominations in their place.[8] He was increasingly aware of the importance of the English appointive power, and in 1752 he complained bitterly about the selection of Peter Wraxall as secretary of Indian affairs and clerk of Albany,

3. Clinton to Lords of Trade, November 30 and September 27, 1747, to Newcastle, September 27, 1747, to Bedford, March 26, 1750, *New York Col. Docs.*, VI, 412, 379, 395, 554; Clinton to H. Pelham, December 8, 1747, Clinton MSS., IV, C.L.
4. Clinton to Thomas Corbett, May 23, 1747, Adm. 1:3818, PRO.
5. Clinton to Dorset, October 30, 1748, draft, Clinton MSS., C.L.
6. Clinton to Lords of Trade, July 24, 1747, *New York Col. Docs.*, VI, 364.
7. Clinton to Newcastle, September 30, 1748, Add. MSS. 32716, fol. 399, B.M.
8. [Clinton] to Bedford, [September 24, 1749, delivered], "State of Disloyal Situation of Affairs in New York," Clinton MSS., C.L.

and of William Kempe as attorney general, having previously nominated his own friends for these posts.[9]

Year after year Clinton repeated the complaint that he was neglected by the ministry and the board of trade. An argument he frequently used was that lack of English approbation caused his candidates to lose assembly elections. In 1751, for instance, he stated that had he received the requested royal instructions, "I made no doubt but the next choice, might have been supplyed by better men." [10] In the later years of his administration, despairing of positive ministerial action in his behalf, Clinton bewailed the absence of *any* communication from England: "What is it possible can their silence mean? or what can occasion it? unless they are determined to leave me to my self, to be made a sacrifice both here and at home." [11] Roused to a fever pitch, Clinton cried out that he was left to the mercy of a mob, and urged his English friends to discover the "sinister persons" who were "the Source of this secret malice against me." [12]

Clinton surely had grounds for complaining about the board of trade's neglect. The board wrote him only once in each of the years 1744, 1745, 1746, 1748, 1750, and 1752, and not at all in the intervening years.[13] The board defended itself, in 1745, by assuring

9. Clinton to H. Clinton, January 20, 1752, Clinton MSS.; Clinton to H. Clinton, May 16, 1753, Clinton MSS., XIII, C.L.

10. Clinton to Holdernesse, November 25, 1751, *New York Col. Docs.*, VI, 751; Catherwood to Clinton, October 10, 1749, Clinton MSS., C.L. Conversely, Clinton believed the ministry's silence permitted DeLancey to win the New York elections by proclaiming that the ministry no longer supported Clinton. Clinton to R. H. Morris, November 28, 1751, R. H. Morris Papers, I, 33, NJHS.

11. Clinton to R. H. Morris, July 26, 1751, Clinton Letterbook, pp. 80–81, C.L.

12. Clinton to Catherwood, July 26, 1752; Clinton to Lincoln, November 26, 1752, Clinton Letterbook, pp. 74, 131, C.L.

13. *New York Col. Docs.*, VI, 252–253, 277–278, 308–309, 427–428, 586–587, 761–762. This was not a new state of affairs. In 1731 F. J. Paris protested that the board of trade failed to act on colonial business because it was "swallowed up in paper" and yet the commissioners sat "but a very few hours on Board Days." F. J. Paris to Alexander, January 31, 1731, Rutherfurd Collection, Small Scrapbook, no. 44, NYHS.

Clinton that "this Board never fails to make an immediate Return to all Letters from Governors, where the Subject appears to require Dispatch." [14] It was in the same letter that they defended their own appointment to the New York council over Clinton's objections on the grounds that the board was not confined by a governor's recommendation. Clinton's retort was to the point: "To be Sure the Ministry have their hands full but notwithstanding that it is absolutely become necessary for them to look this way a little, or by God they will make your hearts aike in England." [15] The board never did provide effective support for Clinton vis-à-vis the assembly, and their unimaginative attitude is characterized by their advice to Clinton in June 1748: "we can only recommend you such moderate and prudent measures as may if possible reconcile these differences, and induce the respective branches of the Legislature to concur in carrying on the publick service, for the mutual support of His Majesty's Government and the good of the Province." [16] Under President John, Lord Monson the board had been slothful, and under Halifax after 1748 it was more concerned to pick up the pieces and start afresh than to shore up Clinton's tottering administration.[17] Halifax's personal advice to Clinton was "to keep strictly to my Instructions (suffering no Innovation upon ye Kings Authority)." [18] His plan for New York, envisioning a new governor armed with stronger instructions, was presented at the conclusion of the 1751 board of trade report on the province, and it shows that Clinton was not so far off when he complained that he was being sacrificed.

The secretaries of state were sympathetic to Clinton, but did as little for him as the board of trade. During the war years, Clinton's patron held the secretaryship, but Newcastle was too preoccupied with the hostilities in Europe to concern himself with the difficulties of a governor in New York. In 1748, when Bedford took over the southern department, he expressed concern over Clinton's plight,

14. Lords of Trade to Clinton, April 5, 1745, *ibid.*, VI, 277.
15. Clinton to Guerin, July 23, 1747, draft, Clinton MSS., C.L.
16. Lords of Trade to Clinton, June 29, 1748, *New York Col. Docs.*, VI, 427.
17. O. M. Dickerson, *American Colonial Government*, pp. 35–36.
18. Clinton to Shirley, July 3, 1749, draft, Clinton MSS., IX, C.L.

and throughout 1749, in interviews with the Governor's agent, he expressed dislike of DeLancey and encouragement for Clinton's challenge to the assembly.[19]

In November 1749 Bedford sent a letter to Governor Clinton in which he mentioned the royal investigation of the situation in New York:

> However, as it will be some time before any Report can be made to the King, upon a Matter of so complicated a Nature, I would no longer deferr assuring you, that if upon Examination, the Facts turn out as you represent them, (as I do not doubt, they will) you may depend on all proper assistance to support the Authority the King has put into your Hands, and which His Majesty will consequently defend from any unjust, or malicious Attacks whatsoever.[20]

This letter was reportedly calculated by Bedford, "to convince the legislature of the Province, that he would endeavour to support you [Clinton] in Maintaining the King's Prerogative upon just Measures." [21] Clinton apparently did not consider such a guarded endorsement sufficient to enable him to persevere in his fight to recover the financial prerogatives of the crown, however, and several years later his comment was that "I have received not one line from the Ministry ever since upon that Subject." [22] At the end of 1749, Bedford was still well disposed toward Governor Clinton. In December John Catherwood reported that Bedford was anxious to aid the Governor, "with the rest of the Kings Servants, but that he could not do it alone, as your Friends were backward to attend; that he would not neglect doing something this Winter." [23] In February 1749-50, however, Bedford's secretary informed Catherwood "that the Ministry are determin'd to settle a general plan for establishing the Kings Authority in all the plantations and this may be a prin-

19. Observations, Catherwood to Clinton, February 27, 1748, February 13, 1749, April 18, 1749, and October 10, 1749, Clinton MSS., C.L.

20. Bedford to Clinton, November 1, 1749, Clinton MSS., IX, C.L.

21. Catherwood to Clinton, May 2, 1750, Clinton MSS., C.L.

22. Observation, Catherwood to Clinton, November 4, 1749, Clinton MSS., C.L.

23. Catherwood to Clinton, December 5, 1749, Clinton MSS., C.L.

cipal reason why your Excellency's affairs have not been taken into consideration separately by themselves." [24] From this time on, Bedford was unresponsive to Clinton's demands.

In the end, then, the imperial administration failed to support its chosen representative. In 1746 Governor Clinton had thought that New York's difficulties could be solved, as they had been in 1736, by the direct intervention of English authorities. He justified his defensive posture by pointing out that he could display to the newly-formed opposition no sign of "His Majestys approbation of my conduct, or displeasure of theirs" and argued that the ministry should act to help him as it had Clarke ten years previously.[25] As the ministry perhaps realized, however, Clinton's problem was not as simple as Clarke's need for an unambiguous statement of his authority to exercise the powers of government. Clinton never could have succeeded in dislodging the DeLancey faction by a mere show of his imperial support. Rather, his only hope of reasserting his and the ministry's authority was to negotiate privately in England for the accomplishment of a series of specific measures. What official action had failed to do, informal politics might.

II

"Connections," "interest," and "influence" were the ingredients of Anglo-American political in-fighting. As contestants for American political power maneuvered for position, their personal channels of access to English officials were decisive. Clinton himself was the first to admit that the status of colonial office did not in itself count for much in London: "one Parliament Man's vote weighs

24. Colden to Clinton, February 12, 1750, Clinton MSS., X, C.L. R. H. Morris, however, thought that Clinton's complaints might have carried more weight with the ministry if the council had joined him in his letters "representing the state of the province." R. H. Morris to Alexander, March 3, 1751, *Cal. Stevens Papers*, II, 6.

25. Clinton to Newcastle, November 9, 1747, *New York Col. Docs.*, VI, 410. See also, Colden to Clinton, November 9, 1749, NYHS, *Colls.*, p. 150.

more than all the American Governour's Interest together." [26]
Clinton also recognized the efficacy of personal solicitations of support at home ("dont doubt upon my coming home here to have the
same interest, for there is nothing like being upon the spot"),[27] but
most American political negotiation in England was necessarily carried on by proxy. The key to political success for those in America
lay in the establishment of an English connection that could exert its
influence in their behalf.

Governor Clinton's superb English connections can have been
matched by few eighteenth-century officials. His strength was, of
course, in his relationship to the Pelham family, especially the Duke
of Newcastle. Newcastle had made Clinton's naval career as successful as his limited talents would permit and had procured the government of New York for him in order to provide a support for his
growing family. As secretary of state for the southern department,
Newcastle was in the best possible situation to help his protégé; as
one Londoner put it, "the Channel of all promotion is all through
the Duke of Newcastle . . . its all in his Breast." [28]

Unhappily for Clinton, however, Newcastle was not in a good
position to help him after 1746, when the Governor was most in
need of aid. From 1746 to 1748 the Secretary was absorbed in the
direction of the French war, and after the war he transferred from
the southern department to the northern, giving up responsibility
for the management of colonial affairs. William Shirley assured
Clinton that Newcastle's transfer was actually a gain, giving him "a
closer and more frequent access to his M———y's Closet," [29] but
this proved of little solace to Clinton. In fact, colonial questions
quickly moved out of the range of Newcastle's concern and control: the Secretary soon fell out with his successor in the southern
department, Bedford, and Halifax's presidency rendered the board
of trade more aggressive and independent than it had been before.

26. Clinton to Colden, May 5, 1752, NYHS, *Colls.*, 1920, p. 324.
27. Clinton to R. H. Morris, January 15, 1751, R. H. Morris Papers, I, 37, NJHS.
28. Collinson to Colden, September 26, 1755, NYHS, *Colls.*, 1921, p. 27.
29. Shirley to Clinton, August 22, 1748, Clinton MSS., VIII, C.L.

Clinton was also disappointed in the performance of Henry Pelham and his nephew, the Earl of Lincoln. His relationship to Pelham, the chief minister of the crown during the years of his New York government, must have seemed very promising. There is evidence that Pelham was willing to help Clinton if he could, but it is also clear that he was not very concerned with the Governor's problems. His indifference was probably reinforced by his quarrel with Newcastle in late 1750 over the marriage settlement of Lord Lincoln,[30] since Clinton was obviously Newcastle's dependent rather than Pelham's. As it turned out, however, Lincoln himself was Clinton's main hope in the later years of his administration.[31] Lincoln was a politician of some weight as Newcastle's heir, and Clinton particularly counted upon Lincoln to rouse his father-in-law Pelham in his favor.[32]

Regardless of the strength of his family connections, any governor needed the almost constant attention of personal representatives in London to look out for his interests generally and to conduct his formal business with the several bodies of imperial administration. Clinton's first and principal agent was John Catherwood, who had come to New York as his private secretary in 1743

30. Newcastle to Lincoln, September 30/October 10, 1750, and February 6, 1751, Add. MSS. 33066, foll. 189, 221–222; Newcastle to Andrew Stone, February 26, 1752, Add. MSS. 33066, foll. 224, 258–266, B.M. See also, *DNB*, XLIV, 246. The brothers also quarreled in 1751 when Newcastle forced Bedford to resign the secretaryship.

31. Sir Lewis B. Namier, "Brice Fisher, M.P.: A Mid-Eighteenth-Century Merchant and His Connections," *English Historical Review*, XLII (1927), pp. 521–523; Namier, *England in the Age of the American Revolution*, p. 382. For an idea of the role Lincoln played in Clinton's English negotiations, see his memorandum to Lincoln, transmitted by Catherwood, June 2, 1750, Clinton MSS., C.L. In the memorandum, Clinton made eight requests. Five were requests for Lincoln to intercede with Henry Pelham: for revoking DeLancey's commission as lieutenant governor; for interceding with Bedford to procure an official letter supporting Clinton as governor; for ending Peter Warren's interference in New York government; for speeding payment of Clinton's accounts; for securing the payment of Clinton's salary. Lincoln himself was to speak to Halifax in support of Clinton's nominations to the New York council, to secure Clinton a naval command and promotion, and to obtain permission for Clinton to return home as governor.

32. Collinson to Colden, July 27, 1750, Emmet MSS., no. 3202, NYPL; Collinson to Colden, October 3, 1750, NYHS, *Colls.*, 1935, p. 78.

and later served as deputy secretary of the colony and captain of one of the Independent Companies in New York.[33]

In 1746 and again in 1748 Clinton sent Catherwood to England with a specific mission: to solicit the crown's payment of the bills of exchange that Clinton had personally drawn upon the treasury and the paymaster general to finance the 1746 expedition against Canada. After the second trip, however, Catherwood remained in London as a permanent agent of the Governor. A detailed list of instructions which Clinton drew up on December 4, 1748, provides a clear statement of his expectations of the agent. The first item instructed Catherwood to induce Lincoln and his uncles to have Clinton put on active duty as an admiral, so that his naval salary would render him independent of the assembly. Secondly, Catherwood was to insist to Newcastle, Bedford, and Dorset that DeLancey's commission as lieutenant governor be suppressed. Finally, the agent was to attempt to have the remaining DeLanceyite councillors replaced by Clinton's nominees. At the same time, Clinton expected Catherwood to aid his English benefactors, to report back regularly, and to carry on a multitude of small solicitations.[34]

Catherwood's responsibilities were great and he worked hard in Clinton's behalf, becoming familiar with the leading figures of the government in the course of his efforts.[35] Characteristically, however, Clinton soon decided that Catherwood was ignoring his interests, debauching at his expense, and even falling into an alliance with Peter Warren against him. He asked Robert Hunter Morris, Henry

33. Clinton to H. Clinton, December 14, 1752, Clinton MSS., XII, C.L.; Board of Trade Report, February 28, 1750, T. 64:44, fol. 56, PRO; *Cal. Coun. Min.*, pp. 349, 354; Clinton to Newcastle, November 28, 1755, Add. MSS. 32861, fol. 123, B.M. Catherwood's appointment as deputy secretary (July 1745–June 1746) was apparently without the knowledge or consent of George Clarke, Jr., the secretary. Clarke determined to recover Catherwood's profits from the office and to protect his patent, and after 1746 Banyar served him faithfully as deputy secretary. Clarke to Banyar, various letters, July 16, 1747, to July 2, 1753, Banyar MSS., NYHS.

34. Clinton's Instructions for Catherwood, December 4, 1748, Clinton MSS., C.L.

35. In 1751, Catherwood stood godfather (by proxy for Clinton) to Lincoln's son, Henry, along with Henry Pelham and the Duchess of Newcastle. Catherwood to Clinton, March 4, 1751, Clinton MSS., C.L.

Clinton, and William Shirley to check on Catherwood, but they all endorsed the agent's conduct and, as far as we can tell today, Catherwood was in fact acting energetically and single-mindedly for Clinton in England.[36]

Suspicious of Catherwood and eager for the help of someone with higher standing, Clinton also enlisted the aid of Robert Hunter Morris, who was going to England in 1749 as the agent of the East New Jersey proprietors.[37] Morris appears to have come to terms with Clinton: he was briefed on the Governor's problems by James Alexander and Colden before embarking from America and Clinton himself booked his passage. Morris, in 1749 the chief justice of New Jersey, had been placed in a weak political position after his father's death in 1746, and it seems likely that Clinton undertook to secure the lieutenant governorship of New York for him if, as seemed increasingly likely, it could not be obtained for Colden.[38]

Morris' chief task in England was to help Catherwood and Henry Clinton prepare memorials to the ministry in the Governor's behalf. He did carry on a certain amount of negotiation for Clinton, however, and reported back regularly on the state of affairs in London.[39] Morris had the experience of his father's 1735–1736 solicitation behind him, of course, but his most valuable connections of those years, Sir John Norris and Sir Charles Wager, were dead. His New Jersey activities brought him into close contact with Thomas Penn, however, and Penn personally introduced Morris to Bedford and Halifax upon his arrival in England in December 1749. He also came to know several members of the board of trade.[40]

36. Clinton to Colden, March 11, 1748, draft, Clinton MSS.; R. H. Morris to H. Clinton, January 13, 1750, Clinton MSS., X; Clinton to H. Clinton, September 20, 1749, Shirley to Clinton, November 30, 1749, Clinton MSS., IX; Clinton to R. H. Morris, February 19, 1752, Clinton Letterbook, pp. 19–21, Clinton to H. Clinton, December 14, 1752, Clinton MSS., C.L.

37. *Board of Trade Journal*, 1750–1753, p. 42; Kemmerer, *Path to Freedom*, pp. 216–220.

38. Keys, *Colden*, p. 233; William Alexander MSS., Box I, 60, NYHS; Smith, *History*, II, 130.

39. Clinton to H. Clinton, November 24, 1752, Clinton Letterbook, pp. 124–125; R. H. Morris to H. Clinton, January 13, 1749, Clinton MSS., X, C.L.

40. R. H. Morris, "Diary," pp. 405–406 (December 16 and 19, 1749); R. H. Morris to Alexander, December 19, 1749, March 24, 1750, January 2, 1750, *Cal. Stevens Papers*, I, 141, 142, 124.

Although Clinton was convinced of Morris' value as an agent, the Chief Justice was more interested in New Jersey than in New York. Certainly when his hopes for the lieutenant governorship faded in 1751 he lost much of his interest in Clinton's problems, and left Catherwood to do most of the work. As we have seen, in January 1753 Morris proposed his brother, Lewis, for the New York council seat left vacant by Warren's death only to find that Clinton had obtained it for William Smith. By the end of Clinton's administration Morris was certainly no longer working closely with the Governor.[41]

Clinton's third important representative in London was Governor William Shirley of Massachusetts, who secured a year's leave to return to England in the summer of 1749. Shirley, like Clinton, was Newcastle's dependent, but unlike Clinton he possessed good political sense and a reputation as one of the most outspoken champions of the empire in America. The two governors came to know one another during their consultations for the 1746 expedition against Canada, and by 1748 they had become steady correspondents.[42]

Clinton attempted to involve Shirley in New York politics in 1748, inviting him to examine the colony for the purpose of informing the ministry of Clinton's plight. The two governors wrote a joint letter to the board of trade in August which presented Shirley's recommendation that Clinton be given additional instructions to oppose the assembly's encroachments. Shirley played a cautious part, however, since he was fearful of compromising himself with the ministry, and he argued to Clinton that Pelham would only accept his recommendations if he appeared to be neutral as between Clinton and DeLancey. It does appear that Shirley was privately responsible for Clinton's 1748–1750 attempts to reassert his gubernatorial authority.[43]

41. Clinton to Colden, [late March or early April 1750?], Bancroft Transcripts, Colden, I, 148, NYPL; *Board of Trade Journal,* 1750–1753, p. 385.
42. Schutz, *Shirley,* esp. chaps. 1, 6, 8.
43. *Ibid.,* pp. 138–140; Wood, *William Shirley,* p. 12; Shirley to Bishop of Lincoln, March 16, 1751, Add. MSS. 32877, fol. 469, B.M.; Osgood, *Eighteenth Century,* III, 567; personal correspondence of Clinton and Shirley, esp. Shirley to Clinton, August 31, 1748, Clinton MSS., C.L.; Clinton and Shirley to Lords of Trade, August 18, 1748, Shirley to Clinton, August 13, 1748, Clinton to Bedford, August 15, 1748, *New York Col. Docs.,* VI, 437–440, 432–437, 428–432.

Shirley offered to aid Clinton against the DeLancey faction ("a factious, vain, upstart Crew") during his stay in England, and Clinton accordingly provided him with letters to the ministry.[44] Shirley subsequently reported that Newcastle, Bedford, Halifax, and Lincoln had all expressed concern, and that Newcastle had promised to have the matter considered as soon as the ministry could be brought together. Having done this, Shirley soon left for Paris as one of the commissaries for settling the boundaries between France and England in America to conclude the treaty of Aix-la-Chapelle. His intervention heartened Clinton and Colden, who assured the Governor in November 1749 that with Shirley's assistance his affairs in England would be settled within six months.[45]

Morris, Shirley, and, above all, Catherwood were Clinton's most effective representatives in London, but he was also aided by a group of relatives and professional solicitors. The Governor's son Henry accompanied Catherwood to England in 1748 to recover his health and to seek a better place for himself. Clinton encouraged the young man to assist Catherwood, but he seems to have spent most of his time alternating between self-indulgence and self-aggrandizement.[46] Clinton, however, was seconded in his solicitations by his brother-in-law, Henry Yelverton, and by his sister, Lady Susannah Booth.[47] He also employed a series of colonial agents throughout his administration: Maynard Guerin, John Sharpe (both of whom had represented Cosby previously), and Ferdinand John Paris (Lewis Morris' agent, who was hired in 1749, probably at the behest of Robert Hunter Morris).[48] Catherwood also consulted a "Mr.

44. Shirley to Clinton, June 26, 1749, Clinton MSS., IX, C.L. Clinton accepted this offer on July 3, 1749. Clinton to Shirley, draft, Clinton MSS., IX, C.L.

45. Shirley to Clinton, November 30, 1749, Clinton MSS., IX, C.L.; Colden to Clinton, November 9, 1749, Bancroft Transcripts, Colden, I, 128, NYPL; Schutz, *Shirley*, p. 153.

46. Clinton to H. Clinton, September 20, 1749, Catherwood to Clinton, May 2, 1750, Clinton MSS., C.L.

47. Clinton to H. Clinton, January 21, 1752, R. H. Morris to Clinton, March 11, 1752, Catherwood to Clinton, May 2, 1750, Clinton MSS., C.L.; Collins, *Peerage*, II, 275.

48. Clinton to Newcastle, December 9, 1746, *New York Col. Docs.*, VI, 312; Henry Walker to Clinton, February 17, 1749, Clinton MSS., IX, C.L.;

Murray," who was probably the same Murray involved in the Cosby-Morris case, and at present was the solicitor general.[49] The Clinton-DeLancey affair did not resolve itself into a quasi-judicial contest, however, as had the New York difficulties of the 1730's. In the end, whatever small success Clinton achieved was due to Catherwood's energy and the Pelhams' authority.

James DeLancey's English connections were fewer and less well known than Clinton's, but their task was easier. Once DeLancey had procured the lieutenant governor's commission, his English tactics were to retain the appointment and to deter the ministry from punishing the New York assembly. He needed to prevent action by Whitehall while Clinton solicited positive steps, a situation in which the inefficiency of colonial administration favored the New Yorker over the Englishman.

For an American, DeLancey was extraordinarily well connected to influential English politicians of the second rank, having exploited his education, commercial interests, and family relationships in behalf of his public career. Consider, for instance, his college tutor at Cambridge, Thomas Herring. At the time of DeLancey's matriculation Herring was an obscure fellow of Corpus Christi, but he later came to the notice of the Earl of Hardwicke, who sponsored his meteoric rise through the Anglican hierarchy, until by 1747 he had become the Archbishop of Canterbury. Herring was an old-fashioned Whig who sorely tried the patience of Newcastle and his confidant, Hardwicke, but he exercised a good deal of influence in English government and throughout his career he maintained his friendship with James DeLancey.[50]

F. J. Paris to Alexander, November 10, 1749, *Cal. Stevens Papers*, I, 138. Guerin was Robert Charles' nephew. Varga, "Robert Charles," *William and Mary Quarterly*, XVIII (1961), p. 212n4.

49. Observation, Catherwood to Clinton, October 10, 1749, Clinton MSS., C.L.

50. On Herring's political stature, see Philip C. Yorke, *The Life and Correspondence of Philip Yorke, Earl of Hardwicke, Lord High Chancellor of England* (Cambridge, Eng., 1913), I, 422–423; Norman Sykes, "The Duke of Newcastle as Ecclesiastical Minister," *English Historical Review*, LVII (1942), pp. 62–63; Herring to Hardwicke, June 16, 1743, Add. MSS. 35598, fol. 19; R. Garnett, ed., "Correspondence of Archbishop Herring and Lord

The extensive fur trading interests of the DeLancey family provided another link to London. The influential London merchants, William and Samuel Baker, were the English commercial correspondents of the DeLancey family, and traded with them in political influence as well as Indian goods. The Bakers were deeply involved in American trade and were specialists in American army contracts,[51] and for this reason Newcastle frequently relied upon William Baker, whom he considered "a strong thinker and often a very free speaker," for advice on American problems. William Baker was also a key figure in the London financial world, and he was therefore a man respected by successive ministries.[52] His services to the DeLanceys were many. He performed a few of the tasks an ordinary agent would undertake, such as presenting to the board of trade a memorial complaining of Horsmanden's suspension from the New York council, and representing James DeLancey before the privy council.[53] He also led the English merchants engaged in American

Hardwicke during the Rebellion of 1745," *English Historical Review*, XIX (1904), p. 529; Herring to Newcastle, June 15, 1747, Add. MSS. 32711, fol. 369; Herring to Hardwicke, October 3, 1749, and September 3, 1750, Add. MSS. 35598, fol. 430 and 35599, fol. 22, B.M.; [Herring] to Newcastle, March 24, 1754, quoted in Namier, *England in the Age of the American Revolution*, p. 128.

For DeLancey's relationship to Herring, see DeLancey to Archbishop Herring, October 15, 1753, William Smith MSS., vol. I, no. 4, NYHS; Herring to Sir G. Heathcote, September 23, 1731, I ANC XI:B:4g, L.A.C.; Rev. Samuel Johnson to Herring, June 29, 1753, *New York Col. Docs.*, VI, 777; Clinton to Bedford, October 30, 1748, *ibid.*, VI, 465; Edward F. DeLancey, "Memoir of James DeLancey," in E. B. O'Callaghan, ed., *Documentary History of the State of New York* (Albany, 1849–1851), IV, 1038.

51. On the Bakers and army contracts, see *Board of Trade Journal*, 1723–1728, p. 15; W. and S. Baker to Warren, March 7 to May 26, 1746, Warren MSS., C.L.; A.O. 17:40, foll. 12–29, PRO; Namier, *England in the Age of the American Revolution*, pp. 280, 281–283.

52. Namier, *England in the Age of the American Revolution*, pp. 280–281; Namier, "Brice Fisher," *English Historical Review*, XLII, pp. 518–519; Namier, *The Structure of Politics*, pp. 52–54, 56–58; W. Baker to Newcastle, November 21, 1750, Add. MSS. 32885, fol. 478, B.M.; John Brooke, *The Chatham Administration, 1766–1768* (London, 1956), pp. 105, 128, 283.

53. *Board of Trade Journal*, 1742–1749, p. 263; *Acts, Privy Coun., Col.*, VI, 269–271, IV, 58. Baker does not seem to have appeared before the board personally in any New York cause.

trade who supported DeLancey's policy, and fought Governor Clinton's efforts to finance the war against the French. Baker was a man of great importance in governmental circles, and Clinton must have winced when Catherwood reported he had "heard that Alderman Baker is greatly your enemy and heard he had lodged complaints against you." [54]

The day by day work of representing DeLancey's interests in London was handled by Robert Charles. Charles had been active in Pennsylvania politics from 1732 to 1738, and later became Sir Peter Warren's private secretary.[55] He was selected as the agent of the New York assembly in April 1748 on Warren's recommendation, and he was ordered by the speaker of the assembly "always to take the advice of Sir Peter Warren if in England." [56] He was a vigorous agent for the colony in dealings with the board of trade, and so persistent that Charles M. Andrews has characterized him as "a conspicuous busybody" before that board. Charles, with Warren, supported the assembly's interests in the New York–New Jersey boundary dispute and in the parliamentary discussions of colonial paper currency.[57]

Clinton had been friendly with Charles as early as January 1745, when he offered to recommend Charles's appointment as agent for himself and the assembly at the next session. He asked him to report on any events in London affecting New York, and arranged introductions to Newcastle and Lincoln.[58] Therefore, when the assembly chose Charles as their own agent, completely independent of the Governor's authority, Clinton felt betrayed.

54. Catherwood to Clinton, January 27, 1750, Clinton MSS., C.L.

55. Lilly, *Colonial Agents*, p. 115n125; Varga, "Robert Charles," *William and Mary Quarterly*, 3rd ser., XVIII (1961), pp. 211–235.

56. David Jones to R. Charles, April 9, 1748, excerpt, William Smith, Jr., Papers, III, 229, NYPL; Colden to Clinton, May 9, 1748, Bancroft Transcripts, Colden, I, 77, NYPL.

57. Andrews, *Colonial Period*, IV, 295; Lilly, *Colonial Agents*, p. 175n23; R. H. Morris to Alexander, January 23, 1750, *Cal. Stevens Papers*, I, 142; *Board of Trade Journal*, 1742–1749, p. 440; Smith, *History*, I, 129; Stock, *Proceedings of British Parliaments*, V, 320n44.

58. Clinton to R. Charles, January 3, 1745, draft, Clinton MSS., II, C.L.; Clinton to Colden, May 16, 1748, NYHS, *Colls.*, 1920, p. 63.

> I have lately discovered the spring of all my disappointments in England by Mr. Charles (upon whome I depended) acting in confidence with Sir Peter Warren, and nothing surprized me more yesterday than the Speaker asking me if I would consent to the giving an allowance of £200 to an agent in England for the service of the Province, & named Mr. Charles to me as recommended by Sir Peter which plainly demonstrates that he has plaid cat in pan with me.[59]

Besides aiding him on legislative matters, Charles helped DeLancey by opposing Robert Hunter Morris' solicitation for the lieutenant governorship, and in general kept the DeLancey party in America informed of proceedings in England. William Smith recognized the underlying reason for Charles's appointment, however, "The Newcastle interest in favor of the possessor [Clinton], had hitherto rendered the colony politics unsuccessful, and there was a necessity for some pointed exertions against him by an agent at court, to improve and give them success." [60]

Family relationships provided DeLancey with his most dependable contacts. We have already seen how well he was served by marriage into the Heathcote family, but by far the most important of his connections was his sister's husband, Admiral Sir Peter Warren. Warren was a gifted Irish naval officer who gained fame and fortune during the War of the Austrian Succession by commanding a fleet that captured the fortress of Louisbourg and took hundreds of thousands of pounds sterling in prizes. A grateful ministry made him a knight of the Bath and promoted him to admiral, and henceforth he began to take an interest in politics in New York, where he was acquiring a considerable estate, and in England. His political influence, which was enhanced by his great wealth, derived from his friendship with Admiral George Anson and Anson's patrons, the Duke of Bedford and the Earl of Sandwich, who secured Warren a parliamentary seat for Westminster in the election of 1747. Warren was, then, very happily placed as DeLancey neared the peak of his

59. Clinton to Colden, April 1, 1748, NYHS, *Colls.*, 1920, pp. 32–33.
60. Smith, *History*, II, 117–118. See also, *ibid.*, II, 145–146.

career.[61] "He now must be one of the richest men in England & not one has done his Country so much Service; he must be worth three or four Hundred Thousand Pounds Sterling, he's Vice Admiral of the White and a Member of Parliament for Westminster, and make no doubt in a very Short time will be a Pier of England, there being no person more Able to Maintain that dignity." [62]

George Clinton and his brother officer Peter Warren had been friendly long before his governorship in New York and, oddly, the Governor continued to think that Warren could be counted on his side even after his break with DeLancey in 1746.[63] Of course Clinton was disabused by the news that Warren had had DeLancey appointed lieutenant governor in 1747; he protested the appointment to Newcastle on the grounds of DeLancey's unsuitability and Warren's partiality, begging that Warren be prevented from interfering further in New York affairs.[64] Characteristically, by March 1748 Clinton was accusing Warren of bribing his dependents and abusing his acquaintance with the Earl of Lincoln to Clinton's detriment. The politic Warren attempted to explain away his procurement of the lieutenant governorship, and by the end of 1748 he had

61. *DNB*, XX, 876–877; Edward Floyd DeLancey, *New York and Admiral Sir Peter Warren at the Capture of Louisbourg, 1745* (n.p., [1896]), pp. 7–9; John Charnock, *Biographia Navalis* . . . (London, 1794–1798), IV, 184–192; [Anon.,] "Biographical Memoir of the Late Sir Peter Warren, K.B., Vice Admiral of the Red Squadron," *The Naval Chronicle*, XII (1804), pp. 257–275 (many inaccuracies); Gerald S. Graham, *Empire of the North Atlantic* (Toronto, 1950), pp. 123, 116–142. For an intensive discussion of Warren's career, see Katz "An Easie Access," pp. 242–257. For Warren's political connections in England, see Sir John Barrow, *The Life of George Lord Anson* (London, 1839), p. 12; Horace Walpole, *Memoirs of the Reign of King George the Second*, ed. Lord Holland (2nd ed., revised, London, 1847), I, 194–195; W. and S. Baker to Warren, April 30 and August 1, 1745, Warren MSS., C.L.; Bedford to Anson, June 20, 1747, Add. MSS. 15955, fol. 141; H. Hale Bellot, "Council and Cabinet in the Mainland Colonies," Royal Historical Society, *Transactions*, 5th series, V (1955), p. 166.

62. Warren Johnson to W. Johnson, September 13, 1747, in Sullivan, *Johnson Papers*, I, 117.

63. R. H. Morris, "Diary," p. 392; Colden to [John Rutherford?], n.d., NYHS, *Colls.*, 1919, p. 311.

64. Clinton to Newcastle, February 13, 1748, *New York Col. Docs.*, VI, 417.

Clinton believing that he might be wooed away from DeLancey.[65]

In fact, however, Warren championed the DeLancey cause in England from 1747 until his death in July 1752. His period of greatest effectiveness was from 1747 to 1749, when he was at the height of his naval fame and a new star on the London political horizon. He used his past friendship with Clinton to ingratiate himself with Newcastle and Lincoln, and obtained the lieutenant governor's commission for DeLancey through their influence. In 1749, however, a series of rumors swept New York that Warren had lost his political power and that the ministry would soon act against the DeLancey faction in New York.[66] What seems to have happened is that Warren's influence in the early years of the Clinton administration depended upon Bedford's assumption of the secretaryship in 1748, and that Warren's decline in power resulted from his quarrel with Anson and Sandwich in 1749. Bedford had known and admired Warren as a sailor and was probably thus open to his suggestions on colonial affairs. Early in 1749, however, Warren led the parliamentary opposition to the new navy bills introduced by Sandwich and Anson, and this must have antagonized Bedford, as the political patron of Sandwich and Anson and the man responsible for Warren's entering parliament.[67] Thus when DeLancey began to muffle his opposition to Clinton after 1750, Warren's standing was much weaker than it had been. But from the Chief Justice's point of view, Warren's decline made little difference. At the crucial moments of DeLancey's career he had singlehandedly provided enough weight in the conduct of colonial affairs to enable DeLancey to challenge the Governor's authority and to overawe the population with his interest and power.

65. Clinton to Colden, March 11, 1748, NYHS, *Colls.*, 1919, p. 364; Peter Warren to Clinton, December 1747, extract, *ibid.*, 1919, p. 432; Clinton's instructions for Catherwood, December 4, 1748, Clinton MSS.; R.,H. Morris to H. Clinton, January 13, 1750, Clinton MSS., X, C.L.; Warren to Clinton, October 18, 1747, G/Am/6, no. 37, Gage MSS., S.A.S.
66. J. Ayscough to Colden, May 9, 1749, Bancroft Transcripts, Colden, I, 101, NYPL; Clinton to Colden, November 6, 1749, NYHS, *Colls.*, 1920, pp. 149–150; R. H. Morris to Alexander, June 6, 1750, *Cal. Stevens Papers*, I, 142.
67. Walpole to Horace Mann, March 4, 1749, in Toynbee, *Letters of Horace Walpole*, II, 364.

The stage is now set for a consideration of the negotiations in England that were to determine the course of politics in New York. The backing of the ministry and the organizations of imperial control, which any American politician needed to dominate the government of a colony, depended on the aid of such relatives and representatives as Newcastle, Lincoln, Warren, Catherwood, and Charles. Clinton's connections ought to have been strong enough to preserve him in his government, but his lack of political ability put them at a disadvantage.[68]

III

The English aspect of the Clinton-DeLancey contest seems chaotic in contrast to the conflict between Cosby and Morris, which had taken on the formality of an adversary proceeding. Frequently, however, the resolution of a New Yorker's problems in England required a series of narrow and seemingly unrelated solicitations, and James DeLancey was a master of the art. His first efforts against Clinton in England were an extension of his opposition to the Governor's war plans in 1746 and 1747.

In response to the Duke of Newcastle's letter of April 9, 1746, the governors of the northern colonies in North America began to raise men for an expedition against the French in Canada. The troops they raised collected in Albany during the summer, and when Governor William Gooch of Virginia declined to assume command, Clinton was left with the problem of commanding and providing for more than 1,600 men. This expedition differed from earlier American military efforts in that the royal government now offered to assume some of the expense. Newcastle suggested that the crown pay the salaries of officers and men, but that the colonies provide for their subsistence.[69]

68. Consider, for instance, the ground Clinton lost during the years he thought Warren and Charles were his English allies.

69. C.O. 5:45, I, foll. 56–57, PRO; T. 64:44, foll. 2–3, PRO; Osgood, *Eighteenth Century*, IV, 185–186. See also, Arthur H. Buffinton, "The Canada Expedition of 1746: Its Relation to British Politics," *American Historical Review*, XLV (1940), 552–580; V. H. Palstits, "A Scheme for the

The New York assembly, however, felt no responsibility for the levies of the other colonies, no matter how poorly they had been equipped and provisioned. The New Yorkers also thought that their Independent Companies ought to subsist out of their own pay and that the crown ought to supply presents for the Indians, though they did provide handsomely for many phases of the expedition.

The assembly suggested that, in the absence of funds from England, Clinton ought to raise money by drawing bills of exchange. Clinton did so, and was forced to pledge his personal estate in order to secure the bills. He ascribed the reluctance of the assembly to underwrite the war to the DeLancey faction's advocacy of the neutrality and their desire to embarrass him personally: if the expedition were to fail because of his lack of leadership and interest, the ministry might recall him in disgrace.[70]

In May 1747, for instance, Clinton notified the assembly that

Conquest of Canada in 1746," American Antiquarian Society, *Proceedings,* New Series, XVII (1905–1906), 69–92.

70. Statement of Case, 1746/7, Clinton MSS., C.L.; Clinton to Newcastle, May 11, 1747, and Clinton to Bedford, August 15, 1748, *New York Col. Docs.,* VI, 340–342, 429–430; Smith, *History,* II, 82–83. Smith contended that Clinton took the assembly's suggestion that he draw bills of credit as a hint, which he "improved greatly to his own emolument." The subsequent history of these bills indicates that they were never fully redeemed, and to the end of his administration Clinton feared that he would be jailed as a debtor and would not be able to raise bail. Clinton to H. Clinton, January 21, 1752, Clinton MSS., C.L. Smith also contended that Clinton's accounts for the expedition were £84,000 sterling (they were closer to £93,000, in fact) and supposed that "the governor returned to England a fortune very little short of that sum." Smith, *History,* II, 159. Labaree (*DAB,* IV, 226) accepts Smith's estimate. Clinton doubtless profited from the sale of military commissions and from granting supply contracts for the expedition, but it is unlikely that his profits were anywhere near so large or that they came from the bills of exchange. In fact, although Clinton financed William Johnson's activities with bills of exchange, he enjoined Johnson not to reveal the fact, in order that the assembly would think Johnson had assumed the expense himself, and would feel obligated to pay him. Clinton to W. Johnson, September 7, 1747, in Sullivan, *Johnson Papers,* I, 114–115. This was not the tactic of a man anxious to draw upon his credit and to proliferate bills of exchange. It may be, however, that Clinton was not fully aware of the consequences of drawing the bills at the outset, for it appears that at least R. H. Morris was in favor of such a procedure. R. H. Morris to Alexander, June 3, 1747, Rutherfurd Collection, IV, 49, NYHS.

the troops at Albany were likely to disband for lack of pay, and asked the representatives to indemnify him against protests of the bills of exchange. The assembly flatly refused, and on May 2 Clinton and the council were forced to accept an agreement, signed by six merchants, to furnish the £5,500 sterling required to pay the troops. The merchants balked at paying the money, however, and on May 5 the council agreed to extend the time for drawing the bills of exchange to ninety days. These merchants, especially David Clarkson and Paul Richard, were among Clinton's stoutest enemies, and he knowingly fell deeply into their debt, acknowledging that "the greatest enemies I had in the Assembly subscribed to get me under their lash and made it a point for nobody to take my bills but them." [71] Clinton secured the loan by issuing bills of exchange on the treasury and the paymaster general, but he was to be personally liable for the amount of the bills if they were not honored, and he would have to pay a re-exchange of 20 percent as well.[72]

The Governor was, very reasonably, disturbed about this personal responsibility for the bills, and he sent Catherwood to England in December 1746 for the sole purpose of obtaining their payment or indemnification. Governor Shirley had approved of drawing the bills, and assured Clinton that they would be paid when parliament provided for the expenses of the expedition. This assurance was encouraging, since Shirley was in charge of liquidating the accounts of the expedition for the treasury, and through the efforts of Catherwood, Newcastle, and Lincoln a considerable number of the bills were paid at this time.[73]

71. Clinton to Andrew Stone, July 24, 1747, *New York Col. Docs.*, VI, 377.
72. *Cal. Coun. Min.*, p. 364; Smith, *History*, II, 101–103. See also, Clark, *The Rise of the British Treasury*, pp. 88–89. The funds were generally raised from merchants who would accept the bills of exchange the governor drew upon the home government. In New York, unlike Massachusetts and other colonies, the assembly refused to indemnify the governor for issuing the bills. An indemnity was a legal exemption from the penalties or liabilities of nonpayment of the bills. The bills were also subject to re-exchange, or the damages incurred by nonpayment.
73. Clinton to Lords of Treasury, December 1746, Clinton MSS., IV; Wraxall to Clinton, October 27, 1747, Clinton MSS., C.L.; Shirley to Clinton, September 27, 1747, extract, *New York Col. Docs.*, VI, 398; Shirley to New-

In the fall of 1748, however, after Catherwood had returned to New York, Clinton suddenly received word that the treasury had stopped payment of his bills. He complained bitterly to William Pitt, the paymaster general, that this action "will embarrass my affairs to that degree that I shall not know how to extricate my-self." [74] The treasury's justification of its action was that Clinton had never submitted to Governor Shirley for their liquidation complete accounts of his expenses, accompanied by proper vouchers.[75] Clinton thereupon sent Catherwood to England once more, and furnished him with fuller accounts. His anxiety to be compensated for his expenses can be imagined when we learn that he had drawn bills for £93,162.16.3, and that payment had been stopped after £56,150.1.3 had been redeemed, leaving Clinton liable for bills worth £37,012.15.0.[76]

The accounts were sent to Shirley for examination and recommendation, but meanwhile the London merchants who had come into possession of Clinton's bills, led by DeLancey's London correspondent William Baker, began to demand immediate payment. The chancellor of the exchequer, Henry Pelham, informed them that no money had been appropriated for this service and that the bills could not be paid immediately since the board of trade, the paymaster general, and the secretary at war had been ordered to consider the merchants' memorial and relevant papers in order to lay

castle, December 28, 1747, C.O. 5:45, I, fol. 101, PRO; Treasury Minute Book, March 24, 1748, T. 29:31, fol. 104, PRO; Clark, *Rise of the British Treasury*, p. 95 and n. 93. In early 1747, Clinton banked heavily on the influence of Newcastle, Pelham, and Shirley to have his bills paid. Since they were the southern secretary, the head of the treasury, and the liquidator of the expedition's accounts for the treasury, he had reason to be sanguine. On the other hand, he also thought Johnson could enlist Warren for the effort, for he had not yet realized the strength of Warren's attachment to the DeLanceys. Clinton to W. Johnson, September 7, 1747, in Sullivan, *Johnson Papers*, I, 114–115.

74. Clinton to Pitt, September 5, 1748, Clinton MSS., VIII, C.L.; Treasury Minute Book, July 13, 1748, T. 29:31, fol. 105, PRO.

75. Treasury Minute Book, November 9, 1748, T. 29:31, fol. 162, PRO; J. West to Clinton, November 22, 1748, Clinton MSS., C.L.

76. Board of Trade Report, February 28, 1750, T. 64:44, foll. 93b–94, PRO.

the question before parliament "for their deliberation and Judgment." [77]

Catherwood applied to Pelham for the payment of Clinton's bills, but was told that he must apply instead to the board of trade, which was considering the matter. Catherwood despaired of the board's activity in mid-summer 1749 and petitioned the Duke of Bedford and Henry Pelham on Clinton's behalf, but they both treated the petition formally and sent it to the treasury. Shirley was convinced, however, that Catherwood was "in a fair way of getting thro your [Clinton's] Accounts." [78]

The board of trade began its extensive investigation of the 1746 expedition on June 28, 1749, and carefully considered the demands of all the colonies for repayment of expenses. Unluckily, Clinton's accounts were mislaid, but duplicates arrived in December. Catherwood appeared before the board (plus Pitt and Henry Fox), as did Shirley and the agents of the other colonies and the English merchants holding the bills. The board compiled a lengthy report, which it presented to the treasury on February 28, 1750.[79]

The report discussed the requests of each colony separately and gave a great deal of attention to New York. Several of Clinton's claims were rejected, particularly those for his own and Catherwood's military salaries, and Shirley's liquidation of Clinton's accounts was accepted. The board thus recommended payment of all but £9,739.1.0 of the full £93,837.9.6 that Clinton had claimed as the expenses for the expedition, which led Robert Hunter Morris to

77. R. H. Morris to H. Clinton, January 13, 1749, Clinton MSS., X, C.L.; Treasury Minute Book, February 9, 1749, T. 29:31, fol. 183, PRO.

78. Treasury Minute Book, April 11, 1749, T. 29:31, fol. 193, PRO; Catherwood's memorial to Bedford on behalf of Clinton, June 7, 1749, C.O. 5:1096, foll. 120, 123, PRO; Catherwood to H. Pelham, [June 9, 1749, delivered], Clinton MSS.; Shirley to Clinton, June 26, 1749, Clinton MSS., IX, C.L.

79. *Board of Trade Journal,* 1742–1749, pp. 429–430, 454–455, 457, 460, 462, 464, 466–471; *ibid.,* 1750–1753, pp. 38–42; Board of Trade Report, February 28, 1750, T. 64:44, PRO. The report was signed by Halifax, J. Pitt, J. Grenville, Dupplin, and Francis Fane of the board of trade, William Pitt (paymaster general), and Henry Fox (secretary at war).

assure Alexander that Clinton had "received his money on his own terms." [80]

Catherwood was not satisfied to leave Clinton with such a large encumbrance, however, and he wrote him that Halifax and Grenville (a member of the board of trade) had taken his part, but that Fox and Pitt were "great sticklers against you." Catherwood also suggested, as Clinton had suspected, that Shirley had sacrificed Clinton's interests in order to have his own accounts liquidated in full. [81] Pelham, the agent thought, was out of humor with Clinton for having granted himself a lieutenant general's pay during the expedition. [82] Nevertheless, by May 1750 Catherwood and Shirley were cooperating to secure the crown's discharge for the amount of their accounts, lest the accounts be "overhall'd" again. [83]

Both Shirley and Catherwood had good cause for concern, for the DeLanceyite New York merchants and their allies in London were pressing the two governors to make good on the bills. The London merchants were led by Samuel Storke and Alderman Baker, who appeared frequently before the treasury, and were told that the Lords could appropriate no more money for the payment of the bills than parliament had already appropriated in accordance with the board of trade report. [84] The treasury suggested to Catherwood that he contact the merchants holding the bills in order to recom-

80. Board of Trade Report, February 28, 1750, T. 64:44, foll. 49–77, passim; R. H. Morris to Alexander, March 3, 1750, *Cal. Stevens Papers*, I, 158.
81. Observation, Catherwood to Clinton, May 29, 1750, Clinton MSS.; Clinton to Catherwood, April 20, 1749, Clinton MSS., IX, C.L. Catherwood and Clinton were not alone in their suspicion of Shirley. Elisha Williams accused the Massachusetts governor of doing "a dirty job" for the ministry, "whose least concern" was of "doing justice." Schutz, *Shirley*, pp. 155–156.
82. Catherwood to Clinton, April 2 and May 24, 1750, Clinton MSS., C.L.
83. Catherwood to Clinton, May 29, 1750, Clinton MSS., C.L. Parliament voted the funds suggested by the board of trade report in mid-1750, but the warrants for payment of New York were not issued until January 8, 1751. Warrants relating to money, Lords of Treasury to Paymaster General, T. 53:43, foll. 476–477; Treasury Minute Book, December 18, 1750, and January 8, 1751, T. 29:31, foll. 334, 337, PRO; Stock, *Proceedings of British Parliaments*, V, 416–417, 425.
84. Shirley to Newcastle, January 23, 1753, Add. MSS. 32731, fol. 100, B.M.; Catherwood to Clinton, March 4, 1751, Clinton MSS., C.L.; Treasury Minute Book, September 12, 1750, T. 29:31, fol. 305, PRO.

mend that they accept partial payment in proportion to the amount voted by parliament. Catherwood did so, but the merchants refused, "being principally supported and advised thereto by Alderman Baker and Storke (two bitter enemies)," who demanded payment in full. Baker reportedly wished that he could throw Catherwood in jail.[85]

Catherwood then asked the treasury to pay the bills to save Clinton from the re-exchange, but was refused on the grounds that such action would make the merchants "murderous." Catherwood was now desperate, but he devised a scheme whereby he could discharge Clinton's remaining debts if he secured £5,000 more than the sum voted by parliament. He solicited Pelham's aid. At the outset the First Lord of the Treasury said he could not act without parliamentary sanction, but he later fell in with the scheme ("by my frequent importunities and other assistance procured"), though he considered it very dangerous. On March 4, 1751, Catherwood announced that Clinton was free from all encumbrances, despite the opposition of "the haughty and imperious Alderman." Catherwood emphasized that the matter must be kept secret, even from Robert Hunter Morris, "unless your Excellency will expose Your self to your own prejudice and my discredit with the Ministry, who are made believe you are to advance £1600 out of your own pocket to make good your bills and certificates besides £3700 of bills disallowed." [86]

The suspicious Governor was not sure that he had really been cleared, however, and he pressed Robert Hunter Morris and his son to check his accounts. He feared that the New York merchants might arrest him as soon as he left his government and throw him in jail for want of bail, and he therefore began solicitations to enter parliament, thinking that this would protect him against arrest for debt.[87] The wheel had come full circle, since Clinton had originally

85. Catherwood to Clinton, March 4, 1751, Clinton MSS., C.L.
86. *Ibid.* The alderman referred to is William Baker.
87. Clinton to H. Clinton, December 16, 1752, Clinton Letterbook, pp. 152–153; Clinton to R.H. Morris, December 25, 1752, Clinton Letterbook, p. 155; Clinton to H. Clinton, January 21, 1752, Clinton MSS., C.L.

sought the government of New York because he was being hounded by his creditors.

Thus DeLancey failed to disrupt the expedition against Canada by inhibiting the assembly's participation, and his influence with Clinton's London creditors also failed to prevent Clinton from discharging his financial responsibilities. But the Chief Justice did make it clear to the Governor that New York was not a profitable post for him, and that an American's resentment could reach into Whitehall. Above all, DeLancey convinced Clinton that he would do well to leave New York.

IV

The selection of his successor in office was one of Clinton's major concerns almost from the moment of his own appointment to the governorship of New York. At first his interest was essentially economic: he wanted to sell the office at a profit in order to return to potentially lucrative wartime naval command. Later, although still determined to improve his fortune in the succession to his government, he also had a political objective, namely, keeping the governorship out of the control of the DeLancey faction. As we have already seen, the struggle for succession largely determined the course of politics in New York, since it revealed where the sympathies of the imperial administration lay in the contest for local political control. Cosby and Clarke had both stabilized their governments only after receiving signs of imperial approval, and the issue between Clinton and DeLancey was to a great extent simply one of whom the ministry would favor in assigning Clinton's successor.

During the first five years of Clinton's tenure, the succession question took the deceptively simple form of the protracted negotiation, already briefly noted, between the Governor and Sir Peter Warren for the sale of the government of New York. From the fall of 1742 until the fall of 1747, Warren made a series of attempts to purchase the office. With the wisdom of hindsight Clinton later observed that "Sir Peter Warren had set his heart on this government, till by his good fortune his hopes was rais'd above it." [88] It seems clear that Warren originally desired the office as a hedge against peace, which might stifle his prospects of naval promotion and profit. After his fabulous prize-taking successes in 1745, however, he continued to solicit for the government, probably both as a mark of his increasing interest in his wife's homeland and as an indication of his newly-elevated status, much as a newly rich London merchant might seek out a landed estate in the English countryside. After 1746, of course, he was also interested in furthering the political prospects of his DeLancey in-laws in New York.

Warren first mentioned his aspiration to be governor in 1742, when he wrote that if Clinton did not consider it worthwhile to come to New York, he would "be glad to make a very advantagious proposal" for the post.[89] So far as we know, the subject was then dropped until April 1745, when Warren began serious solicitations in England for either the government of New Jersey or that of New York. He asked Admiral Anson's aid in obtaining the New Jersey government, which would be a stepping-stone to New York once peace had come. In New York, he asserted, "I shou'd be at the Pinnackle of my ambition and happiness, for I take it to be so slippery as that to which wee aspire, in a Military way, where tho' wee soar very high, wee seldom can support ourselves long." Warren claimed that Clinton endorsed his ambitions and had recommended him to Lincoln and the Pelhams, and that Sir John Norris would also lend him his aid.[90]

88. Clinton to Bedford, August 15, 1748, *New York Col. Docs.*, VI, 429.

89. Warren to Clinton, October 26, 1742, Clinton MSS., I, C.L. At this time Warren was acting as Clinton's New York agent in receiving the £1,200 out of the provincial quit rents directed by royal warrant. He remitted £250 with this letter.

90. Warren to Anson, April 2, 1745, Add. MSS. 15957, foll. 152–153, B.M. Warren recommended his appointment to a colonial government on the grounds that sea officers made the best governors by reason of their knowledge of the colonies and the vulnerability of the colonies to attack by sea. Warren solicited Newcastle's aid at this time, as well. Warren to Newcastle, June 18, 1745, quoted in Stokes, *Iconography*, IV, 590. See also, Warren to Anson, June 19, 1745, Add. MSS. 15957, fol. 158, B.M.

William and Samuel Baker handled the negotiations in England, and spoke to Newcastle and Anson on Warren's behalf, soliciting his promotion to an admiralcy and his nomination to an American government. His success in taking the fortress of Louisbourg rendered the ministry especially anxious to please him, and in August 1745 the Bakers were able to report Henry Pelham's assurance that Warren could have the New Jersey post when it came vacant and his opinion that he could gain New York through his friendship with Clinton. They advised him, however, to concentrate on promotion to a flag as being the best route to further perferment.[91]

Meanwhile Clinton was increasingly dissatisfied with his situation in New York: "Whilst I am fatiguing and fretting myself to peaces about a stubborn Dutch Assembly, who cant get to do any one thing they should either for themselves or to assist our neighbors, the Flags and Commids. [Commodores?] are making immense fortunes." [92] Once he found that Warren had taken prizes worth £50,000, Clinton determined to succeed him in the command of the North American squadron, which would be more profitable than the government of New York. He began negotiations with Warren in hopes of selling his post for £5,500 and returning to the fleet.[93]

Warren, who now had all the money he would ever need, offered Clinton "one third of all the Profits of the Government while I shou'd continue there, and in Case Mrs. Clinton shou'd Survive you during that time I wou'd allow her five hundred Pounds a year," and enjoined Clinton to keep the offer a secret.[94] In October 1745, Warren found that he was to be appointed governor of Cape Breton, but wrote Newcastle that he would prefer a naval command or the government of New York or New Jersey. Warren accepted the Cape Breton post, however, and at the same time he rejected Clinton's price for the government of New York as too high, "if I must give up my half pay as an Admiral, which will be dayly growing." The government of Cape Breton was more profitable than

91. W. and S. Baker to Warren, August 1, 1745, Warren MSS., C.L.
92. Clinton to [?], August 27, 1745, incomplete, Clinton MSS., II, C.L.
93. *Ibid.;* Clinton's memo, "A scheme how to get home," Clinton MSS., II, C.L.
94. Warren to Clinton, August 28, 1745, Clinton MSS., II, C.L.

Clinton's, and he would prefer to retire in New York as a private gentleman rather than pay such a sum.[95]

The negotiation lapsed for several months, until Clinton renewed it in April 1746. Clinton rejected Warren's proposal on the grounds that he, too, would lose his admiral's half-pay, and said that only a lump sum of money would satisfy him. He was determined to leave New York, "in case I can get any body to take it off of my hands without being a sufferer which I doubt not," but he preferred that his successor be Warren. On the other hand, if he did not receive a suitable offer, "as much as I dislike the place and ways of the people, yet rather then hurt my family [I] am determined to stay till I have met with an offer worth waiting for." Clinton was anxious that they come to an agreement lest the numerous seekers of the government in England get wind of its availability. Councillor Joseph Murray had already attempted to buy the government from Clinton, who told him it was promised to Warren.[96]

In June 1746, upon receiving word of Governor Morris' death, Warren again applied to Newcastle for the New Jersey government, and asked to succeed Clinton in New York as soon as he was better provided for elsewhere.[97] At this time he altered his terms for the New York job, offering Clinton either the one third share of the profits he had previously mentioned or a lump sum of £3,000. He planned to go to England to recover his health and to solicit one of the governments, but would stop in New York en route.[98] Clinton's reply was that they could settle the terms when they saw one

95. Warren to Newcastle, October 3, 1745, C.O. 5:44, I, foll. 96–97, PRO; Warren to Clinton, October 11, 1745, Clinton MSS., II, C.L.

96. [Clinton] to [Warren], April 24 and 27, [1746], Clinton MSS., III, C.L.

97. Warren to Newcastle, June 7, 1746, C.O. 5:44, I, fol. 51, PRO. Warren stated his desire for "a Government in the Colonys where my Family and Estate lyes." Warren to Thomas Corbett, June 2, 1746, G/Am/6, no. 2, Gage MSS., S.A.S. He also wrote similar letters to the Bakers and Sir John Norris at this time, June 7, 1746, G/Am/6, nos. 5, 6, Gage MSS., S.A.S.

98. Warren to Clinton, June 24, 1746, Clinton MSS., III, C.L. See also, Warren to Clinton, July 14, 1746, Clinton MSS., III, C.L. Warren apparently intended to become an absentee governor if the war resumed, returning to naval service: "for in a Civil Government under regular Laws, there is not the necessity there is in a Military one of the Governours residing." Warren to Sir John Norris, June 7, 1746, G/Am/6, no. 6, Gage MSS., S.A.S.

another, but that he hoped Warren had intended to offer £3,000 sterling. He calculated a third of his profits at £800 a year in New York currency, but admitted that this would greatly increase in peacetime. In any case, he preferred a lump sum of £3,000 sterling to as much as £400 sterling a year during his and Mrs. Clinton's lifetimes and during Warren's term in the government. "I do assure you dear Sir I had an ofer from the Lieutenant Governor [Clarke] before I left England to allow me five hundred pounds a year Sterling and the Cloathing but I was lead to believe the Government was a [?] four thousand pounds a year sterling and I question it wont be more then that shoud there be a peace." [99]

Unfortunately, only two additional letters survive to complete the story of the Warren-Clinton negotiation. In September 1746 Warren wrote the Governor from Boston to apologize that his last letter on the subject of the purchase had been delayed.[100] In October 1747 Warren wrote from England. He said that if Clinton decided to resign the New York government after returning home, "you may depend on my complying with the proposal that we were some time past in treaty about and you will find no difficulty in getting it transferred to me by the interest we can joyntly make here." [101] It appears, then, that the two admirals had come to terms in late 1746 or early 1747, but that Clinton was no longer willing to sell the post to Warren.

Undoubtedly, after the break with DeLancey in mid-1746, Clinton could no longer ignore the political implications of alienating the New York government to a brother-in-law of the Chief Justice. He later tried to convince the ministry that he had remained in his post in order to further the prosecution of the war and the 1746 expedition. He alleged that when Warren and Murray applied for his interest in choosing a successor, the DeLancey faction was in reality attempting "to make my Administration uneasy to me . . . For this Purpose the more effectually to lessen any Influence I

99. Clinton to Warren, [July 1746], Clinton MSS., III, C.L.
100. Warren to Clinton, September 8, 1746, Clinton MSS., IV, C.L.
101. Warren to Clinton, October 18, 1747, G/Am/6, no. 37, Gage MSS., S.A.S.

might have, it was spread abroad, that I designed to leave my Government and that Admiral Warren was to succeed me." At the same time, the DeLanceyites were, he said, attempting to obstruct the expedition against Canada in order to blacken his reputation with the ministry.[102] In short, Clinton's conspiratorial view of politics led him to believe that DeLancey and Warren were in league against his administration, and that Warren's solicitation of the succession was merely a part of the plot, undermining his authority in England and his prestige in New York, where it was being given out that Warren's English influence was greater than Clinton's.[103] From 1747 on, then, the problem of succession to the government of New York was inextricably interwoven with the domestic tangle of New York politics.

V

There were two continuing skirmishes for position in Anglo-American politics during the Clinton administration: Clinton's attempts to secure royal permission to return to England on his own terms, and his campaign to remove DeLancey from office and replace him with a Clinton ally. Each of these struggles extended throughout most of the administration and each was complex enough to demand a separate telling.

Governor Clinton's solicitation to return home began even before DeLancey's defection. The Governor had from the first found New York neither as profitable nor as hospitable as he had hoped, and he came to believe quite fervently that the rigorous American climate would prove the death of his entire family. From the time that Warren's success opened his eyes to the lucrativeness of naval service in wartime, Clinton continually solicited Newcastle and the admiralty for reassignment to naval command. After the break with DeLancey, his desire to return home was intensified and complicated. He was anxious to leave his problems behind him in America, but he was unwilling to abandon the control of New York to De-

102. Statement of Case, 1746/7, Clinton MSS., C.L.
103. Clinton to Bedford, August 15, 1748, *New York Col. Docs.*, VI, 429.

Lancey or to leave while his gubernatorial conduct was misunderstood by the imperial administration.

Clinton's prolonged campaign to secure leave to return to England began in connection with his quest for naval command during the negotiation with Warren for the sale of the New York government. His request was repeated in June and July 1746.[104] From this time until his departure from New York in 1753, Clinton persisted in his attempt, always stressing the need to recover his health and to repair his "private Affairs," by which he meant securing the payment of his bills of exchange and arranging a suitable retirement. Above all, he felt that he had to go to England as governor in order to facilitate the payment of his bills at home, lest he be arrested as a debtor before he could leave New York.[105] Clinton's financial encumbrance from the Canadian expedition had provided the opposition with a powerful lever against him, for he had already experienced the fears of a debtor. He was repeatedly put off by Newcastle and the ministry, and, characteristically, attributed his failure to the wicked designs of his enemies.

Within a few months, however, Clinton achieved an ironic success. In October 1747 he was informed that his nephew Lord Lincoln had secured him permission to return, and on the same day the king's formal leave arrived. Unfortunately, however, the same post contained DeLancey's commission as lieutenant governor of New York and instructions to Clinton to present DeLancey's commission before leaving America.[106] It would appear that Newcastle had arranged DeLancey's appointment on the hypothesis that he was aid-

104. Clinton to [?], August 27, 1745, incomplete, and Clinton's memo, "A scheme how to get home," Clinton MSS., II, C.L.; Clinton to Newcastle, June 10, 1746, *New York Col. Docs.*, VI, 309–310; Clinton to Newcastle, July 24, 1746, draft, Clinton MSS., C.L.; Newcastle to Lincoln, n.d. [1746?], Add. MSS. 33030, fol. 357, B.M.

105. For instance, Clinton to Andrew Stone, July 24, 1747, *New York Col. Docs.*, VI, 377; Clinton to Guerin, July 23, 1747, draft, Clinton MSS.; Clinton to Newcastle, August 1747, draft, Clinton MSS., VI, C.L.; Clinton to Newcastle, May 30, 1747, *New York Col. Docs.*, VI, 351.

106. Wraxall to Clinton, October 27, 1747, Clinton MSS.; Newcastle to Clinton, October 27, 1747, Clinton MSS., VI, C.L.

ing Clinton, for Peter Warren had assured the Duke that Clinton and DeLancey were on good terms.[107]

Newcastle's misguided assistance placed Governor Clinton in a quandry. By leaving the colony he would now surrender the executive to DeLancey, thereby endangering his allies in New York, laying himself open to DeLancey's interference in the payment of his bills, and doubtless losing all the perquisites of government that the lieutenant governor ought to share with an absentee governor. Governor Shirley convinced Clinton that his departure would needlessly play into the hands of the opposition, whereas an open contest might prove profitable to both crown and Governor. Clinton therefore determined to stand and fight—in New York against the aggressions of the assembly, and in England against the grant of the lieutenant governorship to DeLancey. He would remain in New York, he announced to Bedford, "till I can put an end to the present factions which are so Prejudicial to His Majestys authority." [108]

Meanwhile, across the Atlantic, the imperial authorities were rousing themselves to consider the situation in New York. Their concern was stimulated by a fierce controversy that had flared up in 1748 and 1749 over the New York–New Jersey border. A large area was disputed by the adjacent colonies, and land riots had been occasioned by a New Jersey land act setting out a line favorable to the East New Jersey proprietors, who thereupon sent Robert Hunter Morris to England in defense of their interests. Morris was immediately confronted with the opposition of the New York assembly's agent, Robert Charles, for it turned out that Peter Warren and the DeLanceys held title to lands claimed by New York.[109]

President Halifax of the board of trade was exercised over the

107. Clinton to Colden, January 31, 1748, Bancroft Transcripts, Colden, I, 59, NYPL. See also, Colden to Clinton, February 14, 1748, NYHS, *Colls.,* 1920, p. 13.

108. Clinton to Bedford, October 17, 1749, *New York Col. Docs.,* VI, 528. See also, Clinton to Thomas Corbett, June 11, 1749, Adm. 1:3818, PRO; Shirley to Clinton, June 26, 1749, Clinton MSS., IX, C.L.

109. Lilly, *Colonial Agents,* p. 175n23; R. H. Morris to Alexander, January 23, 1750, *Cal. Stevens Papers,* I, 142; *Board of Trade Journal,* 1742–1749, p. 440; Kemmerer, *Path to Freedom,* pp. 214–221.

situation, and suggested to Morris that the solution might be to combine the governments of the two colonies as they had been before 1738, in order to use the Independent Companies of New York for the protection of the New Jersey lands.[110] The board of trade discussed the question, and apparently reported to the privy council their approval of Halifax's plan of union. In the council, however, Bedford and Newcastle clashed over the plan, with Newcastle opposing it. A union of New York and New Jersey would jeopardize Clinton's administration, for the creation of a single government would very likely entail the removal of both Clinton and Belcher and the dispatch of a new governor to New York.[111]

Newcastle saved Clinton from imperial intervention in 1750, but the combination of turbulence in America and uneasiness in England resulted in a flurry of rumors of a change of government in New York. In April 1750 Catherwood wrote that Peter Warren was "soliciting underhand" for the job, and Colden appears to have been taken in by the story that Clinton had agreed to leave the administration to Warren.[112] In September 1750 William Shirley wrote Newcastle from Paris to ask for the New York post, leading Clinton to think that he had been betrayed by his fellow governor.[113] In June 1751 Clinton and some of his friends seem actually to have thought that Warren had been appointed to the governorship. Robert Hunter Morris assured them, however, that Warren had twice

110. Alexander to R. H. Morris, June 5, 1749, *Cal. Stevens Papers*, I, 136.

111. R. H. Morris to Alexander, January 6, 1750, March 24, 1750, March 3, 1751, *Cal. Stevens Papers*, I, 142, II, 6; Catherwood to Clinton, April 2, 1750, Clinton MSS., C.L.; Shirley to Newcastle, September 1, 1750 N.S., Add. MSS. 32722, fol. 212, B.M. For Newcastle's judgment of Bedford, see Newcastle to Pelham, September 2, 1750, in Williams, *Eighteenth-Century Constitution*, p. 82.

112. Catherwood to Clinton, April 2, 1750, Clinton MSS., C.L.; Alexander to R. H. Morris, September 10 and December 4, 1750, *Cal. Stevens Papers*, I, 172, 184.

113. Shirley to Newcastle, September 1, 1750 N.S., Add. MSS. 32722, fol. 212, B.M.; Charles H. Lincoln, ed., *Correspondence of William Shirley, Governor of Massachusetts and Military Commander in America, 1731–1760* (New York, 1912), I, 508–509; Clinton to R. H. Morris, September 8, 1750, and Colden to [R. H. Morris?], October 1, 1750, R. H. Morris Papers, I, 8, 10, NJHS.

been refused the government because of Bedford's opposition to his pretensions and Newcastle's defense of Clinton's interests.[114] It is true, as we shall see, that early in 1751 Halifax and Bedford had intended to send a strong new governor to New York. The change had been averted, however, by the board of trade's sluggishness in compiling the requested report on New York and by the quarrel between Newcastle and Bedford which ended with Bedford's retirement from office in June 1751. Thus the succession to the government of New York remained unaltered, but each report weakened Clinton's position a little more by lending credence to the DeLanceyite assertion that his English influence was declining.[115]

His brief show of strength against the assembly having expended itself, in September 1750 Clinton returned to his solicitations for permission to return home. This time he tried a new tack. He argued that the appointment of a new governor would prejudice his profits and his reputation, and suggested to Newcastle that he be allowed to be an absentee governor, receiving part of the lieutenant governor's salary plus his half-pay as admiral of the fleet.[116] In December 1750 he asked Bedford for a year's leave of absence. The Secretary refused to act, however, until the privy council had considered the board of trade report on New York, even after Lincoln had tried to exert his influence in Clinton's behalf.[117]

By late 1750 it was becoming increasingly apparent that Gov-

114. Clinton to Bedford, June 18, 1751, *New York Col. Docs.*, VI, 712; Alexander to R. H. Morris, June 20, 1751, *Cal. Stevens Papers*, II, 17; Shirley to Clinton, November 9, 1752, Clinton MSS., XII, C.L.; R. H. Morris to Alexander, January 6, 1751, *Cal. Stevens Papers*, II, 2; Alexander to R. H. Morris, September 16, 1750, *ibid.*, I, 172.

115. Thomas Penn to James Hamilton, March 30, 1751, Bancroft Transcripts, Penn, p. 243, NYPL. DeLancey propaganda in England and a growing awareness of the distressed state of royal government in New York began to weaken Clinton's strength at home. In May 1751 Catherwood was concerned to prove to Hardwicke that "the calumnies with which you [Clinton] are aspersed are false and groundless." Catherwood to Clinton, May 25, 1751, Clinton MSS., C.L. See also, below, n. 118.

116. R. H. Morris to Lincoln, July 1751, Clinton to R. H. Morris, September 8, 1750, R. H. Morris Papers, I, 19, 8, NJHS.

117. Clinton to Bedford, December 31, 1750, *New York Col. Docs.*, VI, 606; Catherwood to Clinton, March 5, March 12 and n.d. [March 21?], 1751, Clinton MSS., C.L.

ernor Clinton's fortunes were on the wane. "Clintons affairs in London," confessed Robert Hunter Morris, "are not in the best condition." [118] The Governor's intention to leave New York was well known in the province, and in February 1751 James DeLancey boldly tried to arrange a settlement with him. The Chief Justice offered to agree to any proposals Clinton made if the Governor would leave New York and present him with the lieutenant governor's commission. He boasted that he "could better afford it [the government of New York], for that the Assembly would give him more then anyone else." He also promised to pay Clinton the governor's share of the executive income until Clinton could sell the office and pledged not to displace any officeholder "that the Governor had put in or should put in." [119] DeLancey's offer came to nothing, perhaps only because Clinton could not get the permission necessary to return to England, but it marks a new stage in the history of the Clinton administration. DeLancey had ended his attempts to drive Clinton out and to disgrace him, and had begun to abate the violence of the opposition in New York so that the ministry would not be impelled to quash his lieutenant governor's commission.

In 1751 things continued to go badly for Clinton. By May 18, Bedford had seen the board of trade's report on New York, although it was not discussed by the privy council until August 6. He told Lincoln that the report criticized Clinton "for giving up the powers of the Crown," and declared his unwillingness to act independently of the privy council. Newcastle then requested the king personally to grant the leave to Clinton. He was refused, and this attempt to go over Bedford's head was not calculated to help the Governor with his superior.[120] By June 11, still before the privy council had acted, Bedford gave Catherwood his "final" answer, that he would not petition the king for Clinton's leave.[121]

In June Newcastle drove Bedford from office and chose the in-

118. R. H. Morris to Alexander, March 29, 1750, *Cal. Stevens Papers*, I, 161.
119. Ayscough's memorandum of a conversation with DeLancey, February 19, 1751, Clinton MSS., XI, C.L.
120. Catherwood to Clinton, May 17–18, 1751, Clinton MSS.; R. H. Morris to Clinton, May 22, 1751, Clinton MSS., XI, C.L.
121. Catherwood to Clinton, June 14, 1751, Clinton MSS., C.L.

effective Lord Holdernesse to replace him in the southern department. On July 5, 1751, Catherwood told Clinton that he had obtained his leave of absence, but he must have been mistaken, for in
January 1752 the Governor was still pressing his son to obtain the
leave. He stressed that a new governor's commission ought not to be
published until after he had left New York, lest he be apprehended
for his debts.[122] By this time Clinton had abandoned all thought of
acting as absentee governor, and was merely concerned to escape
from his administration. Lincoln asked Halifax, who by now had acquired most of the power over the administration of the colonies,
not to dispose of the government till Clinton's arrival in England.[123]

Halifax, however, was determined to send out a forceful governor in accordance with the suggestions in his board's report on the
state of New York. Both he and Bedford had been sympathetic to
Clinton in 1748, after he had proved himself a vigorous war governor and had begun to fight the assembly. But in 1750, after he had
given up the battle for the prerogatives of the crown, they began to
realize the true state of affairs in New York, and both decided that
Clinton was not a suitable person to govern there. Clinton was told
that Halifax had resolved that "none but a Nobleman of Fortune,
Integrity and Understanding shall be my successor." Even Newcastle later described the proposed successor as "a proper Person of
Weight." [124]

122. Catherwood to Clinton, July 5, 1751, Clinton to H. Clinton, January
21, 1752, Clinton MSS., C.L.; Williams, *Whig Supremacy*, pp. 322–323; *New
York Col. Docs.*, VI, 757ni; O. A. Sherard, *Lord Chatham: A War Minister in
the Making* (London, 1952), pp. 225–227. Newcastle forced Bedford to resign
by the simple step of persuading George II to remove Sandwich from the
admiralty. His patron, Bedford, then resigned from the ministry in anger.
His successor, Holdernesse, was a man of little political ability and even less
political influence. In May 1751 R. H. Morris reported that all plantation
business had come to a stop due to a "misunderstanding" between Bedford
and Newcastle. The latter had moved in council that a secretary for plantations
be appointed, but Bedford refused to assent to any diminution in his office.
Newcastle offered to change departments with him, Bedford refused, and
nothing more was done. R. H. Morris to Clinton, May 22, 1751, Clinton MSS.,
XI, C.L.; R. H. Morris to Clinton, March 3, 1751, *Cal. Stevens Papers*, II, 6.
123. R. H. Morris to Clinton, March 11, 1752, Clinton MSS., C.L.
124. Observations, Catherwood to Clinton, February 13 and 27, 1748,
December 8, 1749, and June 14, 1751, Clinton MSS.; Bedford to Clinton,

By early 1752 Clinton had decided to flee the province even without the king's permission. When he intimated this to the board of trade, they nervously asked Catherwood when the Governor intended to leave, and told Clinton that they thought it positively improper for him to go until he had the king's instructions as to "what Method of Administration of Government shall take place upon your leaving the Province." [125] In April 1752 Holdernesse forbade Clinton to quit New York without permission, and Clinton interpreted the order as the result of "the gross misrepresentations of my enemies." [126] He resigned himself to remaining, at the urging of James Alexander, who convinced him that his only immediate prospect of getting home, "to quit my Government and Company," was "very probably to a Person, disagreeable to me and my Friends here." [127]

Having resigned himself to wait for his successor, Clinton determined to salvage what he could from his remaining administration. Unlike Cosby and Clarke, he had never involved himself in land speculations, since he was constantly planning to leave the province. Now, however, he began negotiations with Surveyor General Colden to acquire lands in New York. He apathetically continued to request the leave of absence, and retired to contemplate his misfortunes from his "billyard" table.[128]

November 1, 1749, Clinton MSS., IX; Ayscough to R. H. Morris, November 24, 1752, Clinton Letterbook, p. 126, C.L.; Newcastle to H. Walpole, June 29, 1754, Add. MSS. 32735, fol. 598, B.M.

125. Clinton to Lords of Trade, April 8, 1752, *New York Col. Docs.,* VI, 759; Lords of Trade to Clinton, June 16, 1752, *ibid.,* VI, 761–762; *Board of Trade Journal,* 1750–1753, p. 325.

126. Clinton to Lords of Trade, n.d. [post June 16, 1752], *New York Col. Docs.,* VI, 762–763; Clinton to R. H. Morris, July 26, 1752, Clinton Letterbook, p. 71, C.L.

127. Clinton to R. H. Morris, July 1752, R. H. Morris Papers, I, 45, NJHS; Clinton to R. H. Morris, July 26, 1752, Clinton Letterbook, p. 75, C.L. In April the man of war at New York was being outfitted to carry Clinton and his family to England. Alexander to R. H. Morris, April 7, 1752, draft, Rutherfurd Collection, Small Scrapbook, no. 155, NYHS.

128. Clinton to Colden, July 28, 1752, Clinton Letterbook, pp. 77–79; G. Banyar to O. DeLancey, November 5, 1753, in Sullivan, *Johnson Papers,* I, 391–392; Ayscough to Catherwood, December 8, 1752, Clinton Letterbook, p.

Early in 1753 William Shirley put in once more for the administration of New York. The Bakers and other London merchants friendly with DeLancey opposed his candidacy, but Clinton now wished him well: "I hope to God he will Succeed for I dont know a person in the world they [the faction] dread more." [129] Halifax decided against Shirley, however, and on May 29, 1753, the board of trade was ordered to prepare a representation proposing Sir Danvers Osborn as governor of New York in place of Clinton, "who has desired leave to return to England." [130] Osborn was Halifax's brother-in-law, and those New Yorkers who remembered the similarly connected Governor Cosby may well have blanched at the choice.

On November 5, 1753, George Clinton and his family set sail for England. It had taken eight years for the Governor to escape from the province he hated so much, and he departed in defeat. He had not been able to secure permission to come home when he wished, and he was certainly not returning on his own terms. His powerful connection and the energetic representations of Catherwood and Morris had been of no avail, and upon his departure his opponents in New York confidently anticipated their succession to the control of the colony.

VI

Clinton's attempts to control the disposition of the lieutenant governorship and to strip DeLancey of his offices constitute another long and frustrating episode in the Governor's public career. By November 1747 he was complaining to Bedford that his former adviser ought not "to be continued in the employment he now enjoys,

146; Ayscough to R. H. Morris, November 24, 1752, Clinton Letterbook, p. 126, C.L.

129. Clinton to H. Clinton, March 12, 1753, Clinton MSS., XIII, C.L.; Shirley to Newcastle, January 23, 1753, Add. MSS. 32731, foll. 101–102, B.M.

130. *Board of Trade Journal*, 1750–1753, p. 423; Clinton to H. Clinton, May 14, 1753, Clinton MSS., XII, C.L.; Charles letter, June 11, 1753, William Smith, Jr., Papers, III, 231, NYPL. On the other hand, one might accept the sceptical view that Halifax merely desired the New York government "for a sick brother-in-law that needed an easy post." Schutz, *Shirley*, p. 166.

or in any other service under the Crown," [131] and from 1747 to 1753 he single-mindedly fought DeLancey's continuation as chief justice and appointment as lieutenant governor.

Clinton's strategy immediately after the break with DeLancey was to favor the selection of Cadwallader Colden as lieutenant governor. In December 1746 he tried to explain to Newcastle that Colden's appointment would aid the New York administration, reward Colden "for his past Services," and "prevent inconvenient sollicitations on that head." [132] The Governor promised to keep up his efforts for Colden (which he did, from 1746 to 1753) and Colden, in return, professed to think that his appointment would prove that "the King is resolved to support his prerogative in the plantations." [133] Despite Clinton's recommendation, however, DeLancey was appointed lieutenant governor and Clinton's friends were unable to dislodge him from the place.

In 1748 Clinton remonstrated with Newcastle for his appointment of DeLancey. He demanded that he be allowed to stop De-Lancey's commission as lieutenant governor, and leave Colden, as president of the council, in command of the province when he left. He maintained that he would retain his unwelcome post rather than deliver the lieutenant governor's commission to DeLancey as instructed, blaming the election of the heavily DeLanceyite 1748 assembly on the demonstration of the strength of Sir Peter Warren's English influence. Clinton also argued that it was DeLancey's intention to make him so miserable in his government that he would leave, "as he can receive no benefitt by being Lieutenant Governour during my stay here." [134]

By Clinton's admission, the exhibition of English influence was

131. Clinton to Bedford, November 6, 1747, in Lord John Russell, ed., *Correspondence of John, fourth Duke of Bedford* (London, 1842–1846), I, 285–286.

132. Clinton to Newcastle, December 9, 1746, *New York Col. Docs.*, VI, 313.

133. Clinton to Colden, January 22, 1747, NYHS, *Colls.*, 1919, p. 357; Colden to Shirley, July 25, 1749, Bancroft Transcripts, Colden, I, 105, NYPL.

134. Clinton to Newcastle, February 13, 1748, *New York Col. Docs.*, VI, 416–417; Clinton to Newcastle, September 30, 1748, Add. MSS. 32716, fol. 401, B.M.

a crucial factor in the conduct of New York politics and, unhappily for the Governor, the first round had been won decisively by De-Lancey. Warren's emergent interest in London coincided with Newcastle's blunder in providing DeLancey with the promise of the lieutenant governorship. True, Clinton did not have to deliver the commission until he left the province, and there was a chance of having it revoked, but the knowledge that it had been granted was a powerful weapon in DeLancey's hands. As Clinton sadly acknowledged, the commission stifled independence among potential allies of the administration, who feared being abandoned to DeLancey's resentment when the Governor left.[135]

After learning of DeLancey's appointment in October 1747, Clinton was faced with the double problem of invalidating DeLancey's commission and securing it for Colden or another friend. Alexander and Smith assured the Governor of his legal authority to suspend the commission and in February 1749 he notified Bedford that he had found it necessary to do so. Subsequently, however, Governor Shirley dissuaded Clinton from carrying the plan through on the grounds that it ran "a risque of displeasing your friends at home" and he lamely requested Bedford to revoke the commission himself in October 1749.[136]

In the fall of 1749 Clinton determined to persuade the ministry to help him out. He had heard that agent John Sharpe, Solicitor General William Murray, and the Duke of Newcastle all thought the home government ought to support him by quashing the commission. He also had reason to be optimistic about Halifax, who he was told "would by no means have the *C.J.* [DeLancey] left to represent you" and would probably support anyone designated by

135. Clinton to Newcastle, May 30, 1747, *New York Col. Docs.*, VI, 351. In effect, DeLancey's relationship to Clinton was like that of the Prince of Wales to the first two Hanoverian kings—the anticipation of future power at Leicester House gave focus and encouragement to the development of an opposition to the incumbent ruler. Clinton to Newcastle, September 30, 1748, Add. MSS. 32716, foll. 399–400, B.M.; Sedgwick, *Letters from George III to Bute,* pp. xi–xix.

136. Clinton to Bedford, February 24, 1749, *New York Col. Docs.*, VI, 475–476; Clinton to Bedford, October 17, 1749, *ibid.*, VI, 528; Shirley to Clinton, January 23, 1749, Clinton MSS., IX, C.L.

Clinton at his departure. Besides, Clinton had come to realize that if he personally suspended the commission, the DeLanceyites "would entertain hopes of having that suspension removed." [137] On the other hand, action by the ministry would restore the faith of New Yorkers in the authority of their governor.

Colden and Clinton broadened their attack against DeLancey by seeking to have him removed from the chief justiceship. As early as March 21, 1748, Colden had advised Clinton to ask for a legal opinion "whether one man can be Governor Chancellor & Chief Justice at the same time." [138] His idea was to demonstrate that if DeLancey were left in command of the province as lieutenant governor he would be in a position unconstitutionally to dominate both the executive and the judiciary. In 1749 Clinton requested the board of trade and Bedford to replace Chief Justice DeLancey with an English lawyer, since the past disorders in New York government, "have proceeded from persons ambitious to have that office, and by the several Relations and Dependencies & Parties, which arise on any party struggle, where, in so small a Country, the Judges commonly take sides, and the Administration of Common Justice becomes precarious." [139]

In 1749 Shirley, who was then in London, informed Clinton that Colden's reputation was very poor. Henry Pelham had been told that Colden was actually "a tool to the C.J. and Sir Peter, under the colours of assisting me [Clinton]." [140] In April 1749, Cather-

137. Catherwood to Clinton, October 10, 1749, Clinton MSS., C.L.; Clinton to Colden, November 6, 1749, Bancroft Transcripts, Colden, I, 124, NYPL; Clinton to Bedford, October 17, 1749, *New York Col. Docs.*, VI, 528.

138. Colden to Clinton, March 21, 1748, NYHS, *Colls.*, 1920, p. 26. DeLancey was later perplexed by the question of whether or not he would be allowed to retain both offices. DeLancey to Archbishop Herring, October 15, 1753, William Smith MSS., I, 4, NYHS. No new chief justice was appointed until after DeLancey's death, but he seems to have been unsure of his status. *New York Col. Docs.*, VII, 370.

139. Clinton to Bedford, July 7, 1749, Clinton to Lords of Trade, November 26, 1749, *New York Col. Docs.*, VI, 515, 537. See also, Colden to Shirley, July 25, 1749, Bancroft Transcripts, Colden, I, 112, NYPL.

140. Clinton to Colden, February 9, 1750, NYHS, *Colls.*, 1920, p. 190. DeLancey's propaganda against Colden in London had succeeded brilliantly.

wood recommended that Bedford appoint John Rutherford lieutenant governor. Councillor Rutherford was a firm supporter of Clinton's, and happened to be in London at the time.[141] In fact, however, Clinton had switched his hopes to Robert Hunter Morris, promising to solicit the lieutenant governorship for him in return for Morris' efforts in England to find the Governor a better job. Clinton offered to put Morris in the government after he had left the colony in exchange for half of the lieutenant governor's salary.[142]

As we have seen in relation to his solicitation to secure a leave of absence, the tide began to run against Clinton in the summer of 1750. The board of trade was investigating New York, and Bedford and Halifax were determined to preserve the *status quo* until the inquiry had been completed. As information was compiled, however, they began to realize the true extent of the disruption in New York government and were less inclined to humor Clinton.[143]

The Governor doggedly held to his course. Early in 1751 he introduced a new tactic, directly petitioning the king to appoint another lieutenant governor or to revoke DeLancey's commission.[144] By May 18, 1751, however, Bedford had seen the board of trade report and declared a plague on both houses: he now approved neither of Morris' appointment as lieutenant governor nor of DeLancey's succession to the administration.[145] Nevertheless, the situation remained extremely fluid. It seems that a commission for Morris had actually been made out and in the summer and fall New York was

---

Even at the time DeLancey's commission as lieutenant governor was issued, Wraxall had reported to Clinton that, "Dr Colden is not well spoke of here." Wraxall to Clinton, October 27, 1747, Clinton MSS., C.L.

141. Catherwood's petition to Bedford, April 20, 1749, C.O. 5:1096, fol. 102, PRO.

142. Smith, *History*, II, 129–130.

143. For instance, Catherwood to Clinton, July 24, 1750, Clinton MSS., C.L.

144. Opinion of the attorney and solicitor general, February 28, 1751, *New York Col. Docs.*, VI, 612–614; Catherwood to Clinton, March 4 and 5, 1751, Clinton MSS., C.L.; Clinton's petition, [February 28, 1751?], *New York Col. Docs.*, VI, 612.

145. Catherwood to Clinton, May 17, 1751, Clinton MSS., C.L.

alive with rumors of his appointment.[146] In July Clinton renewed his plan to suspend DeLancey's commission on his own authority and had a legal document drawn up for that purpose. He notified Bedford that he intended to leave Colden in charge of New York, acting on the Duke's hint to Catherwood that he would not agree to leaving DeLancey with the administration.[147]

Clinton's letter to Bedford must have arrived in England when the privy council was discussing the board of trade's report. At one of their sessions, the council sent for agent Catherwood to ask whether or not Clinton had suspended DeLancey, and whether or not he had the power to do so. Clinton gratuitously concluded from Catherwood's report of the meeting that, "had their Lordships been of opinion, I should not, or could not suspend C. Justice, they certainly would have told Mr Catherwood so, at the time they sent out to know of him, if I had suspended him, or had power to do it." [148]

At this stage, Clinton was tripped up by his own benefactor. Newcastle had been confused by Clinton's threats to suspend De-Lancey, and had told the lords of the privy council that the Governor had actually carried out the suspension. On that basis, the privy council decided to defer the choice of another lieutenant governor or governor until Clinton had come to England. Clinton thought that this decision indicated their approval of DeLancey's proposed suspension, and began to consider how he might accomplish it.[149]

Ironically, Clinton's own allies once again proved a hindrance. The precedent for such an act in New York was Cosby's suspension of Van Dam, which had left the government to Clarke, but Clinton's present adherents (Colden, Alexander, Smith) were the very opponents of Clarke who had charged that Van Dam's suspension

146. Smith, *History*, II, 144; Stokes, *Iconography*, IV, 629; Alexander to R. H. Morris, November 4, 1751, *Cal. Stevens Papers*, II, 23–24.

147. "Reasons for the Suspending of James DeLancey . . . ," July 1751, Clinton MSS., C.L.; Clinton to Bedford, July 18, 1751, *New York Col. Docs.*, VI, 726–727.

148. Catherwood to Clinton, September 13, 1751, and the observation, Clinton MSS., C.L.

149. Catherwood to Clinton, December 3, 1751, and the observation, Clinton MSS., C.L.

had been illegal. They could not in good conscience support a similar suspension against DeLancey: "Now what can they say in contradiction to their former Opinion? unless I can have some Authority to shew them from home, before, I embark." [150] Clinton's problem was complicated by the fact that he was afraid his majority in the New York council would not in any case support him against DeLancey without royal instructions to do so. And even if they held firm, DeLancey might secure a reversal of their opinion after Clinton had left New York, and thus succeed to the government.[151]

In February 1752 Clinton heard that the privy council had made out instructions for him to suspend DeLancey, but nothing came from England and the Governor floundered through his last year in office seeking an orderly conclusion to his dilemma. For one thing, he came to realize that Robert Hunter Morris would not be appointed lieutenant governor. Morris acknowledged in March 1752 that he had given up the solicitation, asserting that he did not think the post worthwhile if he could expect to receive no more support from the ministry than Clinton had. He had, he claimed, sought the government "with no other view but that of supporting the Authority of the Crown against a faction that were trampling it under foot." [152] The Governor was then forced to revert to his plan to leave Colden in command of New York when he left for Eng-

150. Clinton to Catherwood, February 18, 1752, Clinton Letterbook, p. 13, C.L.
151. *Ibid.*, pp. 14–16; Clinton to R. H. Morris, February 19, 1752, Clinton Letterbook, pp. 18–19, C.L. Clinton believed several of his allies would desert him in the New York council: Johnson because of his relationship to Peter Warren, Holland because of "his Relation and Intimacy with Mr. Watts and Wife" (Watts was a brother-in-law of DeLancey), and Kennedy because of "his timorous temper." Colden could not be expected to be present at a discussion of his own authority, and DeLancey and Murray would surely oppose him. Thus Alexander was the only sure vote for Colden. Chambers had not yet received his mandamus as a councillor, but Clinton had turned against him, thinking the DeLanceys had intimidated him, and instructed Catherwood not to press for his appointment. Clinton to Catherwood, February 18, 1752, Clinton Letterbook, pp. 14–16, C.L.; *Cal. Coun. Min.*, p. 384; Clinton to R. H. Morris, January 17, 1752, R. H. Morris Papers, I, 50, NJHS.
152. R. H. Morris to Clinton, March 11, 1752, Clinton MSS., C.L.; Smith, *History*, II, 145–146.

land.[153] He assured the board of trade that President Colden would be well received by the colonists, but the board was dubious that anyone invested with such "a temporary authority" could cope with a bitter faction led by a man who would have to be "set aside" in favor of Colden. In March 1753 the board of trade forbade Clinton to remove DeLancey without the king's express order.[154]

By late 1752 Halifax had decided that the deteriorated situation in New York could be improved only by the direct intervention of the imperial administration. From Clinton's point of view, of course, Halifax was about five years late. Halifax had thought Clinton capable of reasserting his authority in 1748 and 1749, but he ultimately perceived that the Governor's requests for help were justified, coming to agree that James DeLancey's official positions underlay his leadership of the opposition to the royal government of the colony. He therefore opposed DeLancey's suspension as lieutenant governor (destroying Morris' hopes in the same stroke) on the ground that, "had that been granted, the pretended necessity of sending over a man to prevent confusions, would have been removed." [155] He apparently concluded that DeLancey was vulnerable in his chief justiceship, however, and on June 25, 1753, the board of trade requested the attorney and solicitor general for an opinion as to whether Clinton had the power to issue a commission on good behavior and whether such a commission might be revoked by the crown. Perhaps Clinton's rash gift of life tenure might be voided. In July, however, the legal authorities replied in the negative: "the Grant is good in point of law and can not be revoked without misbehavior." [156]

153. R. H. Morris to Clinton, March 11, 1752, Clinton MSS.; Clinton to Catherwood, February 18 and 19–21, 1752, Clinton Letterbook, pp. 13–14, 21–22, C.L.
154. Clinton to Sharpe, April 8, 1752, draft, Clinton MSS.; Clinton to Lords of Trade, August 2, 1752, Clinton Letterbook, p. 95; Clinton to H. Clinton, March 12, 1753, Clinton MSS., XII, C.L.; Lords of Trade to Clinton, November 29, 1752, *New York Col. Docs.*, VI, 770.
155. Clinton's concluding observation on Catherwood's London letters [1753?], and R. H. Morris to Clinton, March 11, 1752, Clinton MSS., C.L.
156. *Board of Trade Journal*, 1750–1753, pp. 441, 455; Report of attorney and solicitor general, July 25, 1753, *New York Col. Docs.*, VI, 792.

In any case, George Clinton's sun had set by 1753. The board was by then primarily concerned to provide the next governor, Sir Danvers Osborn, with instructions that would enable him to restore New York government to its status under Governor Hunter. Halifax envisaged a strong governor, provided with a permanent revenue, who would ally himself wisely and control the assembly, and he hoped that Osborn would be such a man. The board certainly did not intend DeLancey to assume the administration, for that would have continued the existing situation, and they must have been appalled when Osborn's sudden suicide presented the government to the Chief Justice.

In 1750 Clinton had written an agonized letter to Robert Hunter Morris in which he described DeLancey's domination of elections and local government in New York: "By this you will perceive the absolute necessity of your and Mr Catherwood's immediate application to Lord Lincoln, and the rest of the Ministry to either get the C. Justice or my self removed, for it is impossible, that I can maintain his Prerogative, in opposition to the Influence and crafty Wiles of him at the head of the Faction." [157] Clinton pleaded with Morris to convince the ministry that he could not support the king's "authority and right, unless they redress my grievances, by giving me sufficient power to supersede the C.J. from all Offices." This was the root of Clinton's desire to remove DeLancey from the supreme court and the lieutenant governorship, for while DeLancey enjoyed these offices, his authority was greater than the Governor's. Clinton's failure to receive support from the home government put a seal of approval on the hegemony that DeLancey had already acquired by his wealth, office, ability, and connections in New York.

Thus Clinton's failure in England was no less striking than his defeat in America. He had sought the governorship in order to make his fortune, but found that fortunes were hard to come by in New York. He could not administer the province adequately, nor

157. Clinton to R. H. Morris, August 29, 1750, R. H. Morris Papers, I, 6, NJHS.

could he sell the post profitably. Thwarted, Clinton began his quest for endorsement from London, where he managed to avert financial disaster by obtaining repayment for his expenses in the 1746 campaign, but failed to win the succession for one of his friends or quash the pretensions of his principal adversary.[158]

VII

Clinton's difficulties were not all of his own making, however, for a new era was dawning in New York. The colony itself was maturing quickly, as population grew and trade prospered. Communications were improving and New York was coming to be acknowledged as one of the great port cities of the Atlantic world. New Yorkers had outgrown much of the Anglo-Dutch antagonism that marred the early years of the century and the next generation would share a new sense of community identity in the heterogeneous province. The sleepy colony that had greeted Cosby was entering its confident, vigorous, and turbulent period of adulthood.

New York's political life was also being transformed, and the tempo of change was accelerating. During the second quarter of the

158. Clinton fared somewhat better at home. Newcastle provided for the Governor after he had left America by securing him a seat in parliament and his half-pay as an admiral. Clinton had been angling for the parliamentary seat since 1733 and had tried to obtain an important naval command or a pension of £1,200 a year (his half-pay amounted to about £650 a year), but to no avail. "Tho' he is greatly allied—his conduct abroad has lost him all Interest at Home." Until his death Clinton was simply a nuisance to Newcastle and Lincoln. Collinson to Colden, March 13, 1755, NYHS, *Colls.*, 1921, p. 6; Adm. 25:45, fol. 1, PRO; Adm. 25:46, fol. 1, etc., PRO; see various letters from Lady Lincoln and Clinton to Newcastle, 1733–1756: Add. MSS. 33064, foll. 467, 472–473, 477, 479, 488, Add. MSS. 32857, foll. 285, 301, 320, Add. MSS. 32862, foll. 149, 296, Add. MSS. 32861, foll. 47, B.M.; Clinton to Henry Clinton, May 17, 1753, Clinton MSS., XII, C.L. Smith and Labaree state (Smith, *History*, II, 158–159; *DAB*, IV, 226; see also, Stokes, *Iconography*, IV, 644) that Clinton retired to the governorship of Greenwich Naval Hospital. He had been offered the job, but would consider it only if he might have a pension or his half-pay as well, and he is not listed as one of the governors of the hospital. J. Cooke and J. Maule, *An Historical Account of the Royal Hospital for Seamen at Greenwich* (London, 1789), pp. 135–136. See also, R. H. Morris Papers, I, 7, NJHS, and various letters, 1745–1754, in Clinton MSS., C.L.

century, the council declined in importance as the assembly increasingly became the center of conflict. The position of the governor and the prerogative of the crown were corroded as New Yorkers became more experienced and sophisticated in the exercise of power and the practice of politics. After mid-century, the political system became even more self-contained. From 1753 until 1776 the province was almost always under the command of local residents acting as lieutenant governor, so that the crown was even less directly represented than it had been in earlier years. Legislative factions perpetuated themselves over a period of years rather than disappearing shortly after they emerged. Fewer conflicts were resolved in London than previously. Perhaps even more important, the easy interaction of New Yorkers and Englishmen began to disappear. Communication was more formal, administration was more stylized, and there was less room for maneuver.

Some of the reasons for this ossification of Anglo-American politics are not hard to find. The informality of Newcastle's southern secretaryship had given way to the more energetic administration of Bedford and Halifax. In like manner, the calm of Walpolean politics was followed by the less placid era of the Pelhams, and, ultimately, by the rampant factionalism of the early years of George III. An equally significant development was parliament's increasing intervention in the administration of the empire, which reduced the discretionary powers of the imperial officials in executive departments.

More than anything else, however, the situation was drastically altered by the onset of the great war for empire between England and France. Beginning in the mid-1740's, the war demanded increased administrative control over the colonies and required careful planning. Military campaigns had to be designed and coordinated, troops had to be transported and billeted, and supply contracts had to be let and supervised. Moreover, the entire effort had to be financed, and it was this requirement, specifically, which brought parliament more closely into the business of imperial administration, since the conduct of American trade and the care of royal troops were hopelessly intertwined with everyday problems of colonial government. Wartime problems necessitated the formulation and execution of colonial policies that introduced rigid standards for measuring American political behavior, as England was driven to demand men, money, and action of the colonists. And, of course, these very demands provided continuing and divisive issues in American assemblies.

The two lines of development, colonial and imperial, thus came into conflict. During the much-maligned era of "salutary neglect" New York had been permitted to work out her problems with a minimum of imperial supervision. After about 1745, however, the relations between metropolis and colony began to change, as imperial policy transcended minimal trade regulation and new pressures were brought to bear on American officials. No longer were governors free to strike bargains with colonial assemblies and political factions on any mutually advantageous terms, because the requirements of imperial policy formalized their relations with the colonists. Just as fifty years of imperial leniency culminated in the growth of a mature political system in New York, a maturity symbolized by the personal achievement of James DeLancey, a new form of imperial pressure was brought to bear.

The change did not, however, come with the conclusion of the war in 1763 and the subsequent attempt to establish a territorial empire. The crucial decade was that of the 1750's, when New Yorkers were pressed to re-examine the basic premises of their political behavior, and when they first were forced to consider whether there was not, suddenly, some disparity between king and country. The era of Anglo-American politics thus ended precipitately amidst the pressures of international warfare, in an environment understandably hostile to the growth of a new system. Newcastle's era, for all its confusion and inefficiency, was the golden age of imperial politics in New York.

APPENDIXES

BIBLIOGRAPHY

INDEX

Appendix A

Members of the Board of Trade, 1719-1760

There is at present no accurate listing of the membership of the board of trade and plantations, the English council established in 1696 to provide intelligence of the colonies and imperial trade. The following list includes all people who served on the board from Westmoreland's appointment in 1719 to the accession of George III. Persons whose names are italicized served as president of the board. The list is intended merely to identify the commissioners, specify their length of service, and indicate the frequency and timing of changes in membership. It is compiled from the relevant volumes of the *Journal of the Commissioners for Trade and Plantations, 1704-1782* (London, 1920-1938).

Name	Appointed	Departed by reason of:			
		Death	Dismissal	Resignation	Unknown
Thomas Fane, Earl of Westmoreland	1719	—	1735	—	—
John Chetwynd	1714	—	—	—	1728
Sir Charles Cooke, Bt.	1714	1721	—	—	—
Paul Docminique	1714	1735	—	—	—
Thomas Pelham (Sr.)	1717	1741	—	—	—
Martin Bladen	1717	1746	—	—	—
Daniel Pulteney	1717	—	—	—	1721
Edward Ashe	1720	1746	—	—	—
Richard Plumer	1721	—	—	—	1727
	1735	—	—	—	1748
Sir John Hobart	1721	—	—	1727	—
Sir Orlando Bridgeman, Bt.	1727	—	—	1737	—
Walter Carey	1727	—	—	1730	—
Sir Thomas Frankland, Bt.	1728	—	—	1730	—
Sir Archer Croft	1730	—	—	—	1741
James Brudenell	1730	1746	—	—	—
Benjamin Mildmay, Earl Fitzwalter	1735	—	—	1737	—
John Monson, Baron Monson	1737	1748	—	—	—
Robert Sawyer Herbert	1737	—	—	1752	—
Sir Charles Gilmour, Bt.	1743	—	1745	—	—

Appendix A

Name	Appointed	Departed by reason of:			
		Death	Dismissal	Resignation	Unknown
Benjamin Keene	1741	—	—	1745	—
Sir John Phillips, Bt.	1745	—	—	1745	—
John Pitt	1745	—	—	1755	—
Baptist Leveson Gower	1745	—	—	1749	—
James Grenville	1746	—	—	1755	—
Thomas Hay, Lord Dupplin	1746	—	—	1754	—
Francis Fane	1746	—	—	1756	—
George Montagu Dunk, Earl of Halifax	1748	—	—	1761	—
Sir Thomas Robinson	1748	—	—	1749	—
Charles Townshend	1749	—	—	1754	—
Andrew Stone	1749	—	—	1761	—
James Oswald	1752	—	—	1759	—
Richard Edgecumbe	1754	—	—	1755	—
Thomas Pelham (Jr.)	1754	—	—	1761	—
John Talbot	1755	1756	—	—	—
Soame Jenyns	1755	—	—	—	1780
Richard Rigby	1755	—	—	1760	—
William Gerard Hamilton	1756	—	—	1761	—
William Sloper	1756	—	—	1761	—
Edward Bacon	1760	—	—	—	1765
Edward Elliot	1760	—	—	—	1776

Appendix B

Genealogies

MORRIS[1]

William Morris = ?

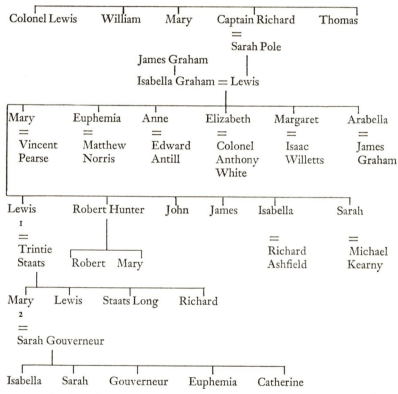

1. John E. Stillwell, comp., *Historcial and Genealogical Miscellany: Early Settlers of New Jersey and Their Descendants* (New York, 1903–1932), IV, 14–34. The genealogical charts in this appendix have been simplified and are intended only to indicate the most important family relationships described in the text.

Appendix B

DeLANCEY [2]

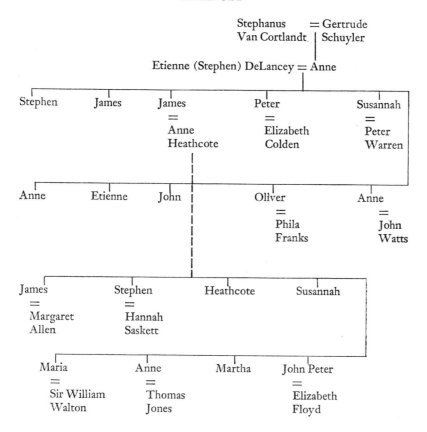

2. D. A. Story, *The DeLancey's: A Romance of a Great Family* [London, 1931], pp. 18, 173.

Appendix B

HEATHCOTE [3]

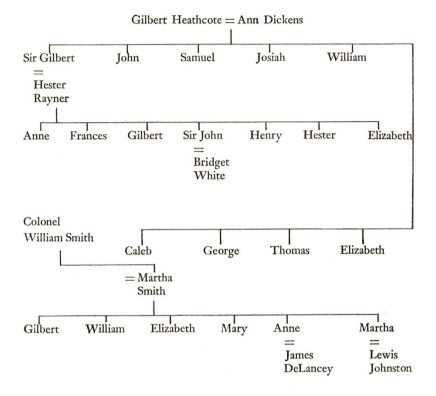

3. Evelyn D. Heathcote, *An Account of Some of the Families Bearing the Name of Heathcote* (Winchester, Eng., 1899), pp. 68, 78.

Appendix B

WARREN [4]

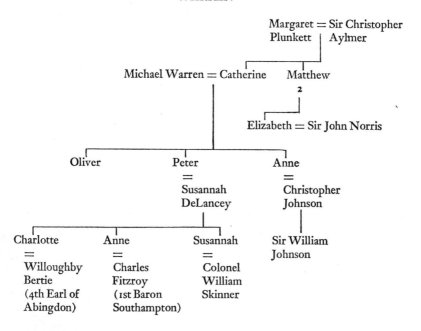

```
                                        Margaret = Sir Christopher
                                        Plunkett  |  Aylmer

              Michael Warren = Catherine      Matthew
                                                  2

                                    Elizabeth = Sir John Norris


        Oliver            Peter              Anne
                            =                 =
                        Susannah          Christopher
                        DeLancey           Johnson

  Charlotte        Anne          Susannah      Sir William
     =              =               =          Johnson
  Willoughby     Charles         Colonel
  Bertie         Fitzroy         William
  (4th Earl of   (1st Baron      Skinner
  Abingdon)      Southampton)
```

---

4. DNB, XX, 876–877; *Burke's Genealogical and Heraldic History of the Peerage, Baronetage and Knightage*, ed. L. G. Pine (London, 1959), p. 123.

Appendix B

COSBY[5]

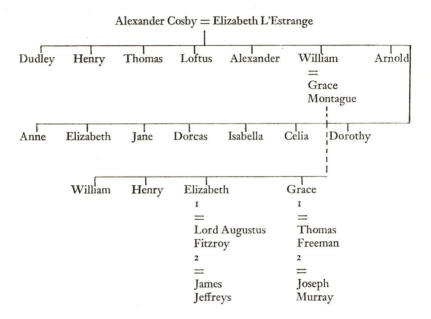

Alexander Cosby = Elizabeth L'Estrange

Dudley   Henry   Thomas   Loftus   Alexander   William   Arnold
=
Grace
Montague

Anne   Elizabeth   Jane   Dorcas   Isabella   Celia   Dorothy

William   Henry   Elizabeth   Grace
                    1   1
                    =   =
                    Lord Augustus   Thomas
                    Fitzroy   Freeman
                    2   2
                    =   =
                    James   Joseph
                    Jeffreys   Murray

5. Sir Bernard Burke, *Genealogical and Heraldic History of the Landed Gentry of Ireland,* ed. L. G. Pine (4th ed., London, 1958), p. 181.

Appendix B

MONTAGUE [6]

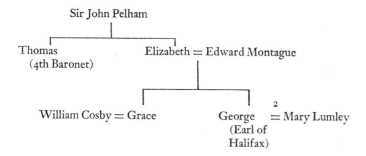

FITZROY [7]

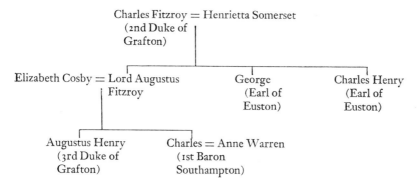

6. Mark Antony Lower, *Historical and Genealogical Notices of the Pelham Family* ([London?], 1873), p. 46; [George Edward Cokayne, ed.,] *The Complete Peerage of England, Scotland, Ireland, Great Britain and the United Kingdom Extant, Extinct or Dormant by* **G.E.C.**, ed. Vicary Gibbs et al. (new ed., London, 1910–1959), VI, 246–247.

7. Burke, *Peerage* (1959), p. 974.

Appendix B

CLARKE [8]

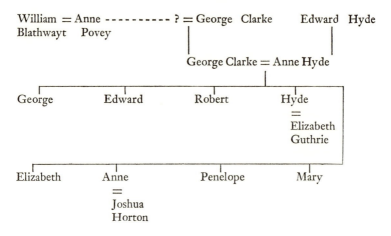

8. John and John Bernard Burke, *A Genealogical and Heraldic Dictionary of the Landed Gentry of Great Britain and Ireland* (London, 1847), I, 224; *DNB*, II, 668.

Appendix B

CLINTON[9]

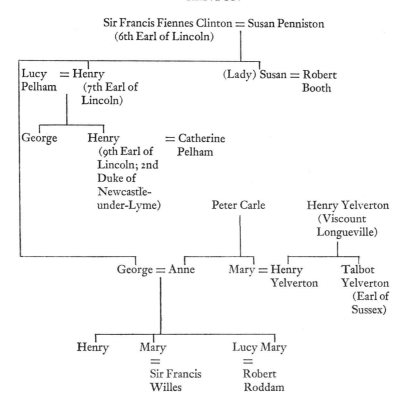

Sir Francis Fiennes Clinton = Susan Penniston
(6th Earl of Lincoln)

Lucy = Henry
Pelham (7th Earl of
Lincoln)

(Lady) Susan = Robert
Booth

George   Henry   = Catherine
          (9th Earl of   Pelham
          Lincoln; 2nd
          Duke of
          Newcastle-
          under-Lyme)

Peter Carle   Henry Yelverton
                   (Viscount
                   Longueville)

George = Anne   Mary = Henry   Talbot
                        Yelverton   Yelverton
                                     (Earl of
                                     Sussex)

Henry   Mary   Lucy Mary
         =   =
         Sir Francis Robert
         Willes   Roddam

9. Burke, *Peerage* (1959), p. 1663; G.E.C., *Complete Peerage*, IX, 532–533.

Appendix B

PELHAM [10]

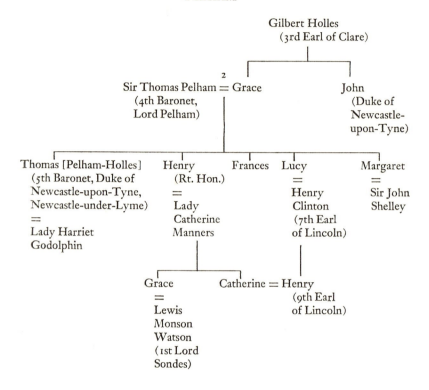

10. Lower, *Pelham Family*, pp. 48–51; G.E.C., *Complete Peerage*, IX, 529–532; Burke, *Peerage* (1959), pp. 449–450.

Bibliography

The recent bibliography of the history of pre-revolutionary New York is small and can be taken note of briefly. Lawrence H. Leder's *Robert Livingston, 1654–1728, and the Politics of Colonial New York* (Chapel Hill, 1961) is the best treatment of the first quarter of the eighteenth century, although its biographical organization restricts its scope. The same may be said for Philip L. White's *The Beekmans of New York: In Politics and Commerce, 1647–1877* (New York, 1956). My introduction to James Alexander's *A Brief Narrative of the Case and Trial of John Peter Zenger* (Cambridge, Mass., 1963) deals with some of the events of the Cosby administration. Milton M. Klein's introduction to William Livingston, *The Independent Reflector* (Cambridge, Mass., 1963) and his unpublished dissertation "*The American Whig: William Livingston of New York*" (Columbia University, 1954) provide the best study of the 1750's and, especially, of the King's College controversy. Two unpublished dissertations remain the standard accounts: Beverly McAnear, "Politics in Provincial New York, 1689–1761" (Stanford University, 1935) and Nicholas Varga, "New York Politics and Government in the Mid-Eighteenth Century" (Fordham University, 1960). McAnear's work is an exhaustive study focused on the assembly, and it remains the leading authority for the colonial period even though it is written with a political bias characteristic of the 1930's. Varga's dissertation, which will soon appear in print as *Governor*

259

Bibliography

George Clinton and the Politics of Pre-Revolutionary New York, is a careful assessment of the American sources for New York history in the second quarter of the century which comes to conclusions somewhat different from my own.

All in all, it would appear that the most obvious need for further research in political history is for accounts of the first sixty-five years of English rule in New York, for an analysis of the political importance of the fur trade, and for studies of particular areas (regions, counties, manors, towns) within the province. Although very little fresh manuscript material has come to light in recent years, practically all of New York's political history needs to be rewritten in the light of the fresh insights of recent work in the colonial field. As matters stand, Herbert L. Osgood's discussion of provincial New York in his *The American Colonies in the Eighteenth Century* (New York, 1924) is still the standard account in print. So far as Anglo-American politics are concerned, there is at the moment no bibliography for New York and very little more for the other English colonies.

A. *English Manuscripts*
British Museum (London)
  Additional Manuscripts 15955–15957. Admiral George Anson Papers, 1743–1759
    Letters received by Anson from Vere Beauclerc, Bedford, Hardwicke, Sandwich, and Peter Warren. A large number (Add. MSS. 15957, foll. 147–312) are from Warren.
  Additional Manuscripts 28130–28133, 28143–28146, 28150. Sir John Norris Papers
    Letterbooks and journals, 1715–1743. Relatively little personal information on Norris or his friends, but a great deal of material on his diplomatic missions.
  Additional Manuscripts 28726–28727. Letters to Peter Collinson, 1725–1790
    Letters from Wager, Henry Fox, Lord Petre, and others.
  Additional Manuscripts 35359, 35376, 35387, 35431, 35598, 35599, 35889, 35605. The Hardwicke Papers
    Only the volumes actually consulted have been cited. This vast collection throws light on the careers of Admiral Anson, Archbishop Herring, and, of course, Newcastle and Hardwicke.
  Additional Manuscripts 32686–33003, 33005–33025, 33028–33030, 33038–33041, 33044–33048, 33054–33057, 33062, 33064–33078, 33082–33083. The Newcastle Papers
    This enormous group of papers was the basic source on English politics for this book. It contains abundant material on such important figures as Governors Cosby, Clarke, De la Warr, and Clinton. Clinton is especially

well represented. Above all, the Newcastle Papers are perhaps the most important source for material on the administration of the colonies and on the use of colonial patronage. The size of the collection creates problems for research, and I used the papers in two ways: specific references from other sources and from the *Catalogue of the Additions to the Manuscripts in the British Museum, 1882–1887* ([London,] 1889) were looked up, and the domestic papers were read seriatim for a few significant periods of time. Add. MSS. 32686–32737, 32860–32879, and 33064 were particularly useful.

Public Record Office (London)

A thorough check was made of important items printed in O'Callaghan's *New York Col. Docs.* and, while omissions were found, they were not generally of great significance. The obvious exception to this statement is the large number of items in the Admiralty and Treasury series which were not included in O'Callaghan. The single most fruitful category for scholars of American colonial history is the Treasury 1 series, the "in" letters of the treasury, which are organized only in a very rough chronological manner. The following are some of the many series consulted, with a few specific items of importance.

Colonial Office Papers 5

The colonial office papers referring to America and the West Indies.

Colonial Office Papers 324:48

Four small volumes used by the board of trade to record nominations for colonial councillors, the names of those making the nominations, and the eventual appointees. I, 1706–1715; II, 1737–1751; III, 1760–1768; IV, 1768–?

Admiralty Papers

Provide information on the lives of naval men such as Clinton and Warren.

Treasury Papers

T. 1 contains valuable material on the intended expedition of 1746 against Canada. T. 64:44 is comprised of the board of trade's report on the expenses incurred by the intended expedition. T. 29 (treasury minute books), T. 53 (warrants relating to money), and T. 27 ("out" letters) were also useful in studying the plans for the expedition.

Privy Council Papers 2

The registers of the privy council, which contain little material not found in *Acts., Privy Coun., Col.,* but do add the names of the councillors attending each session.

State Papers (Domestic) 36

Miscellaneous items received by the secretaries of state and other officials.

War Office Papers 34

The papers of Sir Jeffrey Amherst, valuable for his correspondence with American politicians and merchants.

PRO 30:8

The Chatham Papers.

The National Registry of Archives (London)

The Registry is the survivor of the Historical Manuscripts Commission, located in Quality Court, just off Chancery Lane. While it does not actually possess any manuscripts, the Registry is an invaluable guide to collections in private hands and in small depositories. Lists of hundreds of such collections are available in the London office, so the scholar can quickly determine the sources available for his research.

The Bodleian Library (Oxford)

Rawlinson Manuscripts A 272

The Champante Papers. Correspondence of John Champante, an early agent of New York in London.

The Central Library (Sheffield)

Wentworth Woodhouse Manuscripts

The correspondence of Charles, second marquis of Rockingham, which is important for the study of American history after 1750.

Lincolnshire Archives Committee (Lincoln)

Ancaster Papers

The first Deposit (1 ANC XI:B:1–5) contains correspondence and other papers relating to the bequest of William Heathcote to the children of Caleb Heathcote, and correspondence between James DeLancey and the English Heathcote family, 1732–1735. This valuable group of papers has never previously been consulted by students of colonial American history. Material relating to Heathcote political activities in England can be found in 1 ANC XIII:B and in the Third Deposit (3 ANC IX:1).

Monson Papers

The correspondence of John, Lord Monson, which unfortunately sheds little light on the administration of politics of the board of trade.

The University Library (Cambridge)

Chomondeley-Houghton Manuscripts

The papers of Sir Robert Walpole. The correspondence, constituting a separate section of the manuscripts, is magnificently indexed, chronologically and by sender and receiver. There are relatively few items written by Walpole, but many of the letters to him are useful. Sir Charles Wager is particularly well represented, as is William Heathcote.

William Salt Library (Staffordshire Record Office)

Dartmouth Manuscripts

This collection is calendared in three volumes by the Historical Manuscripts Commission, but includes many uncalendared items which have come to light since the deposit of the papers in the William Salt. The

material is of course especially valuable to the American historian for the
period when Dartmouth was the first lord of the board of trade.
Sussex Archaelogical Society (Lewes)
 Gage Papers
  G/Am 1-66 contain Sir Peter Warren's papers before his death in 1752,
  while G/Am 67-338 relate to the history of the Warren estate in New
  York from 1752 well into the nineteenth century. G/Am/6 is a fools-
  cap book containing Warren's "Private Letters," 1746-1747. The collection
  contains several other items relating to New York history. I have used
  the calendar prepared by the Society as well as transcripts provided me
  by Professor Jacob Judd and Sleepy Hollow Restorations, Tarrytown,
  New York.

B. *American Manuscripts*
New-York Historical Society (New York City)
 Alexander Papers
  A large collection of the papers of James Alexander and his son William,
  the *soi-disant* Earl of Stirling. James Alexander's papers are mostly re-
  lated to business and law, although there are drafts of letters on political
  subjects. The William Alexander papers include large numbers of personal
  papers (especially volumes I to III) which are valuable for the period
  after 1750, and particularly for the information on the execution of the
  supply contract for the 1755 and 1756 military expeditions against the
  French.
 Banyar Papers
  These are the papers of Goldsbrow Banyar, the deputy secretary of New
  York. They are largely the correspondence of Banyar with George Clarke,
  Jr., the nonresident secretary. The earliest items are from 1746, however,
  and the bulk of the collection dates from the period after 1760.
 DeLancey Papers
  Miscellaneous papers and deeds.
 Horsmanden Papers
 John Jay Papers
 Livingston Papers
 Rutherfurd Collection
  A magnificent collection deposited by John Rutherfurd, Jr., in 1966. Six
  bound volumes and two scrapbooks of letters and documents, largely the
  drafts of letters by James Alexander and letters received by Alexander
  from Governors Hunter and Burnet, Cadwallader Colden, Lewis Morris,
  Lewis Morris, Jr., William Smith, Ferdinand John Paris, and a number
  of New Jersey politicians. There is a large body of material on the
  Zenger trial, an entire scrapbook on New Jersey affairs, especially the
  Elizabethtown land riots, and a quantity of correspondence relating to

the supply of the military expeditions of 1755 and 1756. Several of the items in this collection have appeared in print in *N.J. Arch.*, vol. V, and in the *Governor Lewis Morris Papers*. All in all, the collection is the richest single source for the history of New York and New Jersey politics in the 1720's and 1730's.

Sir Peter Warren Papers
Largely commercial papers and Warren's will.

John Watts Papers.

New York Public Library (New York City)

James Alexander Papers
Several items of importance relating to the Zenger trial.

Bancroft Transcripts
Colden Papers: several items which are not printed in the NYHS edition. Livingston Papers: correspondence of Robert R. Livingston, for the most part. Thomas Penn Letters: correspondence with James Hamilton.

Emmet Collection

Myers Collection

William Smith Papers
The manuscript of Smith's *History*, the "Historical Memoirs," and many other items of political interest, especially extracts of letters to and from the New York agent, Robert Charles (vol. III, 229–237).

New Jersey Historical Society (Newark, New Jersey)

East Jersey Manuscripts

Robert Hunter Morris Papers
The collection contains Morris' correspondence, 1734–1758, including several letters to and from Governor Clinton.

New Jersey Manuscripts

Ferdinand John Paris Manuscripts
A large group of papers, 1744–1755, mainly concerned with New Jersey boundary difficulties, which can now be supplemented by the materials in the Rutherfurd Collection, NYHS.

Rutgers University Library (New Brunswick, New Jersey)

Nicholas Bayard Papers

Morris Papers
A large and especially valuable collection which has not been sufficiently explored in the past. For the present topic, the pertinent portions were: Box 1 (Lewis Morris), Box 2 (Robert Hunter Morris), Box 3 (Robert Hunter Morris), and the folder of the papers of John Morris (R. H. Morris' younger brother). This is the largest single source on Lewis Morris' career in New York politics. Other notable items are letters written from London by Euphemia Norris, Matthew Norris, and R.H. Morris.

Franklin Delano Roosevelt Library (Hyde Park, New York)

Livingston-Redmond Papers

Bibliography

The NYHS microfilm copy of these papers was used. This vast collection extends in time from Robert Livingston (1654–1728) to Johnson Livingston (1817–1911). The material on the first Robert Livingston is particularly rich, although much of it (the correspondence with his wife, Alida Schuyler) is in Dutch. Lawrence H. Leder of Louisiana State University (New Orleans) possesses a translation of these items. For the purposes of this book, the correspondence of Philip Livingston (1686–1749) was especially valuable. The papers provide a full picture of the Livingston family's participation in politics and trade, and also contain untapped resources for the study of the fur trade and Albany politics.

William L. Clements Library (Ann Arbor, Michigan)

George Clinton Papers

This is a superb collection which provides an unparalleled source for the portrait of a colonial governor. There are 22 folio volumes of manuscripts, 13 of them chronological arrangements of correspondence, a letter book for 1752, and a great quantity of financial records. The correspondence relates to every aspect of Clinton's political activity in New York. The most important items for the present study were the letters sent to Clinton from R. H. Morris and John Catherwood in London and the letters Clinton sent to his son in London. The most valuable single item was a précis made by Clinton (?) of the letters received from Catherwood from February 27, 1748, to December 3, 1751. This was completed in late 1752 or early 1753 and contains Clinton's "observations" on Catherwood's reports.

Peter Warren Papers

A large number of financial papers and several letters, supplementing the Clinton-Warren correspondence in the George Clinton Papers. The letters from William and Samuel Baker, Warren's English agents, are of particular importance.

Henry Clinton Papers

An extremely large collection, mostly pertaining to Clinton's later military career. There is a considerable discussion of young Clinton's attempts to salvage something of value from his father's estate, however.

Massachusetts Historical Society (Boston, Massachusetts)

William Livingston Papers

Letter-Book A contains material on the King's College controversy.

C. *Public Records: England*

Acts of the Privy Council, Colonial Series. W. L. Grant and James Munro, eds. 6 vols. Hereford and London, 1908–1912.

Calendar of State Papers, Colonial Series, America and West Indies. W. N. Sainsbury, J. W. Fortescue, and Cecil Headlam, eds. 42 vols. London, 1860–1953.

Bibliography

Calendar of Treasury Books and Papers, 1729–1745. William A. Shaw, ed. 5 vols. London, 1897–1903.

The Eighteenth-Century Constitution, 1688–1815. E. Neville Williams, ed. Cambridge, 1960.

Journal of the Commissioners for Trade and Plantations, 1704–1782. 14 vols. London, 1920–1938.

Proceedings and Debates of the British Parliaments respecting North America. Leo Francis Stock, ed. 5 vols. Washington, 1924–1941.

Royal Instructions to British Colonial Governors, 1670–1776. Leonard W. Labaree, ed. 2 vols. New York, 1935.

D. *Public Records: New York*

Calendar of Council Minutes, 1668–1783, New York State Library, *Bulletin,* 58 (1902). Berthold Fernow, ed. Albany, 1902.

Calendar of New York Colonial Commissions. E. B. O'Callaghan, comp. New York, 1929.

The Colonial Laws of New York from the Year 1664 to the Revolution. 5 vols. Albany, 1894–1896.

Documents Relating to the Colonial History of the State of New Jersey. 1st series. vol. V: *1720–1727.* William A. Whitehead, ed. Newark, 1882.

Documents Relating to the Colonial History of the State of New Jersey. 1st series. vol. IX: *Newspapers and Newspaper Extracts, 1704–1739.* William Nelson, ed. Paterson, 1894.

Documents Relative to the Colonial History of the State of New York. E. B. O'Callaghan and Berthold Fernow, eds. 15 vols. Albany, 1856–1887.

Ecclesiastical Records of the State of New York. E. T. Corwin, ed. 7 vols. Albany, 1901–1916.

Journal of the Legislative Council of the Colony of New York, 1691–1775. 2 vols. Albany, 1861.

Journal of the Votes and Proceedings of the General Assembly of the Colony of New-York [1691–1765]. 2 vols. New York, 1764–1766.

Minutes of the Common Council of the City of New York, 1675–1776. 8 vols. New York, 1905.

Names of Persons for whom Marriage Licenses Were Issued by the Secretary of the Province Prior to 1784. E. B. O'Callaghan, ed. Albany, 1860.

E. *Other Printed Primary Sources*

[Alexander, James, and William Smith.] *The Arguments of the Council for the Defendant, . . . Rip Van Dam . . . in the Supream Court of New-York.* New York, 1733.

——— *The Complaint of James Alexander and William Smith to the Committee of the General Assembly of the Colony of New York, etc.* New York, [1736].

Bibliography

[Anon.] *An Essay Upon the Government of the English Plantations on the Continent of America.* Louis B. Wright, ed. San Marino, Calif., 1945.

—— *Of the American Plantations* (1714), William L. Saunders, ed., *The Colonial Records of North Carolina*, Raleigh, N.C., 1886–1890, II, 154–166.

"The Aspinwall Papers," Massachusetts Historical Society, *Collections*, 4th series, IX (1871).

[Colden, Cadwallader.] *The Colden Letter Books, 1760–1775*, New York Historical Society, *Collections*, IX–X (1876–1877), New York, 1877–1878.

—— *History of Gov. William Cosby's Administration and of Lt.-Gov. George Clarke's Administration through 1737*, New-York Historical Society, *Collections*, LXVIII (1935), pp. 283–355.

—— *The History of the Five Indian Nations of Canada.* New York, 1904.

—— "Letters on Smith's History of New York, [1759]," New-York Historical Society, *Collections*, I (1868), pp. 181–235.

—— *The Letters and Papers of Cadwallader Colden*, New-York Historical Society, *Collections*, L–LVI, LXVII–LXVIII (1917–1923, 1934–1935), New York, 1918–1937.

Garnett, R., ed. "Correspondence of Archbishop Herring and Lord Hardwicke during the Rebellion of 1745," *English Historical Review*, XIX (1904), 528–550, 719–742.

Historical Manuscripts Commission. *First Report, Appendix, Port Eliot, Cornwall, the Seat of the Earl of St. Germans.* London, 1870.

—— *Ninth Report, Appendix, Part III, The Manuscripts of Mrs. Stopford Sackville of Drayton House, Northamptonshire.* London, 1883.

—— *Eleventh Report, Appendix, Part IV, The Manuscripts of the Marquess Townshend.* London, 1887.

—— *Fourteenth Report, Appendix, Part IX, Onslow MSS.*, pp. 458–469. London, 1895.

—— *Fourteenth Report, Appendix, Part X, The Manuscripts of the Earl of Dartmouth.* vol. II: *American Papers.* London, 1895.

—— *Fifteenth Report, Appendix, Part IV, The Manuscripts of His Grace the Duke of Portland.* vol. IV: *The Harley Letters and Papers, 1700–1711.* London, 1897.

—— *Report on the Manuscripts of His Grace the Duke of Portland.* vol. V: *The Harley Letters and Papers, 1711–1724.* London, 1899.

Historical Records Survey. *Calendar of the Stevens Family Papers.* 2 vols. Newark, 1940.

Kennedy, Archibald. *An Essay on the Government of the Colonies.* New York, 1752.

Lincoln, C. H., ed. *Correspondence of William Shirley, Governor of Massachusetts and Military Commander in America, 1731–1760.* 2 vols. New York, 1912.

[Livingston, William.] "A Review of the Military Operations in North America from the Commencement of the French Hostilities on the Frontiers of Virginia in 1753, to the Surrender of Oswego, on the 14th of August, 1756; in a Letter to a Nobleman, [20 September 1756]," *Massachusetts Historical Society, Collections*, 1st series, VII–VIII (1801–1856), pp. 67–163.

McAnear, Beverly, ed. "R. H. Morris: An American in London, 1735–1736," *Pennsylvania Magazine of History*, LXIV (1940), pp. 164–217, 356–406.

[Morris, Lewis.] *The Opinion and Argument of the Chief Justice of the Province of New-York, concerning the Jurisdiction of the Supream Court of the said Province, to determine Causes in a Course of Equity*, New Jersey Historical Society, *Proceedings*, LV (1937), pp. 89–116.

——— *The Papers of Lewis Morris, Governor of the Province of New Jersey from 1738 to 1746*, New Jersey Historical Society, *Collections*, IV (1852), New York, 1852.

[Morris, Lewis ?] *Some Observations on the Charge Given by the Honourable James DeLancey, Esq, Justice of the Province of New-York, to the Grand Jury, the 15th Day of January, 1733*. New York, 1734.

[Morris, Robert Hunter.] "Correspondence Relating to the Morris Family," New Jersey Historical Society, *Proceedings*, n.s., VII (1922), pp. 41–48.

[Murray, Joseph.] *Mr. Murray's Opinion Relating to the Courts of Justice in the Colony of New-York* . . . [New York, 1734].

New York Gazette.

New-York Weekly Journal.

O'Callaghan, E. B., ed. *Letters of Isaac Bobin Esq., Private Secretary of Hon. George Clarke, Secretary of the Province of New York, 1718–1730*. Albany, 1872.

——— *Voyage of George Clarke, Esq. to America*. Albany, 1867.

The Proceedings of Rip Van Dam, Esq; in order for obtaining Equal Justice of His Excellency William Cosby, Esq. New York, 1733.

Russell, Lord John, ed. *Correspondence of John, fourth Duke of Bedford*. 3 vols. London, 1842–1846.

Rutherfurd, Livingston. *Family Record and Events, Compiled Originally from the Original MSS in the Rutherfurd Collection*. New York, 1894.

Scull, G. D., ed. *The Montressor Journals*, New-York Historical Society, *Collections*, XIV (1881), New York, 1882.

Sedgwick, Romney, ed. *Letters from George III to Lord Bute, 1756–1766*. London, 1939.

——— ed. *Lord Hervey's Memoirs*. London, 1952.

Smith, William. *The History of the Province of New York From its Discovery, to the Appointment of Governor Colden, in 1762*, New-York Historical Society, *Collections*, 1st series, IV–V (1826), New York, 1829.

——— *Mr. Smith's Opinion Humbly Offered to the General Assembly* . . . New York, 1734.

Bibliography

—— "Observations on the Loss of the American Colonies," Oscar Zeichner, ed., *New York History*, XXIII (1942), pp. 324–340.
Sullivan, James, and Alexander C. Flick, eds. *The Papers of Sir William Johnson*. 14 vols. Albany, 1921–1965.
Toynbee, Mrs. Paget, ed. *The Letters of Horace Walpole, Fourth Earl of Orford*. 19 vols. Oxford, 1903–1925.
Walpole, Horace. *Memoirs of the Reign of King George the Second*. Lord Holland, ed. 2nd ed., revised. 2 vols. London, 1847.
Watts, John. *Letter Book*, New-York Historical Society, *Collections*, LXI (1928), New York, 1928.

F. *Secondary Works*
    This list represents a small selection of those books and articles that have been of general value. For more specialized references the reader should consult the footnotes to the relevant portions of the text.

Andrews, Charles M. *The Colonial Background of the American Revolution*. Revised ed. New Haven, 1937–1938.
—— *The Colonial Period of American History*. 4 vols. New Haven, 1934–1938.
Bargar, B. D. "Lord Dartmouth's Patronage, 1772–1775," *William and Mary Quarterly*, 3rd ser., XV (1958), pp. 191–200.
Barrow, Thomas C. *Trade and Empire: The British Customs Service in Colonial America, 1660–1775*. Cambridge, Mass., 1967.
Basye, Arthur Herbert. *The Lords Commissioners of Trade and Plantations, Commonly Known as the Board of Trade, 1748–1782*. New Haven, 1925.
Baugh, Daniel A. *British Naval Administration in the Age of Walpole*. Princeton, 1965.
Beatson, Robert. *A Political Index*. 3rd ed. 3 vols. London, 1806.
Becker, Carl. "Growth of Revolutionary Parties and Methods in New York, 1765–1774," *American Historical Review*, VII (1901–1902), pp. 56–76.
—— *The History of Political Parties in the Province of New York*. Madison, Wis., 1960.
—— "Nominations in Colonial New York," *American Historical Review*, VI (1900–1901), pp. 260–275.
Beer, George Louis. *British Colonial Policy, 1754–1765*. New York, 1933.
Bellot, H. Hale. "Council and Cabinet in the Mainland Colonies," Royal Historical Society, *Transactions*, 5th series, V (1955), pp. 161–176.
Bond, Beverly W., Jr. "The Colonial Agent as a Popular Representative," *Political Science Quarterly*, XXXV (1920), pp. 372–392.
Brooke, John. *The Chatham Administration, 1766–1768*. London, 1956.
Buffinton, Arthur H. "The Canada Expedition of 1746: Its Relation to British Politics," *American Historical Review*, XLV (1940), pp. 552–580.

Bibliography

Burke's Genealogical and Heraldic History of the Peerage, Baronetage and Knightage. L. G. Pine, ed. 102nd ed. London, 1959.

Burke, Sir Bernard. *Genealogical and Heraldic History of the Landed Gentry of Ireland.* L. G. Pine, ed. 4th ed. London, 1958.

Burke, John et al. *Genealogical and Heraldic History of the Extinct and Dormant Baronetcies of England, Ireland, and Scotland.* London, 1841.

Burke, John and John Bernard. *A Genealogical and Heraldic Dictionary of the Landed Gentry of Great Britain and Ireland.* 2 vols. London, 1847.

Burns, John F. *Controversies Between Royal Governors and Their Assemblies in the Northern American Colonies.* Boston, 1923.

Charnock, John. *Biographia Navalis; or, Impartial Memoirs of the Lives and Characters of Officers of the Navy of Great Britain, from the year 1660 to the Present Time.* 6 vols. London, 1794–1798.

Clark, Dora Mae. *The Rise of the British Treasury: Colonial Administration in the Eighteenth Century.* New Haven, 1960.

Clarke, Mary Patterson. "The Board of Trade at Work," *American Historical Review,* XVII (1911), pp. 17–43.

[Cokayne, George Edward, ed.] *The Complete Peerage of England Scotland Ireland Great Britain and the United Kingdom Extant Extinct or Dormant by G. E. C.* Vicary Gibbs et al., eds. New ed. 14 vols. London, 1910–1959.

Arthur Collins's Peerage of England . . . Greatly Augmented, and Continued to the Present Time. Sir Egerton Brydges, ed. 9 vols. London, 1812.

Crary, Catherine Snell. "The American Dream: John Tabor Kempe's Rise from Poverty to Riches," *William and Mary Quarterly,* 3rd series, XIV (1957), pp. 176–195.

DeLancey, Edward Floyd. "Memoir of James DeLancey," *Documentary History of the State of New York,* E. B. O'Callaghan, ed., Albany, 1849–1851, IV, 1037–1059.

Dickerson, O. M. *American Colonial Government, 1696–1765. A Study of the British Board of Trade in Its Relation to the American Colonies . . .* Cleveland, 1912.

Dillon, Dorothy Rita. *The New York Triumvirate.* Columbia University Studies in History, Economics and Public Law, no. 548, New York, 1949.

Donnan, Elizabeth. "Eighteenth Century English Merchants: Micajah Perry," *Journal of Economic and Business History,* IV (1931), pp. 70–79.

Dunbar, Louise B. "The Royal Governors in the Middle and Southern Colonies on the Eve of the Revolution: A Study in Imperial Personnel," *Era of the American Revolution,* Richard B. Morris, ed., New York, 1939, pp. 214–268.

Edwards, George W. *New York as an Eighteenth Century Municipality, 1731–1776.* New York, 1917.

——— "New York City Politics Before the American Revolution," *Political Science Quarterly,* XXXVI (1921), pp. 586–602.

Bibliography

Feiling, Keith Grahame. *The Second Tory Party, 1714-1832.* London, 1938.

Flexner, James Thomas. *Mohawk Baronet: Sir William Johnson of New York.* New York, 1959.

Flick, Alexander C., ed. *History of the State of New York.* 10 vols. New York, 1933-1937.

Foord, Archibald. *His Majesty's Opposition, 1714-1830.* Oxford, 1964.

Fox, Dixon Ryan. *Caleb Heathcote.* New York, 1926.

—— *The Decline of Aristocracy in the Politics of New York.* Columbia University Studies in History, Economics and Public Law, no. 86, New York, 1919.

Fox, Edith M. *Land Speculation in the Mohawk Country.* Cornell Studies in American History, Literature and Folklore, no. III, Ithaca, 1949.

Gipson, Lawrence Henry. *The British Empire Before the American Revolution.* 9 vols. Caldwell, Idaho, and New York, 1936-1956.

Goebel, Julius, Jr. "Some Legal and Political Aspects of Manors in New York," Order of Colonial Lords of Manors in America, New York Branch, *Publications,* no. 19 (1928).

Goodwin, A., ed. *The European Nobility in the Eighteenth Century.* London, 1953.

Graham, Gerald S. *Empire of the North Atlantic.* Toronto, 1950.

Greene, Evarts B. *The Provincial Governor in the English Colonies of North America.* New York, 1898.

Greene, Jack P. *The Quest for Power: The Lower House of Assembly in the Southern Royal Colonies, 1689-1776.* Chapel Hill, 1963.

Guttridge, G. H. *The Colonial Policy of William III in America and the West Indies.* Cambridge, Eng., 1922.

Haffenden, Philip. "Colonial Appointments and Patronage under the Duke of Newcastle, 1724-1739," *English Historical Review,* LXXVIII (1963), pp. 417-435.

Handlin, Oscar. "The Eastern Frontier of New York," *New York History,* XVIII (1937), pp. 50-75.

Harrington, Virginia D. *The New York Merchant on the Eve of the Revolution.* Columbia University Studies in History, Economics and Public Law, no. 404, New York, 1935.

Haydn, Joseph. *The Book of Dignities.* 2nd ed. London, 1841.

—— *The Book of Dignities.* Cont. by Horace Ockerby. 3rd ed. London, 1894.

Heckscher, Eli F. *Mercantilism.* Mendel Shapiro, trans. E. F. Söderlund, ed. Revised ed. 2 vols. London, 1955.

Hunt, N. C. *Two Early Political Associations: The Quakers and the Dissenting Deputies in the Age of Sir Robert Walpole.* Oxford, 1961.

Hutchins, S. C., comp. *Civil List and Forms of Government of the Colony and State of New York.* Albany, 1869.

271

Bibliography

Ilchester, Earl of [Giles S. H. Fox-Strangways]. *Henry Fox, First Lord Holland*. 2 vols. London, 1920.

Innis, Harold A. *The Fur Trade in Canada*. New York, 1930.

—— "Interrelations between the Fur Trade of Canada and the United States," *Mississippi Valley Historical Review*, XX (1933-1934), pp. 321–332.

Jacobsen, Gertrude Ann. *William Blathwayt: A Late Seventeenth Century English Administrator*. New Haven, 1932.

Jones, Thomas. *History of New York During the Revolutionary War*. Edward Floyd DeLancey, ed. 2 vols. New York, 1879.

Judd, Gerrit P. *Members of Parliament, 1734-1832*. New Haven, 1955.

Keith, Arthur Berriedale. *The Constitutional History of the First British Empire*. Oxford, 1930.

Kemmerer, Donald L. *Path to Freedom: The Struggle for Self-Government in Colonial New Jersey, 1703-1776*. Princeton, 1940.

Keys, Alice Mapelsden. *Cadwallader Colden*. New York, 1906.

Kippis, Andrew. *Biographia Britannica*. 2nd ed. 4 vols. London, 1778-1793.

Klein, Milton M. "Democracy and Politics in Colonial New York," *New York History*, XL (1959), pp. 221–246.

—— "Politics and Personalities in Colonial New York," *New York History*, XLVII (1966), pp. 3–16.

Labaree, Leonard. "The Early Careers of the Royal Governors," *Essays in Colonial History Presented to Charles McLean Andrews by His Students*, New Haven, 1931, pp. 145–168.

—— *Royal Government in America*. New York, 1958.

Lamb, Mrs. Martha J. *History of the City of New York*. 3 vols. New York, 1877.

Leder, Lawrence. "Robert Livingston: A New View of New York Politics," *New York History*, XL (1959), pp. 358–367.

Levermore, C. H. "The Whigs in Colonial New York," *American Historical Review*, I (1895-1896), pp. 238–250.

Levy, Leonard W. "Did the Zenger Case Really Matter? Freedom of the Press in Colonial New York," *William and Mary Quarterly*, 3rd series, XVII (1960), pp. 35–50.

—— *Legacy of Suppression: Freedom of Speech and Press in Early American History*. Cambridge, Mass., 1960.

Lilly, Edward P. *The Colonial Agents of New York and New Jersey*. Washington, 1936.

Lincoln, Charles Zebrina. *The Constitutional History of New York*. 5 vols. Rochester, N.Y., 1906.

Lunn, Jean. "The Illegal Fur Trade Out of New France, 1713-1760," *Canadian Historical Association, Report*, 1939, pp. 61–76.

McAnear, Beverly. "Place of the Freeman in Old New York," *New York History*, XXI (1940), pp. 418–430.

Bibliography

McIlwain, Charles H., ed. *Peter Wraxall's Abridgment of the Indian Affairs.* Cambridge, Mass., 1915.

McManus, Edgar J. *A History of Negro Slavery in New York.* Syracuse, N.Y., 1966.

Mark, Irving. *Agrarian Conflicts in Colonial New York, 1711–1715.* New York, 1940.

Murray, Sir Oswyn A. R. "The Admiralty," *The Mariner's Mirror,* XXIII (1937), pp. 13–25, 129–147, 316–331, XXIV (1938), pp. 101–104, 204–225, 329–352, 458–478, XXV (1939), pp. 89–112, 216–229, 328–338.

Namier, Sir Lewis B. "Brice Fisher, M.P.: A Mid-Eighteenth-Century Merchant and His Connections," *English Historical Review,* XLII (1927), pp. 514–532.

—— *Crossroads of Power: Essays on Eighteenth Century England.* New York, 1963.

—— *England in the Age of the American Revolution.* London, 1930.

—— *Personalities and Powers.* London, 1955.

—— *The Structure of Politics at the Accession of George III.* 2nd ed. London, 1957.

—— and John Brooke. *The History of Parliament: The House of Commons, 1754–1790.* 3 vols. London, 1964.

Naylor, Rex M. "The Royal Prerogative in New York, 1691–1775," *New York State Historical Association, Quarterly Journal,* V (1924), pp. 221–225.

Newman, A. N. "Political Patronage of Frederick George, Prince of Wales," *Historical Journal,* I (1958), pp. 68–75.

O'Callaghan, E. B., ed. *Documentary History of the State of New York.* 4 vols. Albany, 1849–1851.

Owen, John B. *The Rise of the Pelhams.* London, 1957.

Palstits, V. H. "A Scheme for the Conquest of Canada in 1746," American Antiquarian Society, *Proceedings,* new series, XVII (1905–1906), pp. 69–92.

Pares, Richard. *War and Trade in the West Indies, 1739–1763.* London, 1936.

—— and A. J. P. Taylor. *Essays Presented to Sir Lewis Namier.* London, 1956.

Pargellis, Stanley M. *Lord Loudoun in North America.* New Haven, 1933.

Parker, Charles W. "Lewis Morris, First Colonial Governor of New Jersey," New Jersey Historical Society, *Proceedings,* new series, XIII (1928), pp. 273–282.

Penson, Lilian M. "The London West India Interest in the Eighteenth Century," *English Historical Review,* XXXVI (1921), pp. 373–392.

Peterson, Arthur E. *New York as an Eighteenth Century Municipality prior to 1731.* New York, 1917.

Plumb, J. H. *Chatham.* London, 1953.

—— *The First Four Georges.* London, 1956.

Bibliography

—— *Sir Robert Walpole*. 2 vols. London, 1956–1960.

Pole, J.R. "Historians and the Problem of Early American Democracy," *American Historical Review*, LXVII (1962), pp. 626–646.

Pound, Arthur, and Richard E. Day. *Johnson of the Mohawks*. New ed. New York, 1930.

Ruppel, George Joseph. "The Council and Its Activities in Business, Politics, and Law in New York, 1664–1760." Unpublished Ph.D. dissertation, University of Pittsburgh, 1955.

Rutherfurd, Livingston. *John Peter Zenger*. New York, 1904.

Sachse, William L. *The Colonial American in Britain*. Madison, Wis., 1956.

Schlesinger, Arthur Meier. *The Colonial Merchants and the American Revolution*. New York, 1918.

Schutz, John A. *William Shirley: King's Governor of Massachusetts*. Chapel Hill, 1961.

Seybolt, R.F. *The Colonial Citizens of New York City*. Madison, Wis., 1918.

Smith, Joseph Henry. *Appeals to the Privy Council from the American Plantations*. New York, 1950.

Sosin, Jack M. *Agents and Merchants: British Colonial Policy and the Origins of the American Revolution*. Lincoln, Neb., 1965.

—— *Whitehall and the Wilderness: The Middle West in British Colonial Policy, 1760–1775*. Lincoln, Neb., 1961.

Spencer, Charles Worthen. "Land System of Colonial New York," New York State Historical Association, *Proceedings*, XVI (1917), pp. 150–164.

—— *Phases of Royal Government in New York, 1691–1719*. Columbus, O., 1905.

—— "Sectional Aspects of New York Provincial Politics," *Political Science Quarterly*, XXX (1915), pp. 397–424.

Stillwell, John E., comp. *Historical and Genealogical Miscellany: Early Settlers of New Jersey and Their Descendants*. 5 vols. New York, 1903–1932.

Stokes, I.N. Phelps. *The Iconography of Manhattan Island, 1498–1909*. 6 vols. New York, 1915–1928.

Sutherland, Lucy S. *The City of London and the Opposition to Government, 1768–1774: A Study in the Rise of Metropolitan Radicalism*. London, 1959.

—— *The East India Company in Eighteenth-Century Politics*. London, 1952.

—— and J. Binney. "Henry Fox as Paymaster General of the Forces," *English Historical Review*, LXX (1955), pp. 229–257.

Sykes, Norman. "The Duke of Newcastle as Ecclesiastical Minister," *English Historical Review*, LVII (1942), pp. 59–84.

Tanner, Edwin P. "Colonial Agencies in England during the Eighteenth Century," *Political Science Quarterly*, XVI (1901), pp. 22–48.

Thomson, Mark A. *The Secretaries of State, 1681–1782*. Oxford, 1932.

Turner, Gordon B. "Governor Lewis Morris and the Colonial Government Conflict," New Jersey Historical Society, *Proceedings*, LXVII (1949), pp. 260–304.

Bibliography

Varga, Nicholas. "Election Procedures and Practices in Colonial New York," *New York History*, XLI (1960), pp. 249–277.

——— "Robert Charles: New York Agent, 1748–1770," *William and Mary Quarterly*, 3rd ser., XVIII (1961), pp. 211–235.

Venn, John and J. A. *Alumni Cantabrigiensis: A Biographical List of all Known Students, Graduates and Holders of Office at the University of Cambridge, from the Earliest Times to 1900*. 10 vols. Cambridge, Eng., 1922–1954.

Wagner, Anthony Richard. *English Genealogy*. Oxford, 1960.

Walcott, Robert. *English Politics in the Early Eighteenth Century*. Oxford, 1956.

Watson, J. Steven. "Arthur Onslow and Party Politics," *Essays in British History Presented to Sir Keith Feiling*, H. R. Trevor-Roper, ed., New York, 1965, pp. 139–171.

——— *The Reign of George III, 1760–1815*. Oxford, 1960.

Werner, Edgar A., comp. *Civil List and Constitutional History of the Colony and State of New York*. Albany, 1884.

Wickwire, Franklin B. *British Subministers and Colonial America, 1763–1783*. Princeton, 1966.

Williams, Basil. *The Whig Supremacy, 1714–1760*. Oxford, 1949.

Wilson, James Grant, ed. *The Memorial History of the City of New-York*. 4 vols. New York, 1892–1893.

Wood, George Arthur. *William Shirley, Governor of Massachusetts, 1741–1756*. Columbia University Studies in History, Economics and Public Law, vol. XCII, no. 209, New York, 1920.

Yorke, Philip Chesney. *The Life and Correspondence of Philip Yorke, earl of Hardwicke, lord high chancellor of England*. 3 vols. Cambridge, Eng., 1913.

Index

Index

Wars, 171-173, 182-185, 192, 201, 243-244

Watts, John, 239n151

Westmoreland, Thomas Fane, Earl of, 19, 120

Wileman, Isaac, 140

Willes, Sir John, 115

Wilmington, Spencer Compton, Earl of, 109, 110, 113, 115, 121, 123, 124, 130

Wraxall, Peter, 196

Yeamans, John, 98, 100, 107

Yelverton, Henry, 206

Zenger, John Peter, 74, 95, 137, 139, 152, 154; trial of, 76-77, 80, 109. *See also New-York Weekly Journal*